INVITATION TO
PHILOSOPHY

INVITATION TO PHILOSOPHY

EPISTEMOLOGY AND METAPHYSICS

Peter James Dyer

PARTRIDGE
A Penguin Random House Company

To order additional copies of this book, contact
Toll Free 800 101 2657 (Singapore)
Toll Free 1 800 81 7340 (Malaysia)
orders.singapore@partridgepublishing.com

www.partridgepublishing.com/singapore

What is Philosophy?

This is already a philosophical question. Its literal translation from Ancient Greek (*philein*, and *sophia)* is 'love of wisdom'. But what is love and what is wisdom? Two more philosophical questions. Philosophy is perhaps best seen as asking and attempting to answer 'difficult' questions in a search for the 'truth'. From this perspective, it can be regarded as the mother and father of all other disciplines.

Historically, when in philosophy there has seemed to be a set of answers to some difficult questions in a particular area, this has broken off to form a field of endeavor on its own.

For instance, many of the questions in the philosophy of nature (or 'natural philosophy') became the natural sciences. Isaac Newton when identifying the mathematical properties of the 'laws of nature' was engaging in natural philosophy and so viewed as a 'natural philosopher' – there was no term 'scientist' in the 1600s.

A problem arising with such developments is that as new disciplines establish themselves many of the 'difficult' questions, the questions that it is not easy to set about answering, are left behind in philosophy. To continue with the offspring analogy, philosophy can, in these circumstances sometimes play a role akin to an annoying parent, checking up on the behavior of their children and reminding them of where they came from.

There are some, perhaps many, who go straight into natural sciences (or some other branch of learning) with little or minimal exposure to philosophy and come to view it as an activity serving little purpose since it seems always to be asking impossible questions.

Such an attitude says rather more about the person making such a suggestion than it does about philosophy. This is at least because it was only by asking 'impossible' questions that natural science (or some other discipline) was created in the first place, and it maybe that only by asking such questions that any fruitful changes in direction in a discipline (or collection of disciplines) can be made.

It was, for instance, only by the Ancient Greeks asking the (impossible?) question, 'what is *change*?' that the idea of atoms was developed.

It may now be that asking how we can have 'knowledge' of atoms at the quantum level will produce different ideas on what reality can consist of.

The latter, of course, may involve a journey back to the considerations of our Ancient Greek forebears, the shapers of our intellectual context, to see what else they have to offer, to see what other difficult questions can be asked.

It should be noticed from the above, then, that philosophy is not like other types of enquiry because it is not always about finding answers to given questions.

It is often more about exposing, asking and appreciating the significance of difficult questions and by this activity developing understanding.

These difficult questions may also serve to expose structural weaknesses in ostensibly flourishing disciplines, weaknesses many practitioners may want to forget or at least keep hidden; hidden from themselves perhaps, as well as from public scrutiny.

Philosophy, then, can be viewed as being concerned with identifying and facing up to some difficult questions in an effort to improve understanding and *sophia* or wisdom.

It can do this by exposing complexity and problems where none are obviously visible and have not been seen (or at least not been seen for a long time).

To provide an introductory illustration, a difficult question for modern science is considered briefly below.

A difficult question for science:

It is a principle of science that claims to knowledge should be based on evidence as compared with, say, knowledge supposedly gained by faith.

Richard Dawkins, perhaps the loudest cheerleader for science at the present time, mentions that belief based on absence of evidence is 'delusion', as in his 2006 book 'The God Delusion'. The belief in the existence of God he considers not being based on evidence.

If science holds that knowledge must be evidence based in order to be science, however, it has significant problems.

One of these, revealed by Scottish philosopher David Hume in the 18th century, is the 'problem of induction'. Hume exposes the point that it does not seem there can be any evidence that the future will be like the past.

This is because there is no evidence of future events, since these events lie in the future and the future cannot be known as it has not yet happened.

It follows, therefore, that it must be the case that there can be no evidence that the 'scientific' laws of nature will continue to hold into the future – either the near future or the far future.

There can be no evidence that gravity will continue to operate as it does, or electrons will continue to behave as they do.

The predictions of science rely on the assumption that the laws of nature will continue to hold. However, as there can be no evidence for this assumption, it violates its own key principle (highlighted for us by Richard Dawkins) that knowledge must be evidence based.

If belief in God is a 'delusion' because it lacks evidence, then the belief in the continued operation of natural laws, and the scientific explanations based upon this, must also be a 'delusion' since this too must lack evidence.

To respond to this challenge, incidentally, by citing the fact that laws of nature have been shown in the past to hold into the future is no solution.

This is because such cannot count as evidence for the future being like the past.

The question still remains open - what evidence is there that that what happened in the past will continue to the future?

To cite (yet) again as 'evidence' that it has always happened like this in the past continues to leave the question open – what evidence is there that what happened in the past will continue to happen in the future?

No matter how many times the past is cited, it cannot amount to evidence of what will hold in the future since it relies on an assumption the future will be like the past - the very thing evidence is needed for.

Given this lack of evidence, and given the (scientific) principle that knowledge must be evidence based, the difficulty for science is that it is forced, so to speak, to have a *faith* that the laws of nature will continue to hold in the future, for a few minutes, hours, days, millennia or whatever. And this violates its own principle that (scientific) knowledge must be evidence based.

It appears, then, that at its core a necessary condition for the operation of science is a *faith* that the future will be like the past, a faith that the laws of nature will continue to operate as they have before. (Has Richard Dawkins been keeping this need in science to have *faith* that the future will be like the past hidden from public scrutiny and/or himself?)

If no evidence about God amounts to a 'God Delusion' then we might, as noted, reasonably ask of scientists like Richard Dawkins, employing their own principles, are they guilty of an 'Induction Delusion' because there can be no evidence that laws of nature will continue to hold in the future, only a *faith* that they will.

Does science, then, cut its legs from beneath itself by espousing the principle that knowledge requires evidence, since its very core it relies on a belief that has no evidence to support it (i.e. that laws of nature will continue to operate as they have in the past).

A more colorful example may make David Hume's exposure of this problem a little clearer for those still unconvinced. The twentieth century English philosopher and mathematician Bertrand Russell offers a story of a turkey kept at a farm. Every morning, as the sun rises, the turkey hears the rattle of a bucket, and soon after it finds that food appears. This happens every single day in the same way.

If the turkey were sophisticated enough, 'laws of nature' connecting bucket rattle with food appearance might be constructed and predictions about feeding based on them confirmed by experience and experimentation. 360 days of this sunrise - bucket rattle -food arrival takes place. It has happened like this for so long that the turkey now regards it as matter of 'knowledge' that this is the way its turkey universe behaves (always has and always will). On the 361st day, however, the sun rises, the bucket rattles but the turkey's throat is cut. (It is Christmas Day, and the turkey is to be eaten).

The question follows, then, are we no more than sophisticated turkeys (in a human universe)? And one day, metaphorically speaking, could our throats be cut as well?

And so the whole of science and scientific method seems here exposed by David Hume as being based on a *faith*, even though science, in principle, rejects faith as a source of knowledge because it is not evidence based.

Hume's discovery of the 'problem of induction' has been described as 'one of the most important advances in the whole history of thought' and it perhaps remains so. [1]

This brief introductory discussion surrounding science, knowledge and what can be known, belong to Part I 'Epistemology'. Further difficult questions revealed as still with us lie in the realm of what is called 'Metaphysics' in Part II of this book.

In Metaphysics we have questions concerning 'existence'. What *can* exist and what *must* exist? *Can*, for instance, any, none, or all of the following oft presumed features of reality exist. God? Electrons? Consciousness? Free willing? (and more)? *Must* any of these (and more) exist?

Part III provides an invitation to learn more about Plato's epistemology and metaphysics. Alfred North Whitehead, influential 20th century American philosopher and mathematician famously regards the western intellectual tradition as a series of footnotes to the writings of Plato.

Whitehead was co-author with Bertrand Russell, mentioned just previously, of a three-volume work 'Principia Mathematica' (published in 1910, 1912 and 1927) on the foundations in formal logic of mathematics. This work echoed and complemented the 17th century great work 'Principia' by Isaac Newton, on the mathematical foundations of natural philosophy.

Whitehead regards the whole agenda and conceptual framework within which we operate and/or react to as traceable back to Plato. As a consequence, an understanding how our epistemology and metaphysics owes its origin to Plato is needed to comprehend the presuppositions shaping our modern science, and those shaping our religious beliefs as well. An appreciation of Plato would then seem entirely necessary if all that comes after him is a series of footnotes to his ideas.

CONTENTS

PART I

EPISTEMOLOGY

(What is knowledge? What can we know?)

PART 1

EPISTEMOLOGY

INTRODUCTION

Epistemology is concerned with fundamental and difficult to answer questions about the nature and extent of human knowledge, questions that have perhaps always been with us. What can be known? What is knowledge? How might it be secured?

Take a simple question such as 'What is the point of studying cosmology?' To answer this we might pose further questions. 'What is it for something to have a point in life?'

Soon we might pass on to 'How could we come to have *knowledge* about having a point in life?' Must it be in the same way as we come to have knowledge of the cosmos? 'Is it even possible to have 'knowledge' about what it is to have a point in life?' Is the cosmos pointless? Is life as part of the cosmos pointless?

How to find knowledge about such things? How could we come to know the meaning of life? How, could we come to know the meaning of 'meaning'? (What is it to *mean* something?)

Questions about our world and our place in it eventually end up as questions about 'knowledge': What is it to know about what is being considered? Can we have 'knowledge' of what is being considered? Can we really know anything or is certain knowledge always slightly out of reach?

Such difficult questions are why epistemology is fundamental and always lies beneath any attempt to understand our life our past, our planet, the universe and anything 'beyond'.

Leaving reference to the first chapter of Part I Epistemology until end of this introduction, the second chapter of Part I Epistemology is entitled, 'Reasoning and Experience'. It addresses the 'How can we know?' question by looking at the prime candidates for sources of knowledge, our reasoning and our experiences.

In the third chapter 'Knowledge of the External World' reasoning and experience are exposed as unable to provide support for many of those things we think we know best about ourselves and the world outside us.

This raises concerns about where knowledge can come from, and if it is possible at all. If we cannot even be sure we have knowledge of what we think we know best about ourselves and the world outside us, can we be sure about anything?

These long standing troubles are perhaps now complicated further by developments in Psychology in our modern era. It used to be held in intellectual circles that we know (have 'knowledge' of) what we think we know. I know I *think* I exist, for example, and I know I *think* a world outside me exists.

Even if I can doubt that the world exists or even doubt that I exist, at least I know what I'm *thinking* about it. My mind is transparent to itself as it were.

If Sigmund Freud (1856-1939) is right about the existence of the unconscious, however, we don't even have secure knowledge of what we are thinking - we can have thoughts we are unable to think about, so the mind it not transparent to itself.

This may sound strange, but the modern Western culture, at least, is now generally comfortable in accepting the idea of an unconscious element to cognition, and comfortable with the notion that the unconscious can shape what we believe to be the case and so shape our behavior in response to such beliefs.

A traditional epistemological problem is directed at finding out if what I *believe* to be the case about the world outside me, actually *is* the case. If the idea of the unconscious is accepted, I am moved a step backwards, concerned to find out first if what I believe I am thinking about the world, *is* actually what I think about the world.

Judging from this, epistemological questions appear to be becoming *more* difficult to answer rather than easier as time passes and new ideas emerge.

To digress for a moment, the modern acceptance of the idea of the unconscious, incidentally, has political as well as epistemological implications. If our beliefs and behavior are shaped by unconscious thought processes we have no control over or even access to, then democracy is exposed as making little sense.

The (Ancient Greek) idea of democracy depends on the assumption humans are rational animals able in principle (even if not always willing) to make rational deductions on what a best course of action might be in a situation, and acting on this reasoning.

The acceptance of the existence of a Freudian unconscious in all of us renders humans slaves to unconscious thinking which is often *irrational* and which we have no control over, or even access to – our hidden irrational longings, hatreds, our 'heart of darkness' as Joseph Conrad puts it in his well-known (1899) book of that title.

Accepting the existence of an unconscious element to mind exposes the a situation whereby the key presupposition supporting democracy - humans as rational animals - could be false, and perhaps (ironically) we are in Freudian 'denial' if we pretend to ourselves it isn't; the ramifications of consciously accepting this death of democracy perhaps being too disturbing for us to face.

Plato reasoned that democracy was the worst form of government, although it was in situ in Athens during his time. This was because, for Plato, it placed power with the majority and only a minority would be likely to understand how to exercise power for the good of all; democratic decision-making was as absurd to Plato as calling on a majority to navigate a cruise ship.

Plato powerfully degrades democracy but now Freud has perhaps destroyed it altogether. In both cases power is located in about the worst place possible; in the irrationality of the majority for Plato and in the irrationality of the unconscious within the majority *and* within the minority for Freud.

Back now to epistemology: These questions about the implications of unconscious thoughts flag up another connected point. What would it be for me to know or not to know what I am thinking? What are and what must be the criteria for knowledge, for knowing that something is the case?

An influential attempt to answer the question, what is knowledge?' is examined in the final chapter (chapter five) in this Part I Epistemology. Consideration this definition of knowledge is technical but one with important implications. If we cannot say when something amounts to knowledge, then how can we to 'know' when we have knowledge?

It might be considered we need to know what knowledge is to be able to answer a question like, 'Should a piece of experimental physics count as knowledge, or a piece of theoretical physics count as knowledge, or both count as knowledge?' Should scientific *faith* that that the laws of nature have always existed and will continue to exist count as knowledge, or indeed religious *faith* that God has always existed and will continue to exist count as knowledge? Can faith (scientific or religious or whatever) ever amount to knowledge, or must it always fall short, and are both best exposed as such?

Philosophy, as is hopefully being revealed, can often help with such activities of exposure, and thereby increase wisdom and understanding. Even if it is disturbing the peace, greater understanding of the true extent of a complexity where none was seen before is to increase wisdom.

The fourth chapter in this Part I is called 'Idealism'. Like chapter two on reasoning and experience it is an effort to establish certain 'knowledge' of what exists in reality given that all that can be known are our *ideas* or thoughts about what is the case.

The first chapter in this Part I Epistemology yet to be mentioned in this introduction concerns the challenge of 'skepticism'. Skepticism argues that knowledge in the end is impossible, and we should come to terms with this fact. Some might say, "Face it. At bottom all can only ultimately be just a matter of opinion", opinion about what there is and about what ought to be.

This is a popular point of view. There seem to be things the skeptics amongst us, however, need to come to terms with as well. It appears, for instance, the skeptic must always allow that *some* knowledge is possible. If he/she does not allow some knowledge then the claim (the *knowledge* claim) that 'knowledge is impossible' collapses – if it is true, it is false.

If the claim 'knowledge is impossible' is a piece of knowledge, then, so to speak, it can't be a piece of knowledge; if the claim that 'all is opinion' is true, then *all* is not opinion.

The central task for epistemology now raised by this apparent exposure of extreme skepticism seems to be searching for what can count as knowledge, as some things must count as knowledge for the skeptic to 'know' that something is *not* the case – like knowing that 'knowledge is *not* possible'. Thus, it appears there must exist criteria for what counts as knowledge and what does not count as knowledge.

CONTENTS PART I

1

THE CHALLENGE OF SKEPTICISM

(Is certain knowledge impossible?)

Skepticism forms part of the subject matter of epistemology. Epistemology, as mentioned in the introduction to this Part I, investigates the nature and extent of human knowledge: What can be known? How can we know it? What is knowledge?

Skepticism amounts to the denial that knowledge in various forms, or even *all* forms, is possible. One of the core activities in epistemology is to try and answer the skeptic; to demonstrate that knowledge is possible and show what forms such knowledge can take.

There exists one school of thought in opposition to the skeptic which suggests that knowledge is possible but we are born a 'blank slate' or blank piece of paper (or empty word-processing document). As a consequence anything which counts as knowledge can only be acquired through <u>experience</u> 'writing' something on that blank slate. Another contrasting school also opposing the skeptic, while usually not denying that most types of knowledge are gained through experience, suggests that *some* knowledge can be gained by thinking alone, by <u>reasoning</u>. These two potential sources of knowledge, experience and reason, are the subject matter of the next chapter. Before we can consider how reason and experience might operate to answer to the skeptic, however, we need to look more closely at exactly what skepticism is and the force of its arguments.

Skepticism:-

'Skepticism' is derived from the Ancient Greek language and originally meant 'to reflect on', or 'to consider'. What is sometimes called 'philosophical skepticism' is now the view that knowledge of something, or perhaps even everything, is impossible. In ordinary non-philosophical usage, to be 'skeptical' about something simply means to have doubts about it. We are thus led to a distinction between, say, *ordinary* doubt (or skepticism) and *philosophical* doubt (or skepticism).

To establish that something is certain knowledge, we would seem to have to consider what knowledge amounts to, a key project of epistemology.

A distinction between local and global skepticism may also be drawn in this context. 'Local' skepticism accepts that knowledge is possible within particular fields but says that there are certain things that are impossible for us to know. It questions our ability to gain certain knowledge in a particular area. For example, a certain type of *local* skeptic might hold that scientific beliefs can become knowledge, that knowledge is possible within the sphere of science, but that religious beliefs cannot amount to knowledge.

'Global' skepticism questions our ability to gain *any* certain knowledge. According to the global skeptic *none* of our beliefs are indubitable (immune from all doubt), and therefore certain knowledge of any kind is impossible.

Global skepticism:

The Ancient Greek philosopher Sextus Empiricus (AD c.200) argued that we cannot be certain that *any* of our beliefs are true – all of them can be doubted – and so we should try not to believe anything at all. This state of 'suspension of judgment' was called '*epochē*' in Greek. In his 'Outlines of Pyrrhonism' written late in the 2nd century, Sextus Empiricus formally provides five arguments (or 'modes') for the position that all beliefs can be doubted.

Mode 1: *The existence of disagreement*

Given any subject area that we might consider, there will always be someone who disagrees with what our beliefs in this area are. Disagreement can be found in science, mathematics, morality, religion and so forth. Sextus Empiricus is not simply arguing that because there is always disagreement, we should suspend judgment just because we cannot be sure our beliefs are true.

We should suspend judgment, he says, because disagreements in beliefs can never be completely resolved. He argues this in the 2nd, 4th, and 5th modes.

Mode 2: *Infinite regress*

To settle disagreements between beliefs in a particular subject area, we normally cite reasons to justify our beliefs. But Sextus Empiricus points out that any reason cited for a belief will be another belief. This belief to will also need to be justified by appeal to reasons, and these too will be further beliefs in need of justification. Ending disagreements by citing reasons in support of beliefs is impossible because it leads to an infinite regress. Citing the existence of miracles as a reason for my belief in God, for example, just leads to the need to cite reasons for beliefs in miracles, which leads to the need to cite reasons for those beliefs, and so on...

Mode 4: *Hypothesis*

A way of stopping the infinite regress described above might be to state a belief is just self-evidently true. It does not require any further reasons to support it; explanations have to stop somewhere. The trouble is that what is self-evidently true for one person might not be for another and so disagreement still remains a possibility and the infinite regress problem remains.

A hypothetical belief might be that schizophrenia is a type of insanity – something has 'gone wrong'. Some forms of insanity may, however, instead be viewed as a sane response to insane world; a world where a lie is given the status of truth, where injustice can be called justice and where what is of little importance (celebrity gossip?) is often regarded as of immense importance, and so forth.

Mode 5: *Circularity*

This involves the error of trying to end the infinite regress of justifying a particular belief by appeal to another belief, which also purportedly justifies the first belief. If I claim that my belief in the existence of God is supported by what is written in some Great Book and that my belief in the truth of what is written in that Great Book is justified by the fact that God exists, then my reasoning is 'circular' and both beliefs *still* stand in need of justification.

Mode 3: *Relativity*

Mode three considers beliefs that are ostensibly justified by appeals to sensory experience, e.g., 'I believe the tower is circular because I can see it.' However, if someone stands in a different place they might see the tower as not circular at all (rectangular, perhaps). How things are sensed depend upon, and so are *relative* to, the conditions the perceiver is in. Therefore, Sextus Empiricus is saying, we should suspend judgment on such beliefs.

Sextus Empiricus' conclusion from the Five Modes is that we should suspend judgment because we cannot be sure that any of our beliefs are true. This position is an example of global skepticism. It says that *none* of our beliefs have the certainty required for knowledge.

Is global skepticism possible?

The global skeptic claims that certain knowledge in any field is impossible. A more modern expression of this view heard often is something like "all is just a matter of opinion, so no-one has the 'right' to tell anyone else what is the case." The global skeptical position, however, has its own core difficulty. Its claim that knowledge is impossible ("all is just opinion") seems to be contradictory.

If I know that 'knowledge is impossible', I know something, which means the proposition that 'knowledge is impossible' must be false. The attempt to deny the possibility of knowledge seems only to involve affirming that it is possible (at least in one case), and to affirm there are criteria for deciding what is and what is not knowledge.

It may be that a 'local' skepticism, involving the acceptance that *some* knowledge in exists, is a more tenable position. The problem then becomes finding out exactly where and what this particular knowledge is. One attempt to carry out this search for where knowledge could be found was undertaken by René Descartes (1596-1650). His project is described next.

René Descartes and Methodological Doubt:-

The philosophical writings of French mathematician René Descartes' (1596-1650), have played an influential role in the history of human thought ever since the 17th century.

Those familiar with graphs will recognize the term 'Cartesian coordinates' revealing Descartes' place in the creation of graphical representation. He made many contributions to algebra as well, and to optics, such as his study of the reflection and refraction of light. His work in these areas was known to and respected by Isaac Newton (1643-1727).

Descartes employs an extreme version of philosophical doubt, the questioning of even the most basic of his beliefs, as a *method* to search for knowledge. He uses this method to assess everything he had been formally taught and everything that was considered to be true at during his time to find out what, if anything, could amount to knowledge. What would be incapable of being doubted and so withstand the challenge of the skeptic?

Descartes realized that time would not allow him to test each and every single belief to see which are immune from doubt, so instead he questions the foundations of his beliefs. If, for example, the grounds for a set of beliefs could be doubted he had reason to reject the entire set. Approaching the project in this way Descartes employed three key arguments, the illusion argument, the dream argument and the evil genius argument.

Illusion Argument:

This is similar to Mode 3 used by Sextus Empiricus noted above. Descartes' illusion argument amounts to the following

- I have often been deceived by the senses in the past. For example, I sense I am moving forward in a train but it turns out it is the carriage next to me moving backwards. Straight sticks pointing up in water are seen as bent, I sometimes hear the alarm clock ring when it doesn't actually ring (and so on).
- I cannot be sure that I'm *not* being deceived now.
- Therefore, knowledge gained through the senses is not completely certain.

Scientific 'knowledge' relies on information gained through the senses of course, and so must be open to doubt using the Cartesian method, because the senses often deceive us. Visual illusions are also instructive in this regard.

Consider this well-known snake illusion by Akiyoshi Kitaoka, Professor of Psychology at Ritsumeikan University, Japan

It is difficult not to occasionally perceive movement here when all the time there is, in reality, no movement (which strongly suggests the immediate object of our perception, the moving snake, cannot be of what is in the world since the image in the world is not moving). Suppose too something seen for the first time through a microscope, or in distant space appears to be moving. When and how can we be sure any perceived movement is 'out there'? And, similarly, when and how, then, can we be sure there is *no* movement, when we sense no movement? Collecting valid data from what is experienced is not a straightforward task in scientific investigations of this kind.

Descartes' Dream Argument:

This amounts to the following.

-   I cannot be certain that I am not dreaming.
-   Therefore, it is possible that what I think I am now experiencing is a dream.
-   Therefore, what I think I'm experiencing might be false and so it is not completely certain that what I think I am experiencing is actually the case.

Descartes' Evil Demon Argument:

There appear to be some beliefs that are certain, if sleeping or if awake. Geometrical truths for instance: Even in a dream, triangles have three sides. Therefore, although the dream argument makes it possible to doubt all of our 'perceptual' beliefs, it seems to leave untouched the certainty of various mathematical and geometrical beliefs. Descartes' final skeptical argument, however, allows that it is just possible that even the latter may be subject to doubt.

Descartes says it is just *possible* that an evil demon exists who is of the utmost power and cunning and has employed all his energies in order to deceive him.

Descartes is looking for knowledge that is so certain it can stand up to even this extreme possibility.[2]

A modern version of the evil demon argument is called the 'brains in vats argument'. In place of the evil demon, it supposes that we might simply be disembodied brains suspended in vats full of liquid, and wired up to a supercomputer that feeds us experiences by electrically stimulating our brains. The movie 'The Matrix' is a version of 'brains in vats argument' (albeit an inconsistent one).

- It is just possible that experiences I have are placed in me by an evil demon (or a Matrix).
- This possibility means, therefore, all my mathematical beliefs as well my perceptual beliefs are susceptible to doubt.

The introduction of the *possibility* of a powerful evil demon seems to subject *every* belief to doubt, which leaves us with global skepticism. Certain knowledge does not appear to be possible if a deceiving evil demon is possible, and so it appears the challenge of the global skeptic cannot be answered. Descartes does have an answer though.

'Cogito ergo sum':

The evil demon hypothesis appears to remove the possibility there exists any knowledge that cannot be subject to doubt. However, Descartes points out that even if an evil demon (or Matrix.) exists who plants thoughts in me is possible, I can still be certain that I exist. This is because to doubt the belief you exist (e.g., "I wonder if an evil demon has planted this thought in me?") is to exist.

This conclusion, which is expressed in the famous tag *'cogito, ergo sum'* (Latin for 'I think, therefore I am'), seems to be certain. Global skepticism holding that *all* beliefs are subject to doubt is, on this reasoning, false – I can at least have certain 'knowledge' that I exist.

So far in this chapter the problem of 'skepticism' within the domain of epistemology has been introduced. Descartes use of skepticism as a *method* for searching for knowledge has been described and his final acceptance of the belief that he thinks he has established *some* certain knowledge (that he exists) by <u>reasoning</u> alone. Just by thinking Descartes appears to have established that he has 'knowledge' that he exists. This is an example of what is known as the 'rationalist' approach to the problem of skepticism – rejecting skepticism by using reason alone; by showing reasoning can be a source of some of our knowledge. Rationalism is considered again in the next chapter.

Problems for Descartes and an Invitation to Ludwig Wittgenstein:-

Ludwig Wittgenstein is generally held by those in the Anglo-American tradition (at least) to be the most important philosopher of the 20th century. Sigmund Freud is thought by many (for good or ill) to be the most influential 'intellectual' of the 20th century but it may be that he must be counted as a psychologist rather than a philosopher. Either way, the influence of both continues and is set to continue. Like Freud (1856-1939) Wittgenstein (1889-1951) was Austrian. He moved to England as a young man and later became a British citizen. He worked as an academic in Cambridge and was buried there. (Freud also moved to England late in his life).

Wittgenstein will return again several times in this book. He will return, for instance, in Part III as a rejection of Plato's epistemology. It may be remembered from the introduction to this book how mathematician and philosopher Alfred North Whitehead regards the history of Western thought since Plato as footnotes to Plato. If Wittgenstein is right in his critique of Plato, the history Western thinking founded on this Platonic tradition could be based on a centuries-old fundamental error. More of this in Part III 'An Invitation to Plato'. For now, though, Wittgenstein's view of Descartes' method of doubt is in the spotlight.

Descartes is using a method of doubt to search for certain knowledge, rejecting anything as counting as certain knowledge that can be subject to doubt of any kind, and ending in what he thinks is the knowledge that he must exist, since this is immune from doubt (as because to doubt one exists, is to exist). Wittgenstein rejects all this, and more, exposing Descartes as mistaken in thinking that because he cannot doubt that he exists, he must exist.

Wittgenstein's work has a focus on how language 'works' and, as we often (perhaps always?) think in a language, also has a focus on how thinking 'works'. One key thematic point Wittgenstein makes is that thinking often fails to operate properly because of a failure in understanding how language operates. And this is where Descartes goes wrong.

Descartes' view is that something is *certain* if there is no possibility of doubting it. This is why he thinks he is certain that he exists since it cannot be doubted (even if an evil demon thought-controller exists).

Wittgenstein rejects this way of thinking in his last work, Philosophical Investigations' published posthumously in 1969. In it he distinguishes between 'subjective' and 'objective' certainty, and considers how language works in relation to certainty and doubt.

To say "*I* am certain" is to deliver a 'subjective' certainty. It is to express the psychological *attitude* that I have no doubt about it.

I also know, however, that I could still be mistaken. I could say 'I am certain that Peter will arrive in a minute' as an expression of my (subjective) psychological attitude (but know, still, that it could in the end turn out that Peter does not arrive).

When Descartes says "*I* am certain that I exist" it is also an expression of a psychological *attitude*. And if this is all it is - a 'subjective' certainty - it may turn out, not to be 'objectively' certain, as in the 'I am certain Peter will arrive in a minute' case just mentioned.

Descartes, of course, wants to say more. He wants to say that "I am certain that I exist" is more than a mere *subjective* expression of his psychological attitude. He wants to claim it is 'objectively' certain that he exists.

To say "It is certain" - an 'objective' certainty - is not simply to express a psychological attitude. It is to state a truth.

In a situation (of 'objective' certainty) like this, it makes no sense to say 'it is certain that X is the case, but X is the case may still turn out be false'. It would be like stating it is (objectively) certain that X is the case *and* it is *not* ('objectively') certain that X is the case.

Doubting a claim to 'objective' certainty is not how language works – "It *is* certain, but it may still turn out not be" makes no sense as it is like saying "it is certain that 2+2 = 4 but we can still doubt that it is". It is like saying "it is certain *and* it is not certain that 2+2=4".

Similarly, if it makes no sense to be mistaken or in doubt about an 'objective' certainty, then words like 'therefore, I *know* it' don't belong either.

In the expression 'It is certain that 2+2= 4, therefore I know it', 'therefore I know it' doesn't belong.

This, however, is exactly what Descartes attempts to do.

He is saying. 'It is certain that I exist, therefore I know it'.

This knowing 'X is the case' is already established by the proposition 'it is certain that X is the case',

The knowing that I exist is already established by the proposition 'It is certain that I exist,' ('therefore I exist' does not belong here).

Wittgenstein moves on even further from this to suggest that, in the end, 'objective' certainty, actually collapses into 'subjective' certainty (but Descartes must still be wrong).

'Objective' Certainty collapsing into 'subjective' Certainty:

We have just seen how Wittgenstein's exposes the point that when one's certainty of something is 'objective', (i.e. 'X is certain'), it makes no sense to doubt it.

We have also seen how Wittgenstein exposes the point that it is inappropriate to then say as well (as Descartes does), 'therefore I know it. 'Therefore I know it' does not belong here – the proposition that I know it is already contained in the statement 'it is certain' – like 'it is certain that 2+2= 4' does not require, 'therefore I know it'.

But Wittgenstein goes on to explain that a judgment that something is 'objectively' certain, so that it makes no sense to doubt it, may *still* turn out to *not* to be true – unlike Descartes who is, of course, saying that it is the certainty of something that *makes* it true, (like the certainty/impossibility of doubting 'I exist', makes it true).

Wittgenstein moves to point out how an extraordinary event may occur to shake one's confidence in something hitherto regarded as impossible to doubt – i.e. 'objectively' certain.

The discovery of the behavior of electrons in quantum physics for instance, might amount to this. The discovery that electrons 'in' an atom seem regularly to come from 'nowhere' and go back to 'nowhere' as they leap orbits.

Previously it seemed objectively 'certain' (i.e. impossible to doubt) that it was not possible for something to 'go' to *nowhere* or come back from *nowhere*. This going to *nowhere* and coming back from *nowhere* seems as logically impossible, as round squares seem logically impossible.

At least three responses are available in the face of an extraordinary event (or extraordinary 'discovery') like this: And these responses are all in the realm of 'subjective' certainty.

1. The objective certainty is replaced by the psychological attitude of doubt. Can I really exist, or continue to exist (since I'm made up of electrons)?
2. I could become completely bewildered and confused, not sure about making any sort of judgment, since I'm not now sure about my continued existence (or the continued existence anything made of atoms/electrons).
3. I could refuse to doubt my continued existence in the face of the extraordinariness of the behavior of electrons.

Either way, 'objective' certainty collapses into 'subjective' certainty. Something that was held to be 'objectively' certain (impossible to doubt) can be called into question via an extraordinary event/discovery and one is bound to adopt a 'subjective' psychological attitude to that event – three (psychological attitude) possibilities being given above.

This idea of 'objective' certainty exposed as collapsing into 'subjective' (psychological) certainty, means that Descartes or anyone else who regards 'objective' certainty (the *impossibility* doubting something) as guaranteeing the truth of that something, no longer holds as well.

2

REASONING AND EXPERIENCE

(How are they sources of knowledge?)

In the previous chapter the approach of skepticism was adumbrated, the position that certain knowledge is not possible. The thinking of René Descartes (1596-1650) was also described whereby he used his reasoning alone to establish the certain knowledge that he exists *is* possible.

The use of reason or reasoning alone to establish certain knowledge forms part of a movement given the name 'Rationalism'. The use of experience to try and establish certain knowledge is called 'Empiricism'.

This chapter will look in some detail at the differences and similarities between these two approaches. Descartes will be mentioned again as an example of a rationalist, but more attention will be given to the work of the empiricist David Hume (1711-1776), a highly influential figure in the history of Western thought, and still very relevant today.

The chapter will end with a look at the work of Immanuel Kant (1724-1804), another important contributor to the Western canon and someone who attempts to address the problems exposed by David Hume.

Experience as a source of knowledge:-

In the previous chapter we saw how Descartes tries to answer the skeptic by means of the indubitable (i.e. impossible to doubt) belief that he exists. He considers he establishes the truth of this belief by reason alone: Descartes does not infer that he exists because of any evidence given to him by his senses (as he thinks the senses cannot be trusted as they have been wrong in the past and so may be wrong now). Rather, reason alone tells him he must exist if he is thinking – that it is impossible that he is thinking (even in doubting he exists) and yet he doesn't exist, because his thinking he holds presupposes his existence.

Descartes' attempt to found knowledge on beliefs that are certified by reason is, as has been said, an example of 'rationalism' (from the Latin 'ratio', meaning 'reason'). This general term applies to the view that some knowledge about the world can be attained through the exercise of pure reason, independent of anything learned via sense experience. 'Empiricism' (from the Greek term 'empeira', meaning 'experience') is the view that sense experience is the ultimate source of any knowledge about what exists.

Care needs to be taken when using the terms 'rationalism' and 'empiricism'. While rationalists think that *some* knowledge of reality can gained through reason alone, most do <u>not</u> think that *all* such knowledge can come through reason alone. Rationalists tend not to deny, for example, that we learn through experience that fire is hot and can burn your skin (children are not born with a fear of fire). And a rationalist would likely accept we come to learn from experience that salt dissolves in water, and so forth.

Most beliefs like this about the world for rationalism *and* for empiricism are derived from observation of the world. Rationalism does hold, however, that *some* knowledge about reality is derived through reason alone and such is *fundamental,* acting as the foundation for all our other knowledge.

More straightforwardly, empiricists argue that *all* knowledge of what exists comes via the senses; nothing about what exists can be known by reasoning alone.

It may be, however, as we will discover, that the number of things that can then (only) be known based on experience is *very* much smaller than we might normally suppose – including the existence of ourselves.

For empiricists like David Hume reasoning does provide *some* knowledge. It can tell us things like round squares are impossible and something cannot both be and not be at the same time, that something cannot be everywhere and nowhere, that something cannot be created from nothing at all. We do not need *experience* to know such matters. (At least we used to think so before quantum physics and the 'discovery' of the strange behavior of electrons).

To be able to go more deeply into the debate between rationalism (reason as a source of knowledge) and empiricism (experience as a source of knowledge) two pairs of technical terms are needed.

A priori and *A posteriori*

'Necessary' and 'Contingent'

A priori and *A posteriori:*

Knowledge acquired via reason alone is called '*a priori*' knowledge.

Knowledge which is gained through experience is called '*a posteriori*' knowledge

As mentioned above, even rationalism accepts that the majority of our knowledge of reality is acquired by means of sensory experience; it is *a posteriori*. For example, our belief that fire is hot or that water freezes at 32° Fahrenheit can only come from experience. No amount of (pure) thinking could establish these facts. These are examples of *a posteriori* knowledge because they come after or *post* experience.

A priori knowledge arrives independently of or *prior* to experience. Mathematical truths are often cited as examples. To know that two things plus two things will equal four things we do not need to count them. We know in advance, independently of and *prior* to experience, that 2 + 2 = 4. Whenever there are two pairs of things we know (*prior* to any sense experience like counting them) there will turn out to be four things in total. And we know it couldn't be otherwise. Reason alone (not experience) tells us this; we do not need the experience of counting all objects to know that 2 objects plus 2 objects will *always* equal 4 objects.

'Necessary' and 'Contingent':

A *priori* knowledge is 'necessarily' true. *A posteriori* knowledge is only 'contingently' true

A priori truths are said to be 'necessary' because it is impossible that they be false. It is impossible using human reason to hold as true, say, that occasionally 2 things and 2 more things will equal 5 things.

A posteriori truths are called 'contingent' truths because it *is* possible they could have been false; they depend, or are contingent on, other states of affairs.

For example, take the *a posteriori* belief that water freezes at 32° Fahrenheit. It is possible that the world was such that water freezes at a different temperature. The truth that water freezes at 32° Fahrenheit depends upon the state of the world.

By contrast, no matter what the world is like, or if there is no world at all, two things plus two more things will always equal to four things.

A priori truths are 'necessary' in this sense and not, unlike *a posteriori* truths, 'contingent'.

Descartes' use of mathematical method:

We have noted that rationalism often holds up mathematical knowledge (e.g. 2 + 2 = 4) as a paradigm example of *a priori* knowledge. Descartes, as mentioned in the pervious chapter, was a mathematician and impressed by the certain knowledge offered by mathematics and the mathematical method.

Mathematics operates with certain fundamental principles ('axioms') whose truth is immediately apparent to reason, and then makes careful deduction of further truths from these first principles, so building up a body of certain knowledge.

Descartes proposed to extend this method beyond mathematics to knowledge in general. For this reason his epistemological approach is often known as a 'mathematical method'. Descartes began with an indubitable (impossible to doubt) truth about the world, such as 'I exist', which could be directly intuited by reason. From this starting point, this first principle or 'axiom', he thought he could deduce further truths that were not immediately apparent to reason and build up a body of certain knowledge.

By means of the rational faculties of 'intuition', with which to arrive at first principles (such as 'I exist'), and 'deduction', with which to arrive at further knowledge, Descartes thought he could arrive at a whole system of necessary and certain knowledge, and thereby thoroughly reject the challenge of skepticism. These faculties of 'intuition' and 'deduction' are considered below.

Intuition and Innate Ideas:

In Descartes' philosophy 'intuition' is a technical term which refers to the way in which we immediately grasp necessary and certain truths through the operation of reason alone. The truths that are apprehended by intuition are *immediate* in the sense that they are not mediated or derived from anything else – from, for example, sense experience or from other ideas.

They are also certain; we cannot be mistaken about them. They are, thus, *a priori* truths. The prime examples Descartes gives of intuitive knowledge is that he exists, and truths of mathematics (like 2+2=4).

t is clear, however, that many beliefs are *a posteriori*, post experience. It is only through empirical observation of the world, for example, that we come to know that fire generates heat (children are not born knowing this).

For *a priori* truths gained via intuition, however, Descartes is suggesting they cannot be traced back to information gained via experience. We know that if there are two pairs of things they will add up to four even though it is impossible for us to experience all the pairs of things, past, present and future.

If some ideas and principles are true *prior* to experience and cannot be derived from experience. Where, then, could they come from? Descartes' answer is that they must then be 'innate'. We are born with them; they must be something we arrive with, as such ideas and principles cannot be picked up from (our limited) experience *after* we are born.

We are not born, then, with minds as 'blank tablets' or pieces of paper waiting to be written on by experience. The mind arrives with some knowledge already written on it, such as knowing that two things plus two more things will *always* equal four things (although it may take time for such knowledge to actually be activated).

This theory of innate ideas (we ae born with certain elements of knowledge) is one of the distinguishing features of rationalism. It is also one that is challenged by empiricism, as we shall see.

Innate ideas and deduction:

The 'mathematical method' was described above whereby deductions can be made from first principles or 'axioms' to build up a body of mathematical knowledge. Any piece of mathematical knowledge can ultimately be traced back to these fundamental axioms. The same method can be applied regarding innate ideas of *a priori truths*.

Discovered by intuition, the innate ideas can act as first principles or axioms, and via making 'deductions', other ideas be generated from them.

'Deduction' is a term from logic which refers to the process by which a proposition is necessarily inferred from others. For example, take the following two premises:

- 'All men are mortal' and
- 'Socrates is a man'

From these a further proposition can be *deduced*

– 'Socrates is mortal'.

'Socrates is mortal' *must* be true if the two premises are true.

Rationalism holds, therefore that we can use our intuitions of *a priori* truths as premises in a deductive argument and, via deduction, expand our knowledge beyond those innate *a priori* truths to generate certain conclusions.

Then more deductions might be drawn from these and so knowledge expanded further while all the time remaining certain, given the truth of the (intuited) first principles to which other knowledge (gained via deduction) can ultimately be traced back to.

In this way, using the 'mathematical method', our non-intuitive (deduced) beliefs are said to be rationally justified by our intuitive beliefs. As long as the intuitive beliefs are certain and we are careful in our deductive reasoning, we can be also certain of the truth of our beliefs based upon them.

Descartes, it may be remembered, thought that some truths about the world (not just mathematical propositions) could be known via rational intuition e.g., 'I exist'. Given such truths about the world, careful deductive reasoning from these should make it possible to generate body of certain knowledge about the world.

And if the first principles can be intuited by reason alone, this body of knowledge about the world can be formulated using reason alone, the 'rationalist' approach; use intuition to gain the first principles and use deduction to formulate more knowledge.

The key features of rationalism can now be listed:

- Mathematical model of knowledge; a unified system based on a foundation of certain basic truths ('axioms').
- First principles known through rational intuition.
- First principles known *a priori* and necessarily true.

- A priori truths intuited in this way are innate; present in the mind from birth (even if not immediately activated).
- A body of knowledge can be derived via deduction and *justified* by ultimate appeal to the necessary truth of the basic beliefs upon which it is founded.
- *Some* knowledge of what exists in the world (not just, say, abstract mathematics and logic) can be established via deduction and justified by ultimate appeal to the necessary truth of first principles.

The Radical Empiricism of David Hume:-

It has just be explained how rationalism holds that reason, by means of the processes of intuition of *a priori* truths and deduction from these, can establish a body of certain knowledge and, as Descartes argues, this knowledge can be about what exists in the world. Empiricism rejects all this. The empiricist attack on rationalism was set down with clarity by David Hume (1711-1776).

You may recall that an *a priori* truth must be 'necessary'. This means that it cannot conceivably be false. 'Barking dogs bark', for instance, is certain (by definition). To deny it, to say that 'barking dogs do *not* bark', would be a logical contradiction. It is true *a priori*, true independently of experience, that 'barking dogs bark'.

However, although it must be certain that 'barking dogs bark', this exercise of reasoning does not, of course, tell us anything about what exists. In particular, it does not tell us whether or not there actually exist any barking dogs.

This, essentially, is Hume's empiricist view. He accepts the rationalist position that all *a priori* truths are necessarily true, but holds that all truths about the world are contingent and *a posteriori* (depend upon or are *post* experience).

The truth of 'dogs exist', for instance, is contingent or dependent upon what is in the world. And it is possible (unlike 'barking dogs bark') that 'dogs exist' could be false – the world *could* be such there are no dogs in it (although the world could never be such that 'barking dogs do not bark').

If Hume is right about this, right about *a priori* truths telling us nothing about reality, then the rationalist claim that *some* knowledge of the world can be gained from reason alone has to be false. Hume's key arguments are given below.

Relations of Ideas & Matters of Fact:

Hume calls the formal *a priori* knowledge made certain by reason a 'relation of ideas'; ideas like 'barking dogs bark' or 'triangles have three angles'. These tell us nothing about reality; whether there are in existence any dogs or triangles.

Knowledge of reality, confirmed by experience (*a posteriori*) he called 'matters of fact'. These include, for example, that 'fire burns', or 'dogs exist'.

These are the only two types of knowledge for Hume. If something claimed to be knowledge cannot be backed up by reason or by experience it can only be, as Hume puts it, 'sophistry and illusion'.

The test for any knowledge claim is to ask whether it is a 'relation of ideas' made certain by reason, or a 'matter of fact' confirmed by experience. If it is neither, it is sophistry and illusion and should be 'committed to the flames' [3].

This test is sometimes known as Hume's 'fork'. Using his test, he proceeds to reject as false some strongly held knowledge claims: knowledge claims about the existence of the self, for instance, knowledge claims about the existence of a world outside us, and knowledge claims about the existence of causes.

The 'problem of causation':

Every time I have experienced a fire I have had a sensation of heat. Because if this I come to regard fire as *causing* the heat. On this basis I feel justified in saying that the next fire I come into contact with will also give out heat (and if it doesn't, it will be some sort of fake fire). In addition, the more times I experience heat coming from fire, the more justified I feel in saying that fire *causes* heat, making it even more likely that the next fire I see will give out heat. The question is what justifies these beliefs?

Hume says that all reasoning about matters of fact (as opposed to relations of ideas) are based on the idea of cause and effect. It is only be employing this concept that we can move beyond the evidence of our senses and our memory. [4]

I believe that the fire I see before me will be hot, because I believe there to be a causal connection between fire and heat. In this case, I am drawing an inference from an observed cause (fire) to an unobserved effect (heat).

Much then depends upon our belief in cause and effect. Applying Hume's test (Hume's 'fork') we must ask if cause and effect is a 'relation of ideas', something established solely by <u>reason</u> *a priori,* or whether it is a 'matter of fact' established *a posteriori* via <u>experience</u>. (And if it is not supported either by reason *or* by experience, then it is nothing but sophistry and illusion).

That causes and effects are not established via <u>reason</u> alone seems clear. No amount of pure thinking about fire will tell you that it is associated with heat. You have to experience it to find that out. In the famous 'Little Albert' experiment by John Watson in the early 20th century, a burning newspaper was placed next to 9 month old boy. It was seen he was not afraid of the flames as Albert reached out several times to grab them. Similarly, we are not born knowing that water can suffocate and one can drown in it. Experience is needed to discover that water can kill.[5]

Causes and effects then (fire causing heat, water causing suffocation etc.) are not then established just by thinking, by reason alone.

Hume, however, also demonstrates that causes and effects are not actually justified by experience either. (And if not supported by being a relation of ideas or by experience, any cause and effect relation must be classified as sophistry and illusion and be committed to the flames).

We might say, for instance, that the movement of one pool table ball striking another 'causes' that other to move.

But Hume notes that if you consider this more closely you will see that all you experience are events. You experience the movement of the first ball (A) and the movement of the second ball (B).

You don't *experience* 'causation'. You experience event A, then event B. And you might experience this many, many times. But this (A then B) is *all* you experience; a constant conjunction between events A and B. You don't experience 'cause'.

It is *possible* in the future that B does not occur after A; *possible* the ball does not move. As has already been mentioned in the introduction to this book, the fact that event B has always occurred after event A in the past (perhaps via a set of scientific experiments even) does not entail in any way that B will *necessarily* follow A in the future.

Nor does it even mean that B will *probably* follow A in the future. This point is elaborated below.

The 'problem of induction':

The issues falling under this heading are closely related to issues of causation.

The following scenario has just be described: Every time I have experienced a fire I have had a sensation of heat. Because if this I come to regard fire as causing the heat. On this basis I feel justified in saying that in the future the next fire I come into contact with will also give out heat (and if it doesn't, it will be a sort of fake fire).

In addition, the more times I experience heat coming from fire, the more justified I feel in saying that fire *causes* heat, making it even more likely that in the future the next fire I see will give out heat. This kind of reasoning from past experience to beliefs about the future is called 'induction'. Hume's attack on it is thus called 'the problem of induction'.

Induction forms the basis of science and scientific experimentation.

The object of an experiment is usually to find out what causes what.

If, by varying one thing only (X) and (while holding all other possible variables constant), something happens (Y), it is inferred that Y can only have been caused by the one changing thing, X.

The more this experiment is repeated with the same result, the more confidence a scientist has in the causal relation X *causes* Y.

If Hume is right in saying this induction cannot be justified, then the standard experimental method of science cannot be justified either.

This bears repeating. If Hume is right, the standard method of using experiments to establish knowledge in science (often what distinguishes science from non-science) *cannot be justified*, either by reason or by experience.

The problem of induction for Hume can also be put like this: Conclusions based on induction rest upon the *assumption* that the future will be like the past. It is only because we make this assumption we argue, for example, that the fact that because a fire has been associated with heat in the past means that it will be associated with heat in the future. But the assumption that the future will resemble the past has no support – it is just an assumption.

Let us subject 'the future will be like the past' to Hume's test (Hume's 'fork'). Is 'the future will be like the past' a relation of ideas made certain by <u>reason</u> alone? No, because it is logically possible that the world be such that fire is not associated with heat, unlike the *impossibility*, that the world be such that 2 things plus two more things does not result in 4 things)

Is 'the future will be like the past' a matter of fact confirmed by <u>experience</u>? Again No. All experience can show is that in the past, the future has been like the past. There is nothing in experience to say that the future we have not experienced will be like the past.

To say, for instance, that 'The future will be like the past because it always has' it a circular argument; it assumes what it is trying to prove. It is like the circular argument religion is often accused of. 'God exists, because it says so in the Bible or other Great Book, and the Great Book is true because God exists'. This leaves the question as to whether God exists or not unanswered. Similarly, to say that 'The future will be like the past because it always has' leaves unanswered the question 'How do you know the future will be like the past?' [6]

We saw in the introduction to this book how Bertrand Russell uses a turkey to illustrate the problem of induction. It also illustrates the related problem of causation above. This turkey story is repeated here. A turkey arrives on a farm on January 1st. It is fed every day at the same time just after sunrise. Just before it is fed it hears the rattle of a bucket and starts to become excited in anticipation of being fed: event Y (feeding), *always* follows event X (rattle of the bucket). The feeding routine goes on for 360 days. On the 361st day just after sunrise the turkey hears the familiar rattle of the bucket as usual and expects food. Then its throat is cut...

It is Christmas Day. Is human reasoning about the future, and (indeed) is reliance on experimental science, anything more than the expectation of a turkey in a turkey universe?

The 'problem of induction' and probability:

You may perhaps be thinking that even though something always occurring in the past (like heat coming from a fire) does not make it *certain* that it will happen in the future, at least it is more *probable* that it will. And the more it occurs, the more probable it becomes. Hume's though, is able to expose that this this is not justified either.

We have no experience of the future whatsoever, only the past. Therefore, as regards the future we have no knowledge at all, not even any *probable* knowledge.

It may be our human habit, like the habit of the turkey just described, to expect the future will (probably) be like the past but this belief is not justified.

This is because our beliefs can only be based on the events in the past and events in the past can never give us knowledge of events in the future unless we *assume* the future will generally be like the past which is to beg the question we are trying to answer – What evidence have we that the future will be like the past, or 'probably' like the past? None, as we only have the past to go on.

Knowledge of the External World:

Much more will be said about knowledge of the 'external' world in the next chapter. For now, though, it is worth noting how Hume's arguments demonstrate that claims to knowledge of the world outside the mind are unjustifiable. Let us apply Hume's test (Hume's 'fork').

Is 'the world exists outside my mind' a relation of ideas made certain by <u>reason</u> alone?

No, because it is logically possible that there be no world out there at all. (It is 'contingent' and not a 'necessary' truth that 'the world exists outside my mind').

Is 'the world exists outside my mind' a matter of fact confirmed by <u>experience</u>?

Again Hume would say 'No', because we do not have direct experience of the world. He says that only have direct access to 'impressions' or 'ideas' of it.

Consider standing in front of a table. If you move away from it the table looks smaller, and as you change your point of view the table changes shape. The actual table cannot change its size or shape in this way, so you cannot be perceiving it *directly*.

What you are directly perceiving is something mental, a sense impression or idea – it is these, we might say, that are the immediate objects of perception not the actual object/table in the world.

Must it still not be the table *causing* these sense impressions that we perceive? We cannot know this, of course, because of Hume's arguments against any experience of 'causation'.

In addition, if all we immediately experience are impressions and ideas in our minds, we can *never* experience the relation between these impressions and ideas and the world.

For all we know from experience, there might be a world that is completely different from the one we perceive via our impressions or ideas and, perhaps no world at all. [7]

Knowledge of the Self:

It might seem that with the rejection of knowledge of causation and knowledge of the external world we are back in a position similar to the one Descartes thought himself in before he found his first certainty; the certainty that all he knew for sure was that he existed. Hume, however, rejects this as well…

Let us apply Hume's test (Hume's 'fork'):

The truth of 'I exist' is contingent, not necessary. It depends upon what is and has been in the world (notably one's parents). It cannot therefore be a relation of ideas confirmable by <u>reason</u>, like X is X.

Is it then a matter of fact confirmable only by <u>experience</u>?

If it is confirmable by neither, then it is nothing but sophistry and illusion.

And so it turns out. Hume explains, we have no experience of our 'self' as a thing that thinks (although it may be our natural psychological habit to regard the situation as such). When we examine our thoughts there is no consciousness of an identifiable self having these thoughts, Although you may assume there *must* be a self to be having the thoughts, but careful examination reveals there is no thought of the self in experience, having thoughts. There are just thoughts.[8]

If we introspect and examine all our impressions and ideas (examine our experiences) all we find are a bundle of constantly changing perceptions. There is no 'I' in our experience distinct from impressions or ideas, and having those impressions and ideas. Try it for yourself. [9]

You might be tempted to assume that there *must* be an 'I' having thoughts or there wouldn't be any thoughts at all! But Hume is only interested in what you *actually* experience, and you don't *actually* experience an 'I' having thoughts – just thoughts.

And if it is not part of experience, it is not justified as knowledge on empiricist grounds as there is no evidence for it.

If Hume is right, any science we care to use has no evidence that there is an identifiable 'I' having 'thoughts. Any belief in the 'I' of I think must merely be a matter of faith (as was the faith at the heart of science that the laws of nature will continue to operate into the near future or into the far future, since both lack the support of evidence from experience).

Reasoning and Psychology:

If Hume's observations are correct, then we have no justification, based on what we actually experience, for believing that events are caused by other events, no justification for believing that there is a world outside our minds, no justification for the belief that the future will be like the past, and no justification, even, for the belief that we exist as a self which is distinct from our ideas and impressions.

Reason cannot give us any knowledge of these 'contingent' facts, and experience provides us with no evidence that might justify such beliefs. All such therefore (on Hume's 'fork') have to be regarded as sophistry and illusion and 'committed to the flames'.

On the basis of Hume's empiricist principles, then, we seem to have arrived back at a position of global skepticism; the view that knowledge is impossible. Should we now refrain from believing anything at all? Is this the only course open to us?

Hume's answer is that it is impossible for us not to believe these sorts of thing. This is because of the way nature has made us. Our *psychological* make-up is such that instinctively we can't help believing that events are caused by other events, the future will be like the past, that the world exists independently of us and that we are subjects in the world having experiences.

We can try and be skeptical in the *philosophical* sense and try to prevent ourselves holding these unjustifiable beliefs (unjustifiable because they lack evidence), but in the end this is impossible and our *psychological* nature prevails.[10]

Hume is able to expose, then, that there is no intellectual justification for assuming, as science does, that the findings from experiments, no matter how often repeated, produce knowledge.

This is because such is not a matter of logical necessity; the future behaviors of things may not be like the past behaviors of things.

It is also because it is not a matter of experience since we have only experience of the past, and neither do we experience causation, just repetition or 'constant conjunction' as Hume calls it.

What holds us to these irrational beliefs, beliefs in the method used by science, is our human *psychological* make-up. Our psychology causes us to think irrationally and to hold beliefs not supported by evidence.

We can't help as 'scientists' believing such things that have no justification in experience or justification from reason.

It may also be perhaps that many can't help believing in an all-powerful god-like figure either, because of a particular psychology, so placing science and religion on a very similar (psychological) footing.

This idea that, like science, religious belief is also merely product of human psychology is examined in Part IIa.

Invitation to Immanuel Kant:-

Immanuel Kant (1724-1804), like David Hume (1711-1776), is another extremely important figure in the history of Western thought. It is generally agreed, incidentally, that there are four truly great philosophers, namely, Plato, Aristotle, Hume and Kant. Who to add to make it a 'top five', however, is often a matter of dispute. Many in the Anglo- American tradition say it must be Ludwig Wittgenstein. For reference, illustrations are provided at the end of the book.

Immanuel Kant was born in Königsburg, a city that became part of the Soviet Union via the Potsdam Conference arrangements at the end of World War II (and re-named Kaliningrad). Kant spent his life as an academic. His intellectual starting point was the disturbance in his thinking caused by the arguments of David Hume, some of which have just been outlined. He famously confesses that it was David Hume's thinking that interrupted his dogmatic slumber and awoke him to the need to find a new alternative to knowledge justified by reason or knowledge justified by experience, as Hume shows neither reason or experience provide support for some of our most firmly held beliefs. Neither supports, for example, the belief there is a world outside us and neither supports the (scientific) belief that knowledge can be gained via experimentation. [11]

The Analytic and the Synthetic:

Previously a distinction was made between *a priori* and *a posteriori* knowledge. It was explained that *a priori* knowledge is 'necessarily' true independently of or *prior* to experience (e.g. two things plus two things will always equal four things).

The truth of *a posteriori* knowledge, however, is 'contingent' and comes after or *post* experience (e.g 'Fire is associated with heat').

To understand Kant's response to Hume, two other terms are needed: 'analytic' and 'synthetic'.

'Analytic' statements are certain independently of experience; they are true *a priori*.

An analytic statement is also a 'tautology'. With a 'tautology', the predicate does not add anything to the subject. The predicate is contained in the subject. This is like Hume's 'relations of ideas': The statement 'X is X', for example, is a tautology. 'A bachelor is an unmarried man' is a tautology as well.

These analytic statements are *a priori* certain: they are true by definition. To deny them would be a logical contradiction (e.g., 'barking dogs do not bark' is a contradiction). Analytic (tautologies) do not, of course, tell us anything about reality – whether there actually are any barking dogs in existence.

'Synthetic' statements do add something to the subject; they are not tautological. For example the proposition that, 'Dogs bark'. Here, that they bark is added to the subject dog. It tells us something about dogs.

This is what Hume called 'matters of fact'. Denying that dogs bark is not a logical contradiction – it is logically possible that the world be such that in it something be a dog and not bark. Therefore, it is not true by definition that dogs bark. It seems that *experience* is needed to tell you whether dogs bark or not – it is *a posteriori*.

We can now say that analytic statements are true *a priori* but synthetic statements can only be true *a posteriori*.

Kant wants to ask, 'Is there a synthetic *a priori*?'

That is to say, is there a truth about the world, a synthetic statement about reality, that we can know independently of (prior to) experience? (Is there, in other words, a synthetic *a priori*?).

Kant's answer to his question is 'Yes'. He seems, therefore, to be adopting the rationalist position that reasoning alone can (*a priori*) provide at least some knowledge of reality.

This support for reason as a source of knowledge about the world, however, is not quite the whole story.

Kant's categories of the understanding:

Take the proposition that 'every event has a cause'. This is synthetic; it is not a tautology, true by definition.

Hume, however, showed that nothing in experience supports the truth of the proposition 'every event has a cause' either.

Is it then, as Hume suggests it must be (re. the application of his 'fork' test), nothing but sophistry and illusion, because it is not supported by reason or by experience.

Kant agrees with Hume that the principle 'every event has a cause' does not make its way into the mind via experience. Nevertheless, he does say that it is a 'category of understanding'.

Kant's way of considering 'every event has a cause' is to say that every event we experience in the world we have to experience in terms of causality. We cannot experience it any other way.

In this sense 'every event has a cause' (although synthetic and not an analytic tautology) is independent of and prior to experience. It is in other words *a priori*.

A 'category of understanding' here is a little like wearing blue tinted glasses which can't be taken off.

We *must* see everything as tinted blue. We *must* see everything in terms of cause and effect.

We must, according to Kant, also see everything in terms of other categories of understanding as well such as 'space' and 'time'.

All our experience is constructed in terms of space and time, but these concepts do not make their way into the mind via experience. They are given independently of and prior to experience; they are *a priori*. [12]

Just as you must experience an object as occupying space, so you cannot, for example, take away time. You must experience things as existing in time. These categories are given *prior* to experience, structure it and make it possible.

We *have* to experience in terms of space and time, and in terms of other categories such as cause and effect.

Kant and Certainty:

Kant's fundamental point, then, is to suggest that the mind does not *passively* receive information from the senses. Rather, the mind is *active* in the construction of experience itself.

The mind acts to impose a structure on the raw data of sensation and 'shapes' it into experience via categories of the understanding such as space, time and causality.

Because experience is in part shaped by the mind, we can know *a priori* (prior to any experience) that it will conform to the structure imposed on it by the mind – just as if you wear blue glasses you know that everything you will see will appear blue.

We know with absolute certainty, for example (*a priori*), that everything that we experience will occur in space and time, and in terms of cause and effect.

Kant points out as well that we need to *have* experience (of course) in order to know how such an experience is framed; to know there exist 'categories of understanding' and what those categories are.

The idea that we have *a priori* certain categories of experience (we know, for example, that all our experience will be in terms of space, time and cause and effect) puts Kant in the 'rationalist' camp.

However, his idea that all experience of reality is structured according these categories makes reference to 'empiricism'.

He seems to have pulled the two approaches of empiricism and rationalism together and allowed for the possibility of synthetic *a priori* knowledge (knowledge about the world *prior* to experience).

This knowledge includes such things as 'every event has a cause' and 'space and time exist'.

Kant described his radical solution to the problem of skepticism as a 'Copernican revolution in philosophy'. Until Copernicus (1473-1543), astronomers assumed that the earth was the center of the universe and the sun and all the other planets orbited around it. Copernicus revolutionized this field by asserting that it is only if we assume that the sun lies at the center and the planets move around this we can account for the observed movements of the planets.

In a similar way, Kant inverted the traditional assumptions of epistemology: Whereas all previous thinkers assumed that knowledge is the result of the conformity of our ideas to objects in the world, Kant shows that it is the objects which must conform to ideas in the mind (conform to the categories of understanding).

We can have *certain* knowledge of the world because this knowledge is something we construct. It is not therefore something 'internal' which has to correspond to something 'external' (the traditional approach which leaves room for the skeptic to raise doubts about ever attaining such a correspondence).

Phenomena and Noumena – The price of the Kantian 'solution':

Science and scientific method is not restored here by Kant after its drubbing at the hands of David Hume.

Kant's 'solution' to the problem of skepticism, comes at a price, a high price. We cannot take off our tinted glasses – the categories of understanding - to see what reality is *actually* like – we cannot know it as it is in itself.

Without these glasses, without categories of understanding, we would in effect be 'blind', unable to experience anything. We can only experience through our conceptual framework, through our *a priori* categories. We can only know reality as it *appears* to us as we experience it via our conceptual framework.

Kant calls this the 'phenomenal' world. Unfortunately, this means we and/ or science can know nothing of reality as it is in itself, what Kant calls the 'noumenal' world. We are always restricted to 'looking through' our conceptual categories.

3
KNOWLEDGE OF THE EXTERNAL WORLD

(What are the immediate objects of perception?)

Chapters one and two of this Part I Epistemology considered skepticism and attempts by empiricism and rationalism to overcome the skeptic's challenge that knowledge is not possible. This chapter three has a particular focus on skepticism with regard to knowledge of the external world. Rationalism, the operation of reason alone, has so far appeared to be able to establish very little about what exists in the external world. Empiricism and knowledge of the external world will now be a focus of attention.

Empiricists already referred to like David Hume will be mentioned here again, as will others including John Locke (1632-1704) and George Berkeley (1658-1753). History has regarded this trio Locke, Berkeley, Hume, as primary exponents of a 'British Empiricism'.

It may be of interest to note that Berkeley University in California is named after George Berkeley (and perhaps of further interest in that the buildings of Berkeley University, according to George Berkeley, could only exist as ideas in the mind).

Three types of empiricist attempt to justify knowledge claims as regards the external world will also be identified in this chapter. These three can be called, direct realism, indirect realism, and idealism.

Knowledge of the External World:-

The empiricist position is that knowledge of the external world is gained through one or more of the five senses of sight, hearing, touch, smell and taste. We formulate beliefs about the world based on information given to us by the senses. I believe there is a table in front of me, for example, because I can see it and I am resting on it.

This view of how we acquire knowledge of the world, however, raises a number of (skeptical) questions. Such include the following.

- Do we experience the external world 'directly' or 'indirectly' (via some intermediate objects of perception)?
- Is there any way we can be sure that the world actually is as it appears to us?
- What is our justification for our belief that objects we experience in the world continue to exist when we are not perceiving them?

There are two major approaches to knowledge of the external world, 'direct' realism (sometimes called 'naïve' realism) and 'indirect' realism (sometimes called 'representative' realism). Each is considered in succession below.

Direct Realism:

Realism is the view that there is a physical world that exists independently of human beings and objects continue to exist in the independent physical world whether or not we perceive them, or whether or not someone else perceives them. Objects are 'out there' waiting to be perceived by anyone.

'Direct' realism holds that the senses put us in *direct* contact with the world 'out there'. I am, for example, perceiving and in direct contact with the table in just in front of me.

I also think that the table here *is* as it appears to be – it appears solid, brown in color, rectangular etc. because it *is* solid, brown and rectangular.

Direct realism may, of course, be thought to be the commonsense view. It is what people normally think when they consider their interactions with the world (although by 'people' here we perhaps do not mean, say, neurologists or physicists).

Problems for the 'commonsense' direct realism view:

Direct realism can be challenged in some fairly damaging ways and, in this context, is referred to as 'naïve' realism. The key point is that there are some well-known aspects of experience which demonstrate we cannot be *directly* perceiving the world (i.e. we cannot be in *direct* contact with the world)

There are two key arguments that challenge the direct realism, commonsense, position. These are i) the 'argument from illusion' and ii) 'the time-lag argument'.

Both these arguments strongly suggest we perceive the world only *indirectly*. The immediate objects of perception are sense impressions or ideas and, at best, we might be able to say these are *caused* by the external world. It is only these intermediate sense impressions we perceive; we never directly experience the world, only the sense impressions or sense data (probably?) caused by the world.

i) 'Argument from illusion'

We have come across this before under skepticism in chapter one with Sextus Empiricus and with Descartes, especially his dream argument. When we have dreams we have the experience of seeing and interacting with objects in the external world, but those objects are not really there. Furthermore, the fact that we think an object is there before us in, say, a dream is precisely because the experience is the *same* as seeing the object when awake and not dreaming.

There seems to be no difference between seeing an object when it is not there in a dream and seeing an object when it is there when awake and not dreaming.

A similar point can be made via the phenomenon of 'phantom limbs'. People who have had to have an amputation of their arm or leg or whatever often continue to feel sensations, such as itches, aches, sometimes extreme pain etc., afterwards 'in' the limb that is no longer there.

There is seemingly is no difference in the experience of itches and/or aches in a limb that is there and one that is *not* there because of amputation.

In both these cases, and with illusions in general, I cannot *directly* be perceiving an object because that object is not there. Yet I still have the experience of perceiving the object, and I think I am experiencing the object.

In both the above cases, and with illusions in general, I must be experiencing something that is 'within me' as there is nothing 'out there' equivalent to it, and I cannot tell the difference between what is just 'within me' and what is 'out there'. This is what makes it an illusion.

We are fooled by illusions because we cannot tell the difference between sense perceptions of objects when they *are* 'out there' and sense perceptions of objects when they are *not*.

The most plausible way of explaining such illusions is to say that sense perceptions are *always* 'within us'. This is what we are directly aware of all the time. Sometimes our sense perceptions are caused by what is 'out there' and sometimes they are not, so accounting for the phenomenon of illusions.

One more example: If a straight stick is placed at an angle standing out of a bowl of water, viewing from a certain position this stick appears bent. The point here is that the stick is not bent, although it is perceived as bent. Therefore the stick cannot be being perceived *directly*. It seems then, because the stick is not being perceived directly (as it appears bent when it is known to be straight), perception must be of something 'between' the perceiver and the actual (straight) stick.

To put it another way, when you are holding a (straight) stick outside a bowl of water you might initially think you directly perceive the stick. When it is placed it in the water, however, it appears to bend and so you know you are not then directly aware of the (straight) stick, as it is not bending.

It is most plausible here to conclude from this stick in the water example that we are only ever aware of sense impressions, and sometimes these accurately represent the objects out there (e.g., a straight stick) and sometimes they do not (e.g. bent stick), leading to illusions like a bent stick in water.

Otherwise we have to explain the events like the illusion of the bent stick in water by suggesting that we are directly aware of the physical (straight) stick before it enters the water and then somehow *switch* to being only directly aware of a mental representation of it *after* it enters the water (and then we switch back again when we pull the stick out of the water).

ii) 'The Time Lag Argument'

This second argument against the view that we *directly* perceive the world requires that we hold (at least partly) the scientific explanation of light and time.

Accepting this, it may be said that light travels at about 186,000 miles per second and so, for instance, it takes about 8 minutes to reach us from the sun. The sun we see, then, is really 8 minutes old. Given the speed of light the sun will always be about 8 minutes old when we see it.

As a consequence, it is impossible for us to *directly* perceive the sun. Direct realism must therefore be false with respect to the sun.

In addition, given that there will always be a time lag of some length (however miniscule) because of the presumed 'gap' between us and objects via which light has to travel, direct realism must be false with regard to *all* (sight) perceptions of the external world.

As with the argument from illusion, this time lag argument demonstrates that it is possible to have a sense impression of something that does not exist. You may, for example, now be looking at a sun that burnt out 8 minutes ago. We again seem to be *directly* aware of mental sense impressions (e.g. of the sun) and not *directly* aware of the objects which (probably?) cause them, such as the actual sun.

We thus appear only to experience the external world *indirectly*, through sense impressions. The (disturbing?) implications for any scientific investigation of reality are perhaps beginning to dawn. How can reality be investigated when we are not actually directly contact with it, only our sense impressions?

Indirect Realism:

This is sometimes known as 'representative' realism. Its starting point is that direct realism is false. We do not immediately perceive objects in the word; our experience of the world takes place 'through' (i.e. is mediated by) sense impressions or sense data so we can only experience the world *indirectly*.

Representative realism is still a form of *realism* because it accepts that there is an external world that exists independently of human beings; objects in an external world are 'out there' waiting to be perceived by anyone.

It is *representative* because it holds that the sense impressions that we experience *represent* what is out there in the physical world. The representative realist would hold that when I see the table in front of me, I do not have direct sensory contact with it. Rather, what I experience is an inner representation of the table.

Indirect/representative realism has an advantage over direct realism in that it is not open to attack by the 'argument from illusion' or the 'time lag argument' both described above.

Direct realism falls foul of the argument from illusion and the time lag argument because in both cases we can experience objects we are not in direct contact with; we can see things that are not there such as a bent stick or a planet/object that no longer exists (so we can't be *directly* perceiving those things).

For the indirect realist, however, the 'argument from illusion' and the 'time lag argument' pose little problem. This is because at any time all we are directly in contact with are sense impressions, inner representations. These might or might *not* have associated objects in the external world that are causing them at a particular moment.

A further support for indirect realism over direct realism is the existence of what can be called 'perceptual variation'.

Indirect realism supported by 'perceptual variation':

David Hume (1711-1776), in particular, makes clear that the existence of perceptual variation means that we cannot be directly aware of external objects, so giving extra support to the indirect realism view.

Hume's argument here runs as follows:

Perceptual variation suggests the object we are aware of appears to change. E.g., as we change our position on viewing a table, we experience size and shape changes (the table appearing to become smaller as we move away etc.).

The real external object does not change (the table does not really become smaller as we move away).

Therefore, we cannot be directly aware of the object (e.g., unchanging table) but must only be directly aware of 'perceptions in the mind' as Hume terms them. [13]

More evidence comes from an example put forward by John Locke (1632-1704)

Suppose you place 2 bowls of water in front of you, one containing cold water and one containing warmer water. If you place your right hand in the cold water and your left hand in your pocket and then place both hands in the bowl of warmer water the temperature of the water should feel hotter to the right hand and colder to the left hand.

The point here is that the actual water in the bowl is not both cold and warm at the same time, but you sense it is warm *and* that it is cool. Our perceptions of the temperature of the water can therefore vary depending upon the circumstances we are in.

Other examples are easy to find. A strawberry, for instance, can taste bitter after eating something sweet and sweet after eating something bitter. We can, then, experience the *same* thing differently at different times and in different circumstances.

This phenomenon of 'perceptual variation' supports the indirect/representative realism position against the direct realism view.

Just because a thing feels, tastes, or looks a certain way etc., does not now mean, because of the existence of the possibility of perceptual variation, that the thing actually possesses these qualities.

Our experience of the external world is only indirect, mediated by our (sometimes conflicting) sense impressions of it. The actual water in the bowl in the external world situation above cannot be understood as being 'out there' as both hot *and* cold in the same moment.

It is just our sense impressions of hotness and our sense impressions of coldness that we are aware of - not an actual object that is both hot *and* cold in the same moment.

Sense data:

The term 'sense impressions' has generally been used so far to describe what we are immediately aware of in our minds (feelings of hotness or coldness etc.). In this we are following David Hume, but you may run across alternative terminologies for the same concept. While Hume uses the term 'impressions,' John Locke (1632-1704) uses the word 'ideas' as does George Berkeley (1658-1753).

Recent debates in this area, following Bertrand Russell (1872-1970) have used the term 'sense data'. So we can have 'sense impressions', 'ideas', and 'sense data'; all being alternative terms for exactly the same thing – the immediate objects of perception in our minds under the indirect realism position.

What we 'see' then is sense data e.g., a certain pattern of colors and shapes etc., and we also *have* a sensation of seeing the sense data, a certain pattern of colors and shapes etc. In terms of 'perceptual variation', the key point is that from different viewpoints I 'see' different sense data as regards, say, a table (i.e. I have 'perceptual variation'). That sense data cannot, however, be identical with the physical object because it (the table) is unchanging.

Primary and Secondary Qualities:

One problem for indirect realism is that it lets in skepticism about the external world. If all we are directly aware of are sense impressions/sense data, to what extent can we know that objects in the world correspond to these impressions, or if there are any objects 'out there' at all causing the impressions?

Given that, in indirect realism, we are directly aware only of our inner sense impressions/sense data, we cannot step outside these to see when, or if at all, they match up with the external world – or find out if there is actually an external world at all beyond our sense impressions.

If indirect realism is an accurate portrayal of how perception operates, then any scientific project that attempts to describe and understand reality 'out there' is doomed from the start since we cannot get beyond sense impressions to what might or might not be 'out there' in the external world.

The major problem is that natural science in most cases *does* want to say that we perceive the world only *indirectly* – natural science does want to say that we are only directly aware of sense impressions in the mind, *not* actual properties of objects in the world.

Natural science also wants, though, to describe and understand reality *outside* our sense impressions. This seems a non-starter, as, by definition, we only have sense impressions to examine.

One response offered by the 'scientific' indirect realist against this skepticism is to distinguish between what are called 'primary' and 'secondary' qualities.

Primary qualities are said to really belong to objects in the external world, but secondary qualities are only products of our minds.

So the primary qualities of objects in the world can be described and understood, but the secondary qualities cannot – since these only exist in the mind.

This, primary-secondary quality distinction finds support in the early 18th century conception of the external world provided by John Locke (1632-1704). Locke sets out the distinction clearly noting that primary qualities of an object, and actually 'in' that object, include extension in space, a shape, a number/ amount. Examples of secondary qualities are colors, sounds, tastes and these are not actually in objects. [14]

This distinction between primary and secondary qualities can be used to avoid the perceptual variation argument against direct realism, mentioned above - objects 'out there' like water mentioned above *cannot* be both hot and cold at the same moment.

Sense impressions of water *can* indicate hot and cold at the same moment, so perception must be of sense impressions not actual objects being hot and cold at the same moment. This is because hotness and coldness are 'secondary' qualities.

To continue on this theme, we saw above that it is possible that, say, a single strawberry can taste both bitter *and* sweet (as water can feel hot *and* cold) to the same person. Secondary qualities are like this. They are qualities such as taste, how the object feels, its color, temperature, smell, etc. They can vary from circumstance to circumstance.

Primary qualities, however, are properties that always seem to be in the object no matter what the circumstance or who the perceiver is. Non-human animals, for example, will sense an object differently than us in terms secondary qualities such as, say, smell, but even to an animal that object will <u>occupy space</u>, will have some kind of <u>shape</u> and be of a certain <u>number</u>.

A strawberry can taste both bitter and sweet depending on the circumstances, but it *always* <u>occupies space</u> (it excludes other things from where it is). It also has a <u>shape</u> (of some type) and it also <u>has</u> a <u>number</u> (one in this case).

The natural science view, then, is that an object really has these primary qualities, but secondary qualities depend upon the circumstances of the perceiver and type of perceiver (human, non-human etc.).

It follows, therefore, that an object can be said to *always* possess its primary qualities whatever the circumstances of its perception, or whether the object it is being perceived at all.

Thus, in response to the skeptic, the scientific indirect realist claims that the sense impressions or sense data of primary qualities of objects in the external world *do* correspond to properties actually in those objects. It is only the sense impressions/sense data of secondary qualities that not so correspond with properties actually in the objects 'out there'. Alfred North Whitehead (1861-1947) remarks that the natural world is a dull affair having no sound, no color and no scent. Birds have no song in reality, flowers have no smell in reality – color, scent and sound are merely the offspring of the human mind.[15]

Problems for Primary Qualities and Indirect Realism:

i) Skepticism regarding the existence of the external world

The move to the primary qualities (properties actually in the external world) causing secondary qualities (existing only the mind) does not save indirect realism from the challenge of skepticism about knowledge of the external world.

It *still* remains for indirect realism that all we are directly aware of are sense impressions or sense data, whether they be of secondary *or* primary qualities.

We cannot, in principle, get beyond our sensory impressions (of primary *or* secondary qualities) to see if they correspond to the external world or if there is an external world at all 'beyond' the sense impressions causing those impressions.

We cannot justify the scientific position that primary qualities are really in objects (while secondary qualities are not) because (as natural science also holds) *all* are still sense data, and we cannot step outside sense data to compare it with what actually exists – sense data will just be replaced by more sense data be it impressions of primary or secondary qualities.

A 'scientific' defense of the position that there exists an external world of primary qualities causing our perceptions of such *and* causing our perceptions of secondary qualities is to claim it is the 'best hypothesis' to explain the facts of experience – the hypothesis of a 'causal' external world of primary qualities.

It may not be a certainty, but resort to the existence of an external world of primary qualities causing our ideas of that external world maybe the best way of explaining the facts of experience.

i) Is the existence on an external world of primary qualities the best hypothesis to explain the facts of experience?

One of the facts explained by the hypothesis of a causal external world of primary qualities is that sense impressions arise <u>independently of our will</u>.

When we open our eyes in daylight it is not in our power to choose whether we see anything or not, or smell anything or not or hear anything or not; sense impressions just seem to enter in. This strongly suggests that the causes of such sense impressions lie outside us.

Impressions of secondary qualities seems to vary, unlike primary qualities, so making the hypothesis that there is an external world of primary qualities causing our sense impressions (of primary and secondary qualities) seem plausible.

In addition to the fact that these experiences arise independently of our will, the fact of the <u>regularity and consistency</u> of our experiences also supports the hypothesis of an external world causing our sense impressions (of primary qualities and of secondary qualities via primary qualities). Bertrand Russell attempts to show how the existence of the external world causing our ideas of it is the best hypothesis to account for the regularity and consistency of sense impressions/sense data. If a cat, say, exists whether it is perceived or not, we can understand from experience how it gets hungry between meals. But if it does not exist when not perceived it cannot become hungry. This is because the cat and its hunger are purely sense data and sense data can no more be hungry than a triangle can play football. [16]

Either the cause of our sense impressions/sense data lies within our minds or lies in a world external to us. The arguments above suggest that the best hypothesis to account for our sense impressions is the latter.

Not only do we seem to have no power over when ideas of the external world enter in, it also seems much more plausible than not accepting the regularity and consistency of our experiences is also determined by an external world; more plausible to believe that our sense impressions are caused by physical objects 'out there' which continue to exist when we are not perceiving them, rather than those objects popping in and out of existence.

ii) Skepticism regarding the nature of the external world (still a problem for science?)

A problem for (scientific) indirect realism still remains. Scientific indirect realism wants to hold, not only that there is an external world which causes our ideas of it, but *also* that this external world is like the way we perceive it – at least with regard to its primary qualities. Nevertheless, even if we accept the existence of the external world as the best hypothesis to account for our sense impressions/sense data, there still remains the problem of investigating this world and knowing just what it is actually like: How can we find out what the world outside our mental sense impressions is really like, since all we have are sense impressions/sense data? Even if we are not in control of when such impressions arise, so suggesting they have an external cause, it still seems impossible to know if our impressions of what is 'out there' actually *represent* what is really 'out there', since (either as scientists or non-scientists) we cannot, in principle, get beyond our mental impressions to see if they match up with the causes of those impressions.

The fact of a barrier to what can be known is perhaps brings to mind again Immanuel Kant's analysis described at the end of the previous chapter. He too had a barrier to what can be known. The world at it is in itself, the 'noumenal' world, forever remains beyond what can be established by investigation, be it a scientific investigation or otherwise.

It would seem, then, that if we accept the dual (scientific) premises that

1. there is an external world *and*
2. we only experience that external world indirectly via our senses,

Then we cannot, in principle, bridge the 'gap' between the way things appear to us and the way they really are.

In order to overcome these skeptical consequences of (scientific) indirect realism one of the above two premises must be rejected. Either we must reject premise 1 the hypothesis that there is a world beyond our sense impressions *or* we must reject premise 2 by saying that *direct* realism is right (that we *do* perceive the external world directly, not just indirectly).

To embrace the latter entails a return to direct/naïve realism and the problems associated with this theory (e.g. the argument from illusion and the time lag argument mentioned previously).

Acceptance of the former, i.e., rejecting the hypothesis that there is an external world, leads us into rejecting 'realism', and to the sphere of *anti*-realism.

Anti-realism the view there is in fact no external world which exists independently of the perceiver, and no perceiver means no external world. It could all be a mental creation rather like the demons, personal voices and other hallucinations experienced by schizophrenics.

Schizophrenics perceive such visual and audible hallucinations as real. There is a regularity to their experience, and the voices etc. are caused by something outside of them, when in fact these are purely a mental creation. Is, then, *anti*-realism correct; are we like schizophrenics and their certain beliefs that the voices and other hallucinations are caused by a reality external to them (as is illustrated quite well by the movie 'Beautiful Mind')?

One famous *anti*-realist theory is known as 'Idealism' and perhaps its most well-known exponent is George Berkeley (1658-1753), whose name is given to the Berkeley University in California. Berkeley's version of Idealism is examined in the following chapter.

4

IDEALISM

(Can physicality only exist in the mind?)

It is sometimes casually written that George Berkeley is not an empiricist like Hume and Locke but rather an exponent of Idealism. This demonstrates a lack of understanding of empiricism and it is false. As empiricists, Locke, Hume and Berkeley start from the point that all that is known about what exists comes from experience and we have, therefore, to examine our experience to find out what we know. Furthermore, if something claimed to be known about what exists cannot be found in experience, that claim as no foundation - and should be 'committed to the flames' as Hume puts it.

Berkeley, then, like Hume and Locke, is in the business of examining experience, to find out what can be known. It follows, therefore, if there is no experience of a world outside our mental sense impressions, then claims to know the existence and content of such a world must also be 'committed to the flames'.

In the previous chapter theories of direct/naïve realism and indirect/ representative realism were considered. The common word *realism* in here refers to the fact that both maintain that the there is a world 'out there' waiting for us to perceive it with our minds.

Direct realism is the view that we directly perceive this external world. It was shown, though, how direct realism finds it difficult to account for the phenomena of illusions and of time lags. Indirect realism holds that there is an external world but we perceive it only indirectly via sense impressions/ sense data - and because of this it could (unlike direct realism) account for the phenomena of perceptual illusions and of time lags.

A problem exposed for indirect realism was that it is vulnerable to a skeptical attack on knowledge of the external world. If, as the indirect realist posits, all we are ever directly aware of is sense impressions/sense data, getting outside these to find out if they actually correspond to the external world or to find out if there is an external world 'out there' at all beyond our sense perceptions seems impossible.

The scientific view that there is an external world out there, but the immediate objects of perception are sense impressions (we only perceive it indirectly) creates the problem that, in principle, the real world as it is in itself can never be fully investigated, since all that can be experienced are sense impressions/ sense data.

One way of side-stepping the skeptic here is simply to say that there is no external world 'out there' independent of our thinking about it. To argue, in other words, that human minds and their ideas are all there is. There cannot now be any skeptical problem of trying to find a way of matching the external world to our ideas of it, since all there is are ideas. This is Berkeley's approach. The issue for an empiricist like Berkeley here is whether or not this denial of the existence of anything outside our minds and their ideas is supported by what is contained in experience.

The denial of the existence of an external world outside our mind is called *anti*-realism and the claim that all that exists are minds and their ideas is called 'Idealism'.

George Berkeley (1658-1753) notes that perceptions of things are clearly ideas of things and ideas cannot exist without minds. [17]. Berkeley moves from this point to, on empiricist grounds, argue that all we know that exists, therefore, are ideas and minds.

Berkeley's argument here runs as follows:

- Ideas exist only in minds (ideas cannot exist without a mind)
- All things we experience are ideas (they are perceptions of, for example, wood, stone, fire, water. . .)

Therefore, (based, on strict empiricist principles) all things we experience (as ideas) can only be said to exist in the mind and not outside it.

This is all the evidence of experience allows us to conclude – that we have ideas (or 'mental impressions')

Berkeley's idealism, then, is based squarely on empiricist principles - what is known depends entirely upon experience. We experience that we have *ideas* of wood, stone, fire, water etc. (i.e., the *idea* of objects in the external world), and this is all we experience, just our ideas of these things.

Berkeley's rejection of the primary-secondary quality distinction:

The (scientific) primary-secondary quality distinction, as described in the previous chapter, holds that secondary qualities such as taste, how the object feels, color, smell, etc. are not in actually in the external world, just in the mind. Primary qualities, on the other hand, like extension in space and shape and number, *are* regarded as part of the external world outside the mind, and these cause the sensations of secondary qualities.

Berkeley's idealism, then, since he wants to say all that our experience can support as existing are ideas in minds, requires him to reject the (scientific) position that the primary qualities in experience exist outside the mind and it is only secondary qualities that do not exist outside the mind).

It was noted previously that the fact that same water can in one moment appear warm to one hand and cold to another means, via the argument from 'perceptual variation', that these temperatures could not both be in the water because the water in itself could not, at the same moment, be cold *and* hot (only our inner *perceptions* can suggest it is cold *and* hot in the same moment).

Berkeley is suggests, however, that primary qualities are *also* open to the very same 'perceptual variation' argument. [18]

Shape, for example, he thinks can be dismissed as actually in the object in exactly the same way as temperatures. So, if the secondary quality temperature is not in the object, then neither is the primary quality shape.

The shape of an object varies with the circumstances of our perspective, such as how close or how far away we are. Therefore, analogous to the water temperature example just given, such an object cannot be many different shapes at a moment in time, just like it cannot be both hot and cold a moment in time. It therefore follows that, if the 'secondary' quality of temperature is dismissed as being in the object on these 'perceptual variation' grounds, then so must the 'primary' quality of shape be dismissed as being in the object.

There are an infinite number of perspectives and so, like secondary qualities, all primary qualities (such as size, position etc.) are also relative to the circumstances the perceiver is in. If the 'perceptual variation' argument establishes that secondary qualities are not in the external world but only in the mind, then it must also establish that (so called) primary qualities are not in the external world but only in the mind as well. And this, of course, is Berkeley's view. All that experience supports as having existence are ideas in minds - and primary qualities, like secondary qualities are also ideas in minds.

It follows from this that the (scientific) idea primary qualities exist in reality and secondary qualities do not is exposed as being without empirical foundation, along with the associated (scientific) notion that it is the primary qualities that cause in us impressions of secondary qualities and cause impressions of themselves.

Some Strengths of Idealism:

i) A reconciliation of direct and indirect realism

Berkeley's idealism is able to reconcile the apparently competing views of direct and indirect realism. This is because it agrees with the direct realists that we do indeed *directly* perceive the external world, *and* it holds with the indirect realists that all we directly perceive are ideas (sense impressions/sense data) in our minds. What we call the external world is directly perceived but what we call the external world is also just is a collection of ideas.

ii) A rejection of skepticism as regards knowledge of the external world

As mentioned above, there need be no skepticism about our normal beliefs under idealism. If, for example, I believe I perceive a tree, then there is an idea of a tree, and there is no room for doubt about it. The skeptic can only mount an attack as regards not knowing what the tree 'out there' is really like if it is assumed that the idea of a tree corresponds to or represents something outside the idea of a tree. But no 'gap' now exists between my idea of a tree and a supposed actual tree; there is just my idea of a tree.

iii) Idealism fits with commonsense

The world is just as we experience it to be. The only difference is that the world consists of ideas; it is mental not physical. This is all the evidence of the content of experience supports.

George Berkeley (1685-1753) was mocked by his illustrious contemporary Dr Samuel Johnson (1709-1784) who famously attempted to demonstrate that idealism did not fit with commonsense by kicking a stone and saying "I refute it thus!". This, of course, suggests that Johnson did not understand Berkeley's idealism. The *idea* of kicking a stone is all Dr Johnson has in his experience and all that can be said based on his experience. Nothing in experience allows him to go beyond this to a stone existing outside the experienced idea of a stone. Berkeley would say that kicking the stone, of feeling the stone against your foot is, like everything else, an idea in the mind - and this idea that might well be followed by another consistent with it such as the idea of pain in the toe.

Idealism and illusions:

Direct realism find it difficult to account for illusions and hallucinations. It seems we cannot be *directly* aware of the external world because sometimes we believe (have ideas that) objects in it are there when they can't possibly be.

Illusions exist in experience, so idealism has to account for them as well. It would seem this is going to be difficult since illusions arise when ideas don't correspond with the real world, and idealism does away with a real world outside our ideas of it (as such is not supported by the evidence of experience).

If I am directly aware of my ideas of objects, and ideas are all there are, how (in idealist terms) can illusions be explained? How can we have an illusory idea of an idea?

Berkeley has an answer.

When perceiving the table in front of me, for instance, I can see that its shape changes as I move around it (e.g., it looks rectangular from above but various types of trapezoid from other points of view). After a little experience of this I can predict and expect these shape changes. There is no discontinuity in the changes; the 'right' one always follows its former, the shapes do not suddenly leap out at me in a surprising way.

The series of my sense experiences of seeing the table follows a pattern. If I combine this with the series of experiences from my other senses such as touch, I soon can put together a large 'family' of interconnected sense experiences. These families of sense impressions are what I generally experience and the table in front of me is just one very particular family, a particular object.

Illusions, Berkeley points out, are just sense impressions that do not belong properly to a particular family. If, for example, in addition to my normal ideas of a the table in front of me I have the experience of passing my hand through it, this would not 'fit' in with the family of beliefs and I would be inclined to think there is something amiss – inclined to think that the table is not really here in front of me in the same way that it usually is.

Truth and Coherence:

Berkeley's explanation of illusions, as not really fitting with a family of experiences, also points to a different way of looking at 'truth'.

For the 'indirect' realist the belief in the existence of the table in front of me is a *true* one (and not, say, an illusion or false one) if actually, in the external world, there *is* a table in front of me – if, in other words, the belief *corresponds* to the actual world. For an idealist like Berkeley, though, my belief/idea that there is a table in front of me is true (and not, say, an illusion) depends internally upon whether or not it 'fits' or *coheres* with my other (families of) beliefs.

The requirement of *correspondence*, it may be remembered, is why indirect realism was left open to attack from skepticism because of the apparent impossibility of stepping 'outside' sense experiences to find out if they do actually *correspond* to the external world.

Berkeley's idealism avoids this skeptical attack, though, because under it he never has to step 'outside' sense experiences to search for correspondence with something beyond those impressions; he only needs to look at a sense experience to see if it 'fits' or *coheres* with others.

'To be is to be perceived' and the external world hypothesis:

For Berkeley, the idealist, physical objects are simply collections or families of ideas. But, like all thoughts, ideas or experiences they can only 'be' when they exist in a mind. If physical objects are experiences and experiences are purely mental, it follows that if there are no experiences (ideas of) physical objects, there are no physical objects. 'To be, therefore, is to be perceived' or *esse est percipi* as Berkeley puts it.

It appears from this definition of existence that if I am not thinking about a physical object (or someone else is) it does not exist. If I go out of the room to make a cup of coffee the table in front of me, on Berkeley's definition of existence, must cease to exist until I return and have an idea about it again.

This takes us back to Bertrand Russell's 'best hypothesis' point described in the previous chapter – the argument that the existence of an external world outside our ideas of it was the 'best hypothesis' to account for the facts of experience; that accepting that an object in the external world, a cat say, continues to exist when I am not thinking about it is the most plausible hypothesis to account for the facts of the regularity and consistency of our subjective experiences of that cat. Berkeley's Idealism looks in danger of not being the best hypothesis to account for the regularity and consistency of our experiences.

Berkeley is well aware of this problem, but he maintains that to be is to be perceived by some mind. Consequently, if an object is are not being perceived, and objects must continue to exist when not perceived, it can only be that objects are being perceived by some *other mind* in order to exist. That other mind, for (Bishop) Berkeley can only be the mind of God.

For Berkeley the cause of all our ideas can only be God as ideas themselves have no causal powers; they are just ideas. God must therefore act directly on all our minds, ensuring the regularity and consistency of experiences for ourselves and for others – acting something like a satellite broadcasting the same program to billions of televisions.

Berkeley argues, then, that objects cannot continue to exist when unperceived by a mind, so if they are not perceived by a human mind, and they continue to exist, they must be being perceived by a non-human mind. God (a non-human mind) must constantly perceive all of the ideas that constitute the world. Physical objects simply are ideas in the mind of God. This view has been expressed in a well-known limerick by theologian Ronald Knox (1888-1957):

There was a young man who said, 'God,
I find it exceedingly odd
That this tree I see should
Continue to be
When there's no one about in the Quad.'

Reply:-

'Dear Sir,
Your astonishment's odd:
I am always about in the Quad.
And that's why the tree

Will continue to be
Since observed by
Yours faithfully,
God.'

Some Problems for Idealism:

i) God Problems

Berkeley's idealism is ostensibly grounded in empiricism, the view that all knowledge of the world is gained via experience. He argues like David Hume that we do not *experience* any objects lying outside our ideas of them which *cause* such ideas. Since we do not experience such objects causing our ideas, we are not (on empiricist grounds) justified in saying we have knowledge of the causes of our ideas.

Berkeley's key point, then, is that in our experience we just have ideas of objects. That's as much as we can say about it and, indeed, all we need to say about it.

Berkeley's resorting to God, however, to account for the regularity and consistency of experience (as noted above) seems to violate his empiricist principles.

Our experiences consist of ideas and we may even have an idea of God. But Berkeley is arguing that God exists outside our ideas and is the *cause* of such ideas. This goes beyond the information given in experience.

Berkeley might instead, as Bertrand Russell did, employ the (best?) hypothesis of actual material objects in an external world *causing* our ideas of them rather than resorting to God.

Using 'God' as the best hypothesis to explain the cause of our ideas also has a problem that using the 'objects in an external world causing out ideas' (best?) hypothesis to explain the cause of our ideas does not have.

This additional problem is that there still remains a 'gap' between our ideas and ideas in God's mind. Our perceptions vary depending upon circumstances. For God, however, perceptions do not presumably vary since, for example, He does not have our limited perceptual apparatus. Therefore, ideas in my mind of objects may not be the same as God's ideas of those objects.

If my ideas are supposed to be 'copies' of God's ideas (albeit inferior copies) then the skeptical problems of indirect realism arise again. We saw how the skeptic could say of the indirect realist, that he/she cannot in principle know that ideas of the external world actually represent the external world, since he/she cannot stand outside them to see if they correspond.

Similarly, the skeptic can, it seems, now *equally* say of Berkeley, that he cannot in principle know his ideas actually represent God's ideas, since he cannot stand outside them to see if they correspond.

ii) 'To be is to be perceived' problem

Berkeley argues that ideas of physical objects cannot be anything other than mental. Experience tells us that an idea of a material object is just that, an idea - without the idea of the material object, there would be no such object – *to be is to be perceived*. Bertrand Russell suggests that this is reasoning is wrong and is based on a misunderstanding.

Perceiving an object as existing is a mental act, but this need not mean that that object is purely mental, and only exists as such. [19]

It is still possible, therefore, that without the idea/perception of a material object, there could exist the object. It may very well be that to exist (to be) in the mind alone is to be perceived – this is an *act* of perception which must be in the mind. However, to exist (to be) as an *object* of perception, it need not be in the mind at all.

Berkeley, is perhaps mixing the an act of perception (which must be mental) with the object of perception (which may not be).

iii) Skepticism about minds problem

Berkeley's arguments denying the existence of a material world could also be used to deny the existence of minds, although ideas in minds are all he wants to exist. Berkeley points out that we have no experience of an external world (only ideas of objects) so we are not justified on empiricist grounds for claiming it exists beyond our ideas.

We saw in chapter 2, however, how David Hume demonstrates we also have no experience of mind either. As a consequence, we also, on empiricist grounds, have no justification for claiming mind exists as well.

It may be remembered that Hume pointed out that if we introspect we find in our experience only fleeting ideas, not 'minds' having those ideas; all we experience are 'bundles' of ideas.

Furthermore, since we also have no (empiricist) reasons to say that ideas belong to minds (we only experience ideas not minds), then there is no need to suppose as Berkeley does that God, the infinite mind, must also exist to have these ideas when we are not attending to them.

iv) Coherence as a criterion of truth problem

For Berkeley my belief/idea that there is a table in front of me is true and not, say, an illusion depends internally upon whether or not it 'fits' with my other (families of) beliefs; whether, that is, the belief *coheres* with my other beliefs.

This, as was noted above, contrasts with the representative realist view of truth as 'correspondence'; i.e., my belief that 'there is a table in front of me' is true and not, say, an illusion if actually in the external world there is a table in front of me – if the belief *corresponds* to the actual world. Coherence as a criterion of truth, however, seems always in danger of collapsing into correspondence.

The sets of beliefs of competing religions, for example, might be thought to each to amount to coherent sets of beliefs because each set 'fits' together. How then can we decide between, say, the truths of different (coherent) religions?

Are we not forced, on such occasions, to slip back into *correspondence* as a criterion? Must the 'true' religion be the one which corresponds with how things actually are?

Furthermore, many coherent networks of scientific explanation which have worked effectively in past ages have been rejected precisely upon these grounds, i.e., that they do not correspond to the way things actually are - the challenge of quantum mechanics to general relativity theory for example, and before this the challenge of general relativity to Newtonian physics.

5

DEFINING KNOWLEDGE

(What is it to know something?)

Difficulties with knowledge and science:-

A number of problems have been exposed so far in this Part I Epistemology as regards a standard science-based approach to knowledge.

David Hume, for example, has shown us that knowledge of what 'causes' what cannot be established via scientific experimental method. This is because science requires that claims to 'knowledge' should be based on the evidence of experience (as opposed to, say, faith).

Hume reveals that there no *experience* of 'causation', only regular conjunctions (perhaps arising from multiple controlled experiments) and nothing in experience establishes that a regular conjunction will continue into the future.

Any (scientific) view that a law-like relation will continue into the future must be more a matter of faith and so is perhaps an 'Induction Delusion', if faith in God can be described as a 'God Delusion'.

Science has also been shown to hold propositions that appear to make it impossible to carry out its project of investigating reality. It holds that experience of reality is not direct; we only experience it indirectly via sense data or sense impressions. If we are locked into sense impressions, it does not seem possible to then examine what is causing these sense impressions.

In the absence of any direct contact with reality it appears impossible to say it is 'known' that the data of sense (which can perhaps be divided into primary and secondary qualities) are generated by primary qualities. It also seems, for the same (lack of any direct access) reason, impossible to say that it is 'known' primary qualities exist outside us (unlike secondary qualities), and impossible to say it is 'known' that in such a reality is composed of atoms and the (causal?) relations between them.

At the quantum level it is said that electrons 'in' atoms 'leap' to 'nowhere' and come back from 'nowhere' defying human logic, and with it, it seems, the power of human thinking. If contradictions are allowed, then something can be *and* not be, or can 'be' here *and* 'be' nowhere at the same time. 'Knowledge' of what is the case in reality does not seem possible if logic has to be abandoned.

An underlying question arising from all these problems (and more) is 'what actually is knowledge?' It would appear we need to investigate more closely what knowledge can be and what knowledge must be in order to properly judge if knowledge is going to be possible; possible via means of science or via means religion or via some other endeavor (art perhaps?). This and related issues are now considered.

What is knowledge?

This is a good example of a 'difficult question' of the type alluded to in the introduction to this book. It is a question that has largely been left in philosophy while various disciplines push on and go about the business of claiming they have found knowledge in various areas and criticizing others for not really having gained knowledge in different or the same areas.

The 'hardest' sciences criticize 'softer' sciences, Ernest Rutherford, for example, is quoted as saying that, "all science is either physics or stamp collecting". And science, in general, often criticizes religious claims to knowledge.

All Such criticisms tend to carry different presuppositions of what knowledge and its acquisition is. The question 'What is knowledge?' perhaps then needs to be considered 'philosophically'. Considered, not simply to find the answer (as the answer is not always easy to find), but at also to understand what an answer might look like and what it can and cannot be.

We have seen previously how skepticism exposes weaknesses in normal thinking about what is generally held to be known. David Hume, in particular, offers strong arguments in support of the view that much of what we think we know best, or claim to know best, we do not really have 'knowledge' of because it is not based on the evidence of experience. The existence of much of what we normally take to be objects and activities in the external world for instance.

Types of knowledge:

In an effort to establish what knowledge is, the existence of different types of knowledge needs to be appreciated. Three of these types are as follows

1. Knowing *that* or 'propositional' knowledge: knowing *that* something is the case such as, I know *that* 2 + 2 = 4, or *that* London is the capital of England.
2. Knowing *how* or 'skills' knowledge: knowing *how* to do something: for example, I know *how* to ride a bicycle, or *how* to play chess.
3. Knowing *of* or Knowledge by 'acquaintance': knowledge *of* something or someone: for example, I might say that I know Peter, or that I know London.

The type knowledge under consideration as regards a description of reality is 'propositional' knowledge. What we want to find out, in particular, given the core themes of this book, is what it is to 'know' *that* something is the case — *that* something in the external world exists, for instance, or *that* it is round, or *that* I exist and so forth.

Defining knowledge - 'truth', 'belief' and 'justification':-

Standard definitions of knowledge, generally emanate from Plato and make use of the concepts of 'truth', 'belief' and 'justification'.

Truth:

For a claim to be counted as 'knowledge' it *must* be true.

I may confidently assert I *know* that Lagos is the capital of Nigeria. But Abuja is the capital of Nigeria, so it can't really be the case that I have 'knowledge' that Lagos is the capital of Nigeria.

I may strongly believe I have knowledge that all swans are white, but the fact that some swans are black means that I do not really have knowledge that all swans are white, because is false.

Before the discovery of Australia in the 17th century, it was held as a truth that all swans were white as no-one outside of Australia had ever seen a black swan.

In times past, part of what was claimed to be known was that the Sun orbited the Earth. Work by Copernicus and Galileo showed that this was false and so not really 'knowledge'. Thus it may turn out that much of what we strongly believe we have knowledge of, from science or from religion or from whatever is not really knowledge at all because it is false.

Belief:

The word 'believe' was just used above in relation to knowledge. A second common feature of the definition of knowledge stemming from Plato is the requirement that in order for something to count as knowledge for me, I must *believe* that something is the case. Having knowledge that Abuja is he capital of Nigeria seems to require that I *believe* that Abuja is the capital of Nigeria. I may well find it difficult to believe that Abuja is the capital of Nigeria (especially after thinking it was Lagos), but if I now have 'knowledge' that Abuja is the capital of Nigeria, I must in some sense believe it to be true.

Part of what it means to claim I have 'knowledge' that Abuja is the capital of Nigeria is that I believe that Abuja is the capital of Nigeria (however strange or embarrassing holding that belief might be).

The work of Sigmund Freud (1856-1939) seems to affect this long held Platonic analysis as I may post-Freud not even know what I believe about certain things. I may not 'know', for instance, that I *believe* I 'killed' my mother by switching off her life support, because this belief' (true or false) is kept locked in my unconscious; kept at an unconscious level by an ego for 'protection' to avoid a crisis of guilt. It may now be suggested, then (post Freud), that we do not even 'know' what we believe on many occasions.

There is a difference in logical status between 'truth' mentioned first above and 'belief' here. The concept of knowledge can be said to logically entail truth. The claim that I have (propositional) 'knowledge' *that* X is the case, is not 'knowledge' if X is not in fact the case – i.e. it is false.

The concept of 'truth', however, does not logically entail belief. We cannot have knowledge that X is the case if it is false but we can, and very often do, *believe* propositions which are false; believe that X is the case, when it is false that X is the case.

If am shown a black swan in the newly discovered Australia, this doesn't necessarily mean that I was wrong to assert that I *believed* all swans to be white. Rather, it demonstrates that my belief was false.

There is no logical contradiction in the notion of a '*false* belief' unlike the logical contradiction in saying there is '*false* 'knowledge'.

We may 'believe' propositions which are either true or false, whereas we can only have 'knowledge' of those which are true.

Given that knowledge entails truth but beliefs may be false, it follows that knowledge and belief cannot be identical 'Believing' that something is the case, is not the same as 'knowing' that it is. It follows that we cannot simply define 'knowledge' as what we believe or most strongly believe.

We do understand, however, that one element of the definition of knowledge at least is that it must be true. Perhaps, then, knowledge could be defined as those beliefs which are true - defined as '*true* belief'?

'*True* belief', plausible as it may be as a definition of knowledge, by itself will not do as a definition of 'knowledge'. This is because knowledge seems to require a 'link' between the belief and its truth. I may, for example, believe that if I blow gently on three standard dice before shaking them they will each turn up revealing a '7' and in fact all three do turn up revealing a 7.

In this case I *believed* that it was the case they would all come up as 7 and it was *true* that they call turned out to be a 7, but it was just luck that the belief turned out to be true. I could not in this scenario be said to have (propositional) *knowledge* that X was the case, actual 'knowledge' that they would all turn up 7.

The reason that true beliefs like this do not amount to knowledge is because the connection between the belief and its truth is accidental or lucky. It seems there needs to be a clear 'link' of some kind between the belief and the truth of that belief. This essential link between a belief and its truth may be described as a 'justification' for believing something is true. This 'justification' as a link between belief and its truth is considered next.

Justification:

The reason for true belief not amounting knowledge in the example just given is there appears to be a lack of justification for the belief. It is a matter of luck that the belief that three 7s will turn up happens to be true.

A lucky guess, however, is not 'knowledge'. That is to say, a belief that X is the case which then happens to be true just by luck is not 'knowledge' that X is the case. Something better than luck (as to truth) is needed to make a belief count as knowledge. Some sort of valid 'justification' for the belief that blowing on dice will lead to them turning up 7 is needed in the above case.

If I thought that blowing on the three dice would activate sensors I had planted in them, this might count as a 'justification' for my belief that blowing on them would cause them to turn up as three 7s – so providing a 'link' between belief and it's truth. When such justificatory reasons are lacking, even if a belief turns out to be true, it cannot be called 'knowledge' because the justificatory link between the belief and its truth is missing.

This requirement of a justificatory link between belief and its truth exposes an significant aspect of knowledge. When we claim to know something we are saying more than that we simply believe it to be true. Our knowledge claim, if it is valid, includes a claim that we are *right* to believe what we do.

This claim to the entitlement of belief may be called a 'normative' aspect of knowledge because it describes not only what we *do* believe, but what we – and others – *ought* to believe.

The Tripartite Definition of Knowledge:-

The three elements mentioned above – truth, belief, and justification – constitute what is known as the 'tripartite definition of knowledge'.

Before this, though, a quick word on propositions is needed. A 'proposition' is where the meaning of a sentence is that something is the case, e.g. 'I believe that I exist'. As a consequence different sentences using different words and different sentences in different languages could express the same proposition that something is the case.

To return to the tripartite definition of knowledge, we can now say

S can be said to 'know' the proposition **p** (*that* something is the case) if and only if:

p is *true*

S *believes* p is true

S's belief p is true is *justified* (i.e., it is not just luck that S's belief in the proposition happens to be true)

According to this (Platonic) tripartite definition, these three elements specify the necessary and sufficient conditions for knowledge. A belief being true is a 'necessary' condition for that belief being knowledge, but it is not 'sufficient' to make it knowledge. The tripartite definition of knowledge claims that knowledge is *justified* true belief. Only satisfaction of all three these conditions is 'sufficient' to make a propositional belief (*that* something is the case) knowledge.

Problems with justification:

Knowledge on the tripartite definition is belief which is true and belief which is not true by luck – belief **p** must be true and must have a justification for being regarded as true. Much then hinges on the word 'justification'. If justification is *never* possible then, on the tripartite definition, knowledge is *not* possible and the skeptic is right. One potential problem for justification, in this regard, is infinite regress.

Suppose A claims to know proposition **p** that 'Ben Nevis is the highest mountain in the UK'. A will have reasons, or evidence (as justification), for this proposition. This evidence will be in the form of further propositions. One such proposition could be that, 'Ben Nevis' is 1344 meters high'. Call this proposition **q**.

Clearly **q** by itself is insufficient to 'justify' the propositional belief that **p** ('Ben Nevi is the highest mountain in the UK')

The argument needs more premises. These premises will be further supporting propositions which will need to show that any other mountain in the UK is below 1344 meters in height. The problem is that each of these supporting propositions will need support from other propositions. That Mount Snowden in Wales, for example, is less than 1344 meters in height, that the method of measurement of mountains produces valid data, and that there are no underwater mountains unaccounted for and so on.

There is, therefore, a danger of an' infinite regress' here of propositions that need support from other propositions.

One way in which beliefs are commonly held to be justified, then, is by their reference to other beliefs that we hold. For example, the propositional belief that the tree in the distance is green may be supported (i.e. 'justified') by the belief that I see it as green, and this belief can be supported by the belief that I am not color blind, and my belief that I am not color blind is supported by the belief that I can trust the results of a childhood eyes test, and so on.

This 'and so on.' is where the problem lies. Only a justified beliefs that something is the case, can justify another belief that something is the case. Further beliefs, though, always seem to be needed to justify an existing belief and the further beliefs require further beliefs to justify them.

If all of our beliefs have to be justified in this way to make knowledge possible then we end up with the infinite regress. Final justification is *never* possible and so knowledge is not possible.

It seems that, for the tripartite definition of knowledge to work, a foundational belief that does not require further justified belief to support it is needed to stop an infinite regress of beliefs and so make knowledge possible. Descartes it may be remembered considered his 'I think therefore, I exist' to be such a foundational belief. This approach to justification can be and is called 'foundationalism'. It is considered next.

Foundationalism:

One way to stop an infinite regress of beliefs in support of beliefs is to say that there is a category of beliefs which do not themselves require further justification. These basic beliefs can thus be foundational, and provide the ground of the justification of all other beliefs. Within rationalist theories of knowledge, like that of Descartes, these foundational beliefs are thought to be those which are gained by rational intuition. The belief 'I exist', for Descartes, does not need further support, because (he considers) doubting the truth of this belief only confirms it.

The empiricist approach also offers up some foundational beliefs which do not require further support. These are generally based on knowledge of one's own mental states. I believe as I am writing I can see a tree. I can question whether there is a tree there at all (I may be day dreaming), but I know that I believe I am seeing a tree and the color green and a shape.

Foundationalism holds that our basic beliefs are infallible (they cannot be mistaken) which is why they don't need to be justified by other beliefs. Truths which are directly intuited by reason or beliefs about our current sensory experiences can count as foundational if they do not need further 'support', If so, they can, in principle at least, provide grounds for all our other beliefs, and so make knowledge (as justified true beliefs) possible, because there need not now be an infinite regress of justified beliefs supporting justified beliefs.

Some Problems with Foundationalism:

According to the foundationalist theory of knowledge, then, a belief is justified and counts as knowledge if it is foundational, either as a belief from experience (say, I know 'I feel it is raining', or a belief whose truth can be rationally intuited (for example, the I know 'I exist' of Descartes).

A belief is justified and also counts as knowledge if it is a non-foundational belief is but inferred from a foundational belief, either directly or via a chain of other justified beliefs.

One problem here, however, is that it seems very little can be inferred from foundational beliefs.

As regards rationalism, foundational beliefs appear to have too limited a content to ground any substantial beliefs about the world. From my foundational belief that 'I exist', say, I can infer very little about anything else. Descartes in the end, has also to rely on other beliefs, 'that God exists' and that 'God is not a deceiver', to put the world back as something that can be 'known'.

As regards empiricism, beliefs about subjective states can be regarded as foundational such as 'I know I feel it is raining' or 'I know what I *believe* is the case'. The difficulty is justifying an inference from such foundational *subjective* states to the existence of an *objective* external world. (How do I get from I *believe* there is a tree here to justified true belief or 'knowledge' that there actually is a tree here corresponding to the belief)?

If, we cannot justify such inferences from the foundational subjective mental states, then basic beliefs about our own experiences will be unable to ground any further beliefs about the world.

Turning to 'Coherence':

These difficulties with foundationalism (citing the existence of foundational beliefs that do not need further justification) suggest it needs to be rejected as a theory of justification; rejected as a way of preventing the problem of infinite regress of justified beliefs supporting justified beliefs.

An alternative is to consider how we go about justifying our beliefs in normal life. We generally do not, for instance, justify our beliefs by inferring them from foundational premises. Our beliefs can be regarded as forming part of a coherent whole of beliefs. They 'fit together' and what on occasion is strange enough not to fit is excluded as part of knowledge (excluded as justified true belief). For example, if a drunk friend says on the our walk home "There are pink elephants in front of us" he must be wrong I think because this belief does not fit with other beliefs; elephants aren't pink, they don't live in the city and there is no circus in town, I can't see them myself, etc.

This reference to the 'coherence' of sets of beliefs has given rise to the 'coherence theory of knowledge', mentioned in chapter 4 with respect to George Berkeley. It can act as well as a contrast to the 'foundationalist theory of knowledge'.

The coherence theory asserts every belief is justified in virtue of its relation to all the other beliefs that a person holds, without any of these beliefs needing to be 'foundational'. It therefore avoids the problem of an infinite regress of justified beliefs, by claiming that there need be no basic, indubitable beliefs in order for all our other beliefs to be justified, since justification relies on 'coherence'.

A particular belief is justified simply if it coheres with all of our other beliefs. If a particular belief doesn't cohere with our other beliefs but instead conflicts with them then it is not justified and cannot constitute knowledge - as in the case of the belief that there are pink elephants in the example above.

The notion of 'coherence' has been defined in different ways by different advocates, but at least one element is generally held to be a necessary condition for coherence (although, as we shall see, it may not be a sufficient condition for coherence).

Firstly, for a set of beliefs to be coherent they must be logically consistent; they must not contradict one another. If I believe, for example, that all philosophers are wise and that Socrates is a philosopher, but I also believe that Socrates isn't wise, then this set of beliefs is logically inconsistent and therefore they cannot *all* be true together (as they do not all *cohere*).

Logical consistency may, then, be a necessary condition for coherence. It is far from being a sufficient condition for coherence, however. This is because a set of beliefs in an array of propositions can be logically consistent in not contradicting each other but still not be justified beliefs. Consider, for example, my beliefs

'John is sitting down'

'2+2=4'

'Tomorrow is Wednesday'.

While these beliefs are logically consistent (do not contradict each other), more needs to be in place if any or all are to be justified since they seem to be too unconnected to support each other.

It may now be seen, therefore, that not only must the beliefs in a coherent system not contradict one another, they must also be 'mutually explanatory'. This means that they must fit together in ways that are connected; ways that let them explain and help support each other.

In the example above, for example, the fact that my friend could see pink elephants could count as evidence that 'he is drunk', and my belief that 'he is drunk' helps explain his seeing of pink elephants.

According to the coherence theory of knowledge, foundationalism is a mistaken idea. Against foundationalism it highlights the point that it makes little sense to ask for an ultimate ground which justifies all of our beliefs because this just is not how people formulate and justify their beliefs. It notes that, instead of a bedrock of absolute certainty, we all have instead a background network of beliefs which we have developed and modified through experience. New situations and experiences are judged against this background web of beliefs. If the beliefs they give rise to are consistent with *and* add to the explanatory power of this system then they are justified.

George Berkeley's idealism is a coherence theory in this sense. Inconsistency in experience, was how Berkeley explained illusions, although (as we saw in the chapter 4), he held that all we experience are ideas in the mind.

To sum up, the 'coherence theory of knowledge' states that:

- Foundational beliefs are not required for ultimate justification of beliefs
- A belief is justified to the extent that it coheres with a system of other beliefs.
- Coherence is defined in terms of logical consistency and (mutual) explanatory power.

Some Problems for coherence:

One of the main objections to coherence theories of knowledge is that it seems to be perfectly possible for our beliefs to cohere with one another without their being *true* in relation to the world. It is then claimed that justification in the coherence sense is not adequate evidence for a belief's truth.

One way in which advocates of coherence have replied to this objection is by offering a definition of *truth* in terms of coherence: a belief is not only justified if it coheres with other beliefs, it is thereby made *true*. (This was also mentioned in the previous chapter Idealism).

If coherence is equivalent to truth then the degree to which a particular belief coheres within the system *is* evidence for its truth. But foundationalism rejects this definition of truth because it leads to *relativism*. This is the position in which the truth of a proposition is defined relative to a system of beliefs, so that the same proposition may be true relative to one system and false relative to another.

Those in the foundationalism camp are *absolutists* (and not relativists) about truth, holding that the truth or falsity of a proposition is independent of all our other beliefs and is judged solely against the way the world is. Because they think that a belief that something is the case is made true by whether or not it corresponds with what is the case in the world and not by coherence with other beliefs. Foundationalistm holds that the coherence of a belief with a system of beliefs is not sufficient to justify it.

Interim conclusions:

In this Chapter 5 'What is Knowlege?' we have examined the concept of knowledge and the criteria for the application for this term. We have seen that knowledge is crucially distinguished from true belief by the condition of justification. True belief only counts as knowledge if it is 'justified'.

Two theories of justification have been outlined:

  i) Foundationalism: a true belief is justified and counts as knowledge if it is either a basic belief which is indubitably true or if it is inferred from such a basic belief either directly or by way of other beliefs.
  ii) Coherence: a true belief is justified and counts as knowledge if it coheres with a system of other beliefs.

We have also seen how the tripartite definition of knowledge has it that truth, belief and justification are the necessary and sufficient conditions for knowledge. This claim is examined further below.

It may be worth noting here, for those perhaps suffering from 'epistemology fatigue', that if we do not understand what knowledge actually is, any attempt, scientific or otherwise, to discover knowledge about reality is without clear purpose.

The Tripartite Definition of Knowledge Again:-

In the previous section the tripartite definition of knowledge was described. According to this a subject **'S'** can be said to 'know' a proposition **'p'** if and only if:

proposition **p** is *true*

S *believes* that proposition **p** is true

S's belief that proposition **p** is true is *justified* (either by citing 'foundational' beliefs or by 'cohering' with other beliefs).

The three criteria justified true belief were said to provide the necessary and sufficient conditions for knowledge. The fact that they are 'necessary' means that, if any of these conditions is not fulfilled, then a person claiming to have knowledge does not have such. (This is why the conditions can be said to be 'necessary' for knowledge).

It has also been said that no further conditions are required for a person to be justified in claiming knowledge (hence the three conditions, justified, true belief, can be said to be 'sufficient' conditions for knowledge). Justified true belief is all that is needed.

In assessing this definition of knowledge, therefore, we must ask whether justified true belief really *is* necessary and sufficient for knowledge.

If there can be cases of knowledge in which one of the conditions is not satisfied then it will have been shown that justified true belief is not *necessary* for knowledge.

And if there can be cases in which all of the conditions are fulfilled but a person lacks knowledge then it will have been shown that these conditions are not *sufficient* for knowledge.

Is justified true belief <u>necessary</u> for knowledge?

In examining whether each of these conditions is 'necessary' for knowledge, we must ask whether there are any cases in which we would allow that a person has knowledge even though one of the conditions is not satisfied. Thus we must establish whether there can be cases of knowledge without one or more of the following:

Truth

Belief

Justification

Knowledge without truth?

Because the concept of knowledge logically entails truth, we must accept that the truth condition in the tripartite definition of knowledge *is* a necessary feature of knowledge. There can be no instances of knowledge without truth.

Knowledge without belief?

The second condition of the tripartite definition *has* been questioned by some. Consider the following often cited example. An unconfident schoolboy has learned the dates of the English kings and queens the night before an important exam. But he is so unsure of himself that in the exam he feels like he has forgotten everything he learned and is just guessing the answers. As it happens, however, he gets all of the questions right.

Now in this case the schoolboy doesn't *believe* that, for example, Elizabeth I died in 1603. However, because his answers are consistently right we are inclined to say that he does in fact *know* this. If this example is accepted, then it would seem that we can have knowledge without belief, and so *believing* that something is the case is not a 'necessary' condition for *knowing* that it is.

The introduction of the possibility of having beliefs that reside in the unconscious complicates this further. If there is such a thing as the unconscious mind, then it is possible not to know what you believe and so, possible to know something, *without* consciously believing it.

Knowledge without Justification?

It has been argued in this chapter that 'justification' is the distinguishing feature of knowledge as opposed to true belief. Without the condition of justification, it appears we have no way of differentiating genuine knowledge from lucky guesses. Nevertheless, there are some cases in which we might want to attribute knowledge even though justification appears to be lacking. An example of such a situation may be taken from a story by D. H. Lawrence, 'The Rocking Horse Winner'.

This story is about a boy who is able consistently to predict the winners of horse races simply by riding a rocking-horse. The fact that the boy always picks the right horse suggests that he does indeed *know* which horse will win the race – he is not just guessing. Yet he is unable to explain *why* he believes that a certain horse will win. If we allow that this is a genuine case of knowledge then it would seem that there can be knowledge without justification. Although this is a fictional, it is perhaps an example of real life situations in which people claim to know that something is the case but are not able being able to provide an explanation for why they think know it. Women's 'intuition' perhaps, or a fireman's just 'knowing' that a particular fire is about to erupt.

Is justified true belief <u>sufficient</u> for knowledge?

In judging whether these three conditions are sufficient for knowledge, we must ascertain whether it is possible for a person to have justified true belief but still lack knowledge.

The most well known attempt to prove that justified true belief is not 'sufficient' for knowledge was given by the contemporary American philosopher, Edmund Gettier (b. 1927). Gettier constructed a series of examples which suggest that a person can have justified true belief that something is the case *without* having knowledge it is the case. He thereby purports to demonstrate that justified, true belief is not 'sufficient' to establish knowledge.

Consider this scenario. Henry is watching television one afternoon in June. It is Wimbledon men's finals day and the television shows Murray beating Djokovic But what Henry doesn't know is that the cameras at Wimbledon have stopped rolling because of rain, and the television is showing a recording of a previous final in 2013. Furthermore, while this is being shown on television Murray has in fact beaten Djokovic in this year's match. Therefore Henry *believes* that Murray has just won this year's Wimbledon final, and this belief is *justified* by the fact that he thinks he has just seen this on television, and this belief is *true* because Murray has just beaten Djokovic in the final. However, we would not say that Henry *knows* that Murray is the new Wimbledon champion, because the fact that his justified belief is true is just a matter of chance.

Murray might have lost the final this year and yet Henry would still have believed that he won. Since this would appear to be a case of justified true belief not leading to knowledge, Gettier claims that these three conditions are not 'sufficient' for knowledge.

From the above it appears possible to argue that justified true belief does not amount to necessary or sufficient conditions for knowledge.

There appear to be cases of knowledge in which belief or justification is lacking (so they are not 'necessary' to make a proposition knowledge).

There also appear to be cases of justified true belief which do not count as knowledge (so all three together are not 'sufficient' to make a proposition knowledge).

How does science stand in relation to 'knowledge'?

Let us say that science holds the belief that X causes Y as a law of nature – perhaps established (ideally) by repeated controlled experiments.

We can now at least ask if this belief is actually true and actually justified. If not it cannot count as knowledge.

David Hume exposes for us the fact that 'causation' does not exist in experience, so our sense impression of constant conjuction of X and Y is not evidence enough to establish the truth of 'X causes Y' and so is no justification of X causes Y.

Furthermore, the belief that a discovered law of nature will continue into the future seems to lack justification as well because of the 'problem of induction' exposed for us by David Hume and, in addition, there is nothing in sense impressions or experience to allow it to be claimed as true that a law of nature will continue into the future.

It seems, then, knowledge established by scientific experimental method fails the test of knowledge as justified true belief.

The significant problem here is that is that this is what science holds knowledge to be. A (propositional) belief that 'X causes Y', is held to be justified because it is evidence based as established (ideally) by repeated controlled experiments, and this also counts as evidence for its truth. David Hume, in particular, is able to expose that scientific knowledge and experimental method, fails by its own criteria of needed evidential support to establish knowledge.

Could knowledge be established in other non-scientific ways? The following Part IIa takes up this question and considers amongst other things the extent to which religious beliefs can count as 'knowledge'.

PART II

METAPHYSICS

(Questions of Existence)

INTRODUCTION

While Part I Epistemology considered questions of knowledge – What is knowledge? What can and cannot count as knowledge? Part II here will consider questions of existence – What is existence? What can and cannot be said to exist? This area of philosophy has the title 'Metaphysics'. The name derives from a translation of Aristotle's work given the title Meta-Physics which literally means 'beyond – physics'. 'Beyond' here might simply mean 'after' physics in a sequence of lectures rather than something profound physicists have not thought about.

The term is used in literature to describe a style of poetry. Samuel Johnson coins the expression 'metaphysical poetry' in his 1781 book 'Lives of the Most Eminent English Poets' to describe a group of 17th-century poets which included John Donne and Andrew Marvell, regarding them as writing in a particular style of wit and imagery often about issues of existence is and what exists.

Often Metaphysics does actually seem to venture into territory 'beyond' the normal concerns of physics. In a way, of course, Epistemology ventures into territory 'beyond' physics as well and many other fields of human endeavor by asking what can be known (if anything) about the natural world or the universe, and what is to count as knowledge?

It would be comforting to be able to say here that Metaphysics starts from the point or an assumption that knowledge is possible and understood. It does not however. Often, via consideration of the elements of what is widely thought to exist, it becomes clear that something cannot exist in this form because descriptions of it contain too many epistemological problems; logical contradictions for instance. And yet a strong urge to regard this something as existing remains, perhaps because of its convenience or predictive usefulness.

Such might be the case in much of quantum physics at present. We have as a scientific fact the proposition that reality consists of atoms (formally proposed in the 4th century BC of by Ancient Greek thinker Democritus incidentally). Atoms are considered to contain electrons. Electrons are said on most introductory physics courses to be 'everywhere' and 'nowhere' in(?) atoms and they leap to no-place and leap back from no-place, so they sort of(?) exist and do not exist. And yet, despite these apparent contradictions, we still have the very strongly held scientific proposition that what exists is made of atoms.

It does not seem from an epistemological point of view, though, that we could have 'knowledge' of atoms if their major component exists and does not exist, not possible we could not have 'knowledge' of that which is everywhere and nowhere. (It is not anywhere long enough to *be* anything!). This is at least partly because we cannot really think that something can be *and* not be, or that something can come from(?) no-place or that something can exist be unless it *is* 'somewhere'.

As will be described in Part III of this book, thinkers before Plato wrestled with this problem, as did Plato, and there are those in the modern scientific community who appreciate the difficulties. A universe described by quantum physics cannot even be *imagined* as existing according to well-known 20th century scientist and science popularizer J.B.S. Haldane. It is akin, perhaps, to trying to imagine reality as populated by square circles or having *faith* in a reality populated by square circles.

It would appear, then, that we are not far off having faith in electrons, perhaps like faith in a god that is spoken of as being everywhere and nowhere (and perhaps cannot be imagined). God is often rejected as something that can possibly exist because the concept (being everywhere and nowhere etc) does not make sense. And so, at best, we can only have faith in the existence of God. Must we also, then, at best, only have faith in the existence of electrons?

We certainly seem to be venturing 'beyond' physics here. Thus the term 'Meta-Physics' is perhaps not such an inappropriate title for this Part II after all. Much more will be said about the existence and idea of God in Part IIa. Part IIb will be concerned essentially with mind and matter.

The contemporary problems of metaphysics often take the following logical form:

- Given we know that X is the case, it does not appear that there can be Y
- But Y appears to be the case as well.
- Therefore, either X or Y (or both) are not the case, or a way has to be found to allow them both to exist.

One example of this is presented by the scientific principle that everything in the world consists of matter in motion governed by the laws of nature. How can we have free will, if this is the case (since we too must be matter in motion governed by the laws of nature)?

That is to say, given X,' all is matter in motion', how can there be Y, 'free will'?

But we also have a strong inclination to believe Y, that we have free will, as this seems to be what we experience when making decisions, as I appear to have freely decided to make this point.

A way needs to be found of understanding how both a material universe governed by the laws of nature *and* the existence of free will can be together, or perhaps one or both of these powerful beliefs has somehow to be rejected.

The question of the existence of free will is also considered in Part IIb 'Metaphysics and Philosophy of Mind'. Part IIb will as well examine the potential need for non-material substance to exist.

It also considers the question of the existence of 'personal identity': we know we are always changing (different experiences, different memories, all the cells in our bodies change every seven years, etc.). We also appear to continue to exist through these changes.

How, if everything is changing, can we retain same identity?

Making use of the above formula, it may be said, given X (that we *change*), how can there be Y, (us having the *same* personal identity over time)?

Prior to IIb, Metaphysics and Philosophy of Mind, Part IIa 'Metaphysics and Philosophy of Religion' considers, amongst other things, the suggestion that God is impossible. If God cannot have God-like attributes and still exist or be known as potentially existing, then the idea of God existing may be an impossible one. If, then, this is avoided by describing God in some other way, without his standard set of God-like attributes, He cannot be God.

To anticipate just a little, I can tie a knot that I can't undo. Can God tie a knot he can't undo? If He can there is something He can't do, namely untie the knot he has just tied. But if He cannot untie the knot, there is something he cannot do and so He is not God – especially because then it would be the case I can tie a knot I can't undo and this is would be something beyond God's powers.

Similar sorts of problem with the traditionally posited attributes of God are also described in Part IIa.

CONTENTS PART II

PART IIA

METAPHYSICS AND PHILOSOPHY OF RELIGION

(Exposing God)

PART IIA

METAPHYSICS AND PHILOSOPHY OF RELIGION

INTRODUCTION

One issue in this Part IIa concerns the question as to whether or not the idea of God is a coherent one and whether God as traditionally described can possibly exist. Is it possible, for example, even just in principle, for God to possess all the attributes (omnipotence, all-knowingness, supreme goodness, and so forth) the traditional idea of God generally posits Him to have? If not, if the attributes cannot fit together, if, say, having one rules out another, such a being possessing all these attributes cannot exist.

And yet, there are 'believers' around the world, who perhaps do not fully appreciate what they believe if they believe in something which cannot possibly exist.

Believing *in* God, however, may well not be the same thing as believing *that* God exists. This, in turn, raises the questions about the nature of the language used religion. Could it be that religious language does not have the usual meanings in the sense of making no factual claims about the world? Do expressions like 'God exists', 'God is great', or 'God is all-knowing', or 'almighty' etc. have no more meaning than say "Hurrah for God" each time they are said?

Such questions, of course, depend on a certain interpretation of what it is to *mean* something, a perspective on what 'meaning' means, so to speak. If meaning can only be of something that is possible, it may be that the word God has no meaning if such is impossible.

If talk of God is empty of meaning because God is impossible, however, then on similar grounds much scientific language must also be empty of meaning. If God is an impossible concept (like a round square) so talk of God has no real meaning, it may also be said if electrons are an impossible concept (like round squares), by the same standard, talk of electrons perhaps has no meaning either.

103

'Electrons exist' may then even mean no more than "Hurrah for electrons". And so we may be left with faith in the existence some impossibilities. God? Electrons? Round squares? etc.

Dismissing religion for being unscientific, as critic of religion Richard Dawkins tends to do (in fairly fundamentalist manner), becomes no easy task if some foundational beliefs of science are as much a matter of faith as any faith expounded by religion. Remember, as well, for example, the 'Induction Delusion' mentioned in Part I Epistemology; the (David Hume) point that we can have no evidence that laws of nature will continue to exist into the far future or into the near future, only a 'faith' that they will.

The above issues and more will be addressed in this Part IIa Metaphysics and Philosophy of Religion. Key arguments for the existence of God presented in history will need to be covered as well, including some that have interested science.

The most well known as regards the latter rests on the fact that the universe appears so precisely set up it is hard to deny the possibility of intelligence behind it. Isaac Newton, arguably the greatest of all scientists, said as much when, in an appendix to the second edition of his 'Principia' published in 1687 he wrote, 'This most elegant system of the sun, planets and comets could not have arisen without the design and dominion of an intelligent and powerful being'.

A modern version of this is to note how improbable it is that the precise arrangement the elegant system of Sun, planets and comets exist. If, for instance, the neutron were not about 1.001 times the mass of the proton, all protons would have decayed into neutrons or all neutrons would have decayed into protons, and there would perhaps be no atoms. [20]

Stephen Hawking is more dubious as regards the existence of God as a designer of the elegant system of the sun, planets and comets and so forth. In an October 2001 interview for the Telegraph Newspaper he says "If you believe in science, like I do, you believe that there are certain laws that are always obeyed. If you like, you can say the laws are the work of God, but that is more a definition of God than a proof of his existence."

It is interesting to note here that, although he has a problem with faith in the existence of God, he has no problem with having faith there are certain laws of nature that are always obeyed: 'faith' because there can be no evidence that the laws of nature will hold into the future as the 'Induction Delusion' described in the introduction to this book exposes (since all possible evidence for the proposition is past).

Moreover, scientific claims are ostensibly all evidenced based, or should be so, which is why the existence of God is rejected by Hawking and Dawkin as lacking evidence to support it - although faith that laws of nature will last into the future is *not* so rejected because of lack of possible evidence.

On the other hand, there are events that appear to occur in the cosmos which challenge the possibility of the existence of God, or at least a traditionally understood God. The problem takes the form, 'if X exists, God cannot exist'.

'Unfair' or 'unjust' treatment in life has been regarded as X here. For example, there are those who work hard to help others, in a war zone say, and yet may be captured and tortured by a terrorist faction. There are more who work hard to build a better world for others to find themselves suffering an agonizing death by drowning in a natural disaster, while those who just take from the world and think only of themselves are often spared in such situations. Old people who have worked saved all their lives for retirement may have their money stolen by a con man who lives happily ever after on his proceeds.

God regarded as all-powerful could intervene to prevent such happenings if He wanted but does not. So either He is not all-powerful (and so not God) or God doesn't care (and so is not God) or He doesn't notice (so is not all-knowing, and not God).

Questions concerning God and His possible and impossible relations to the world are also considered in this Part IIa Metaphysics and Philosophy of

Religion as are questions of the possibility or impossibility of the existence of God.

Issues raised, for the sake of convenience, are placed under three chapter headings given below. There is, of course, an artificiality about this threefold division, the list is not exhaustive and much overlap and interconnectedness lies between them.

CONTENTS PART IIA

1

CAN GOD EXIST?

This title suggests clearly we are in the realm of metaphysics, where metaphysics is regarded as a consideration of existence *per se* and consideration of what exists and what can exist. We have seen in Part I Epistemology a distinction between what *appears* to exist and what in *reality* exists. This distinction obtains in metaphysics as well (of course) so indicating, if such indication were needed, that epistemology and metaphysics overlap.

A standard physical natural science description of what exists is that there *appear* to be many different kinds of things but, in *reality*, all are made of one kind of thing, atoms. Atoms are conceived of as mostly 'empty' and 'contain' protons, neutrons and electrons, the latter of which are described to many students as being 'everywhere and nowhere' and leaping 'from' nowhere and back 'to' nowhere.

As has been mentioned several times, this description of what exists in reality seems at first blush to be impossible. Something needs to be somewhere to exist. How can electrons exist if they are not in any place? Everywhere and nowhere looks to describe something as impossible as a round square. If something is round it cannot be square, and if something is nowhere, it cannot be everywhere as well; if something is not in any place, how can it be in every place?

So what about God? God is often regarded as not existing in a particular place, as being everywhere and nowhere even. Thus if God can exist, something can exist without being in a place, which means is it possible for electrons which do not exist in a particular place to exist as well.

It follows too, for the sake of consistency, that to complain that a religious statement like 'God is everywhere and nowhere' is 'religious' nonsense with no real meaning, as many have done, a statement like 'electrons are everywhere and nowhere' (therefore) has no real meaning as well and so (on grounds of consistency) has to be 'scientific' nonsense.

The Attributes of God:-

A statement that 'God is everywhere and nowhere' may be regarded as a description of one of the characteristics of God. A divine attribute as it were. In most systems of religion God is endowed with characteristics that distinguish Him (mainly a 'him') from other forms of being, particularly human being. In Christianity, Islam, and Judaism, for example, God is considered as all knowing (omniscient) all powerful (omnipotent) eternal, and omnipresent (everywhere and nowhere). [*Omni* here is Latin for 'all']

One issue as regards the title question for this chapter, 'Can God Exist?', is whether the attributes traditionally given as characteristics of God, are coherent? Can they fit together? If they cannot, then the existence of a being possessing all these characteristics is not possible. A key question, then, is to what extent (if at all) does having one particular divine characteristic or attribute rule out having another?

Is it possible, for instance, for a being to be all powerful *and* omniscient *and* eternal? Is it possible, in other words, for God to exist? These issues are considered now.

God as eternal:

St Augustine of Hippo, Northern Africa (354-430) is arguably the founder of Christianity (and, despite many depictions to the contrary, unlikely, incidentally, to possess a white skin). The way Augustine considers God to be eternal is to regard God as standing outside of time – time does not pass for God. Augustine says in his *Confessions* XI, 13 'Thy years do not come and go; while these years of ours do come and go.'

If eternal is taken like this as 'existing outside of time', then the view is in danger of collapse. This is because the meaning of 'existence' appears to become empty. By 'existing' we normally take to mean as continuing to be from one time to another later time. 'Existing outside of time' looks to be in the realms of logical contradiction akin to a square being round.

This problematic use of the language of 'existence' perhaps gives a rise to a role for an interpreter, an educated priest in the early Catholic Church in fact, who could interpret parts of the bible to those finding difficulty understanding it. The role of interpreting the language of a Great Book, of course, exists in many religions.

'Existing outside of time', if this is to have meaning, also creates a difficulty with the language of change. 'Change' is normally taken to involve the passage of time, being something at one time and being something else at a different time. God as outside of time, then, cannot change.

This idea that God is 'unchanging', though, finds no problem fitting into most religions as God is regarded as *perfect* and anything that changed from its perfect state would have then to become less than perfection.

Viewing God as 'unchanging', however, makes it difficult to see how He can interact with us or the world. If He becomes angry because of what we do, for example, or guides us because we are lost, He does not remain unchanging. So an unchanging God would appear to be not one that can connect with the world and what goes on in it.

Eternal as everlasting:

An alternative way of considering God as eternal, instead of viewing Him as 'existing outside of time' (as did Augustine), is to regard Him as 'everlasting'. Broadly speaking, this tends to be the Protestant Christian position. An 'everlasting' God does not exist outside of time. He lives *in* time like the rest of us and He will continue to be around after we have gone.

This makes possible the normal use of the word 'change' and the word 'existence'. The latter being existence from one time to another, unlike as is the case regarding God as 'existing outside of time'. This retention of the normal use of language and meanings of words was one reason the early sixteenth century Protestant movement held that the 'interpreter' priests of Catholicism were not needed and bibles should be translated out of the Latin language and be made available to be read by all.

It also becomes possible, if God exists in time, for God to interact with the world and change from one time to another (which does not appear to be possible if God exists outside of time).

A difficulty, however, is that if God can change, this appears to contradict another traditionally held characteristic of God, that He is 'unchanging, because He is perfect.

A further problem also arises for a God viewed as 'existing in time' in that it does not then appear possible that God could have created time, and so is not the creator of 'everything', another attribute of God held by most religions – the creator of 'everything' including time.

In addition, viewing God as 'existing in time' also seems to make it impossible for Him to be all-knowing (omniscient). For a God existing in time, like the rest of us, the future has not yet happened. Therefore, God cannot know the future, because it has not happened to be known about.

He, like us, cannot *know* how much damage will be caused the arrival of a tsunami next year, or if there will be a tsunami.

This, of course, is why the 'problem of induction' exists for the human discipline of science, as explained in Part I Epistemology. We cannot know if the laws of nature will continue to hold in the future because we exist in time. We can only use past and present events as evidence, and this is what is done. At the risk of laboring the point, to say that events in the past and present can count as evidence for what will happen in the future, requires, again, a *faith* (not a 'scientific' belief based on evidence) that the future will always be like the past – especially as regards the laws of nature continuing to hold.

And so science at its heart is forced to assume what it is trying to prove, and forced to violate its own principle that to count as knowledge a proposition must be backed up by evidence.

Having faith that the laws of nature will continue to hold all the weight of scientific endeavor is perhaps a little like having faith that a rope bridge over a ravine will always continue to hold.

God as All-Knowing/Omniscient:

It has just been described how God regarded as 'existing *in* time', cannot know the future (because for God, like us, it has not yet happened) and so this seems to damage the idea He is knows all or is omniscient.

Conceiving God as 'existing *outside* of time' (as St. Augustine does) removes this difficulty.

If God is outside time He can see our past, present and future simultaneously. To God there will be no past, present and future. He can in this sense 'see' *our* future and the future of the world. He can be all-knowing or omniscient about *our* future and the future of the world

There seems to be a price for God being omniscient in this sense, however, in that that it appears to remove the possibility that 'free will' exists, and God is often thought of as being the creator of beings with free will.

It removes free will because although we may *feel* we choose what we do tomorrow or in the next five minutes, an omniscient God outside of time *knows* it (not simply predicts it with accuracy). It is not possible for humans to have free will if an all-knowing God who (as Augustine has it) exists outside of time exists. For God, the movie of our life, as it were, has already been made.

Many natural scientists would have no problem with the conclusion that free will is impossible, although they would perhaps regard it as so for reasons of their being a mechanistic universe, not because God as existing outside of time knows all. (No free will presumably makes it impossible for me to 'choose' to pursue a career in science or in religion, or both, or neither.)

The issue of the existence or otherwise of free will is considered later in Part IIb Metaphysics and Philosophy of Mind. Mention of it now is necessary, though, because free will may be impossible if there is an omniscient God existing outside of time who knows all about all the events in our lives.

If God is regarded as 'existing *in* time', instead of 'existing *outside* of time', the position as regards free will is different. As God exists in time then, like the rest of us who also exist in time, He cannot know the future because it has not happened. Therefore he cannot know your choices until they are made and free will is still possible.

However, if he cannot *know* the future this then runs counter to the view held in most religions that He is all-knowing or omniscient.

We have now reached a point where, either God is all-knowing and exists *outside* of time but there is no free will, or God is existing *in* time, which still keeps the existence of free will a possibility, but puts limitations on what God can know so suggesting He is not omniscient.

An everlasting God 'existing in time' may, in principle, be able to accurately *predict* what is going to happen next, predict what choices will be made. This however, is not the same as having *knowledge* of those choices, and so accurate prediction does not rule out the possibility of free will. If I, a being that exists in time, can always accurately predict what you, another being existing in time, is going to do in future situations, this does not constrain you in any way. You could still have chosen another course or courses of action.

This you cannot do if a God existing outside of time with no past present or future, has *knowledge* of what you will do in what *for you* is a future – He can, from outside of time, see the movie of your life, and you cannot change or edit it.

Omnipotence:

This is the idea of 'Almighty God'; the idea that God is all-powerful and there is nothing God cannot do.

There are some difficulties with such a position. Can God, for example, tie a knot which he can't undo? Even I can do this, so surely an all-powerful God should be able to. If He can tie a knot he can't undo, however, there is something he cannot do, i.e. untie the knot, and if there is something he cannot do (like untie a knot) He is not all-powerful.

This problem is sometimes presented as God being unable to create a rock he cannot lift. If He can there is something He cannot do (lift a rock) and if He can't, there is something He cannot do, create the said rock.

There may be a confusion of language here, however. God cannot create a rock 'He cannot lift' and then lift it – this is because it would be logically impossible (like God being able to create a 'square' that is also 'round').

Some influential figures, though, have even said that God being 'omnipotent' means he has the power to do what is logically impossible. René Descartes holds such a position noting that to impose any limitation on God is to deny what God is. For Descartes, God should even be able, say, to create a square circle.

This, however, is perhaps just a nonsense statement. If something was a circle it cannot be a square and vice versa. It is more plausible it seems to hold that for God to be all-powerful/omnipotent, He must be able to do anything that is logically possible.

It is, then, still logically possible that God can tie a knot he cannot undo since I can do this myself. There appears still to be a problem, then, as God should be able to do this if I can do it. It is only logically contradictory if it is not possible in any possible universe, like a round square is not possible in any possible universe.

God creating a knot that He can't undo and then being able to undo it, or creating a rock he cannot lift and being able to lift it *is* logically impossible in these senses.

Holding that an all-powerful God is one who has the power to do anything that is logically possible, however, *still* allows for problems. It lets in, for example, acts for God that seem to run counter to what God is. It may be logically possible, for instance, that God commit suicide, since even I can do this. But if He could do this, if God could die, He would not be God.

One way out of all this is to say that God has the power to do anything that is logically possible for God to do – not that which is merely logically possible for humans like ourselves to do.

This then depends upon what God is. As we have seen above, if God is a being that 'exists outside time' He does not change. This would make it logically impossible for Him, therefore, to choose to commit suicide because that would allow change (ceasing to exist in the case of suicide). Alternatively, if God 'exists in time' but is everlasting God can change and so it *is* then logically possible for Him to choose to commit suicide.

We seem to have arrived at two extremes: It appears that regarding God as existing outside time having the power to do anything that is logically possible for God to do restricts Him too much (He does not even have the power to commit suicide, and even I have this power). On the other hand, regarding God as an everlasting God 'existing in time', having the power to do anything that is logically possible for God to do restricts Him too little (since then he has the power kill Himself, and so is not unchanging). Furthermore, tying God to logic at all restricts him too much for some, including René Descartes.

Descartes, however, even though he holds that an all-powerful God need not be restricted by logical possibility, still has something He cannot do. God, for

Descartes, cannot be a *deceiver*. This is because for Descartes and for many religions God is supremely good. If He were a deceiver, He would not then be supremely good and so not be God.

The Euthyphro dilemma:

Descartes, holding that God cannot be a 'deceiver' suggests that standards of right and wrong lie outside God which he can or must conform to – by not being a deceiver. This raises another issue for the existence of God. If God is good because He always does what is right, morality must be independent of God's will.

Such, though, places a limit on God's supposed all-powerfulness, His omnipotence. This is because God on this view cannot make what is 'wrong' into what is 'right' because moral standards seem independent of Him.

One reply to this is to say that what is right is simply what God wills. Something isn't right independently of God, that He must conform to in order to act rightly Himself. He would not be God otherwise.

A problem with this alternative view, however, is that it means what is right or wrong becomes *arbitrary*. Is it then not possible to assess actions or thoughts or whatever in terms of any separate moral standard or right and wrong, because there is no separate standard?

A difficult question but, as mentioned in the introduction to the book, philosophy is about asking the difficult questions, and exposing these as a means to greater understanding, perhaps via the appreciation of a complexity where none is normally seen.

This difficult issue is known as the 'Euthyphro dilemma' after the dialogue 'Euthyphro' written by Plato, where the dilemma was examined. The Euthyphro dilemma is a good lead in to another difficult issue, the 'problem of evil' to be considered next. *Evil* here is regarded as that which does not conform to a moral standard *independent* of God.

The Problem of Evil:-

Evil can be divided into two types. One type is evil that is caused by personal acts, such as torture, murder, war, exploitation and so forth. The second type arises from causes outside personal acts such as suffering caused by natural disasters like earthquakes and erupting volcanoes. The word 'evil' is used because those who suffer, often in extreme ways, generally can be regarded as not deserving of it, and it is difficult avoid viewing this as wrong or unfair, or unjust.

The former type of evil caused by personal acts has been given the name 'moral' evil. The second type, caused by factors outside personal acts, has been given the name 'natural' evil. The distinction between moral and natural evil is becoming less clear cut as events such as droughts, hurricanes, floods and the like, formerly thought to be outside personal acts are today often blamed on reckless human action in creating climate change via global warming. Either way, whatever category an evil falls into the existence of such evil impacts on the question of whether God can exist.

For those who want to hold that God *can* exist, the problem is reconciling the evil that exists in the world with a God who must know about such evil, since He is omniscient (all-knowing). He *can* also do something about it since He is also omnipotent (all-powerful), and *ought* to do something about it as He is ostensibly perfectly good and all-loving.

The problem, then, is how to render God as traditionally understood compatible with the existence of evil. As Hume notes either God is able but not willing to prevent evil or He is unable to prevent evil. Either way, there is a difficulty. [21]

This problem of evil can be used as an argument against the existence of God. The existence of God looks to be made impossible by the existence of evil – it either takes away His omnipotence or His perfect goodness, or both. Evil and God it appears cannot exist together and, since evil exists, God cannot.

In order to retain the possibility of the existence of God, the existence of evil needs somehow to be made compatible with the existence of God with such traditionally held attributes of being all-knowing, all-powerful, all-loving etc.

This, as may be anticipated, is an old problem existing in many religions; the providing of a means to make the existence of evil compatible with the existence of God. In the Christian story this is called a 'theodicy' after the word was used in the title of a book by Gottfried Leibniz (1646-1716), an influential mathematician and contemporary of Isaac Newton (1643-1727).

One approach to a 'theodicy' is to regard the existence of evil as necessary for a 'greater good'. If this can be demonstrated, God can remain omniscient, omnipotent and omnibenevolent as He is creating something better for us by allowing the existence of evil.

This greater good can be difficult or even impossible for us to understand. It may be as a child does not and perhaps cannot understand why his all-powerful mother, who must know it hurts, and who loves him or her, takes them to suffer the pain of an (inoculating) injection - and takes them on perhaps more than one occasion!

One prime candidate for this greater good from the existence of evil is the creation of *free will*. This 'free will defense' of the existence of evil may again be traced back to St Augustine of Hippo in the 5th century. The over-riding point is that free will could not exist if there were no possibility of evil.

God cannot create man with free will and then control his 'choices' (so man never commits evil) without thereby removing his free will; removing his power of choice.

It is not logically possible, then, to create free agents that necessarily are prevented from committing evil acts, as such would not than have free will. The existence of free will carries with it the possibility of making bad choices (as well as good choices), so the possibility of evil can be viewed as the price that must be paid for the existence of free will.

It therefore follows that it is possible God, as traditionally described, could have created beings with free will and so the evil is created as a by-product of this free will. Therefore, the existence God can be compatible with the existence of 'moral' evil (at least) because the existence of the greater good of free will must allow for the possibility of 'wrong' personal choices in order to be free will.

Problems with the free will defense:

One obvious and fundamental problem is that this defense presumes that free will *can* exist. Whether free will can exist or not will be considered from a different perspective in the following Part IIb Metaphysics and Philosophy of Mind. The question now in this Part IIa Metaphysics and Philosophy of Religion takes on some importance for whether God can exist as well as free will.

It has been mentioned above how God conceived as all-knowing and existing *outside* of time means that the existence of free will becomes impossible – although this is not so for a God conceived as everlasting, but existing *in* time, who is not then the knower of all I am going to do (but who may then be thought not to be all-knowing.)

There are other cracks in the free will defense for the existence of evil as well. A person could freely make the 'right' choices all the time and this is perhaps what we should be aspiring to. Free will may require the *possibility* of wrong choices but it doesn't seem to require the *actuality* of wrong choices. God might then be criticized for not making us better at making more 'right' choices.

Perhaps so, but the object of the theodicy is to reveal the *possibility* that the existence of God can be compatible with the existence of evil; to show how it is logically possible that God and evil can exist together (whatever the number of poor choices in practice). This is what the free will defense seems to establish.

The free will defense of the existence of evil seems, at this stage, to refer to 'moral' evil, evil that arises from the personal choices of man. 'Natural' evil, 'unjust' suffering caused by volcanoes, earthquakes, disease etc, is, by definition, not a product of free choosing and so human choosing cannot be responsible for it. Whence, then, does *this* evil come from if not from God? Even insurance companies refer to natural evils as 'Acts of God'. How can

God who is all knowing, perfectly good and supremely powerful allow such (natural) evil to cause so much suffering?

One way to make the existence of God compatible with the existence of natural evil, and so still allow the possibility of God existing together with the existence of natural evil, is (again) to suggest that natural evils allow for the creation of a *greater good* (as with the above justification for 'moral' evil).

The greater good this time is not necessarily the existence of free will. The approach is to suggest, rather, that natural evils make possible the greater good of our own 'personal development' into good people.

If this 'personal development' is a greater good, and if the existence of natural evil is necessary to generate it, then it makes sense for an all-knowing, all-powerful, all-loving God to allow it, and so the existence of God can become compatible with the existence of natural evils. God might be viewed, then, as creating the greater good of 'personal development' by allowing natural evils.

This line of argument appears to owe its origin to Iraneous, an influential monk of the 3rd century from what is now Lyon in France. The method, here, is to suggest that certain evils are needed in order for humans to learn and develop. The world cannot be a better place without the occurrence of some natural evil as without such there would be no opportunity for the behaviors they make possible. These are behaviors like 'compassion' and 'sacrifice for others', and such as these are of the highest sort of moral value. Experience of certain natural evils makes it possible for a person to develop his 'goodness' and in this way develop his 'soul'; indeed, to become closer to God.

This 'soul-making' approach has the added benefit that it can be applied to 'moral' evils as well as 'natural' evils. Experiencing the suffering of innocent victims of, say, acts of torture or acts of personal violence makes possible the development of emotions of sympathy and of compassion.

There are still difficult questions for this 'soul-making' approach though. One issue is whether there needs to be quite *so much* suffering in practice in order to make learning and development of good characteristics possible. Also, the uneven distribution of such suffering seems not to be necessary in practice as well.

There is, in addition, always the on-going potential for *failure* where a person does not develop in the 'right' direction. Someone may learn, for instance, to be concerned only with his own well being when experiencing the undeserved suffering of others.

The point of the 'soul making defense', however, is to establish it is not logically impossible the that God exists even if evil exists; to show that evil is not *necessarily* incompatible with the existence of God described as a being which is omniscient, omnipotent, and omnibenelovent.

And so God (as traditionally described) can still exist, even though natural evil exists, because the existence of such evil might thereby allow for the creation of a situation with the greater good of 'personal development'.

Fyodor Dostoevsky (1821-1881):

Dostoevsky is not impressed with this theodicy. In the 'The Brothers Karamazov' (1880) he notes with great scorn that he'd rather not know about good and evil than pay such a terrible price for such knowledge. [22]

Søren Kierkegaard (1813-1855):

Kierkegaard is equally unimpressed with a view like that of Dostoevsky. Religion for him is a feeling and commitment. There is no passion in simply accepting so called 'proofs' of God's existence or so called 'solutions' to the problem of evil. Such are not only irrelevant to Kierkegaard, they are offensive.

In his, 'Fear and Trembling' (1843), he famously writes that religious belief is about making a 'leap of faith' beyond rational thinking. It is about subjective commitment not about being convinced by objective proofs and rational argument. The point of religion is to *feel* (God) not to *know* (God).

For Kierkegaard, being religious is about confronting the unknown, not what is knowable; not believing because you think you understand, because you think you have (objectively) solved, say, the 'Euthyphro dilemma' or the 'problem of evil', and so forth. This is not, for Kierkegaard, being religious at all – the point of being religious is to 'leap' beyond all this.

2
MUST GOD EXIST?

We are in the world of metaphysics, concerned with existence and what can, must or does exist. So far in this Part IIa Metaphysics and Philosophy of Religion, the (difficult?) question of whether God as traditionally described *can* exist has been considered and most recently if God (as traditionally described) can exist along with the existence of evil. We turn now to arguments which purport to demonstrate that God *does* exist. If He does exist, discussion about whether He *can* exist becomes irrelevant. Most of these arguments for the existence of God are long standing and so the analysis will again include historical as well as contemporary elements.

1. The Ontological Argument for the existence of God:-

This is argument for the existence of God has a considerable lineage. It is found in several different religions and in non-religious domains. In Christianity (as, for instance, by St Anselm (1033-1109) and in Islam, as by Mulla Sadra (1572-1640). A mathematical alternative has been offered by Kurt Gödel (1906–1978), well known for his 'Incompleteness Theorem' of course, and there are other modern approaches such as that by American philosopher Norman Malcom, student and colleague of Ludwig Wittgenstein.

All of these versions generate further difficult questions, but there seems to be something about the ontological argument that attracts powerful thinkers. This is perhaps because, as publicly confirmed by atheist Bertrand Russell (20th century mathematician, philosopher and winner of the Nobel Prize for literature) intuitively something must be wrong with the ontological argument for the existence of God, but it is very difficult to pin down exactly what this something is.

'Ontology' is generally translated from the Greek as 'being' or 'existence'. The ontological argument attempts to move from the idea or concept of God to the conclusion that God exists via reasoning alone. In this way it belongs to the rationalist approach to knowledge mentioned in Part I Epistemology. It may be remembered from this that rationalism takes reason and reasoning to be a source of knowledge. The ontological argument asks us to examine the concept of God we possess, the idea of a perfect being - a being than which nothing greater can be conceived of - and see how it leads to the conclusion that God must exist.

The most cited version of the ontological argument in the Western tradition is that of St. Anselm (1033-1109) sometime Archbishop of Canterbury and regarded by many the most important Christian theologian of the 11th century. The argument is to be found in a composition written around 1077 *Pros logion'* as a 'prayer to God'. The original title of the work is *Fides Quarens Intellectum*– 'Faith Seeking Understanding', so Anselm is aims to use reason to try and understand what he *already* believes via faith. His intention here, therefore, is perhaps *not* to convince those to do not have this belief by setting down a persuasive argument for the existence of God. Nevertheless, it is as an argument for the existence of God that Anselm's work here has generally been portrayed.

The argument in chapters two & three of the *Pros logion* is addressed to the 'fool' of Psalm 14 in the bible (i.e. the atheist) who says there is no God. Anselm's ontological argument here is as follows:

- God is that which nothing greater can be conceived of.
- It is logically impossible to conceive of something greater than that which nothing greater can be conceived of (since that would be a contradiction)
- A being that which nothing greater can be conceived of exists in our thoughts, as a concept, and this includes the atheist's thoughts.
- If a being that which nothing greater can be conceived of was presumed to exist as a thought in the mind alone, this would not be as great as a being who both exists as a thought in the mind *and* in reality.
- Therefore, if a being that which nothing greater can be conceived of exists as a thought in the mind, then (as the greatest being) it must exist in reality as well as in the mind (to be the greatest being)

- Therefore God, that which nothing greater can be conceived of, must exist.

Gaunilo's objection:

You may perhaps have already come up with a type of objection to this ontological argument first mounted by Gaunilo, an 11th century Benedictine monk and contemporary of Anselm. Gaunilo writes a set of replies on behalf of the 'fool'. One of these is that, if Anselm's argument is accepted as valid, we must also accept that *any* concept of which it makes sense to say 'the greatest or most perfect' must also have a counterpart in reality because a non-existent version would not be the greatest or most perfect.

Gaunilo's counter-argument on behalf of the 'fool' used the example of an island: Must, for example, the idea of 'most perfect' island mean that island must exist? Since one that does not exist is not most perfect.

Anselm pays Gaunilo the respect of replying to his challenges and moves to dismiss them. He does this on several counts but most essentially by showing that Gaunilo is not using 'perfect' in the same way when he says 'perfect' island.

A 'perfect' being is one that which nothing greater can be conceived of, and one that depends on nothing at all for its existence; certainly not on the level of the ocean in, say, an age of melting ice caps.

Gaunilo's use of the word perfect' in perfect *island* is different from Anselm's, use of the word 'perfect', therefore, and so 'perfect' island need not entail existence of the island, unlike in the case of 'perfect' being.

Descartes' version of the ontological argument:

The next historically significant version of the ontological argument comes from mathematician René Descartes (1596-1650). Descartes sets his ontological argument down in the *Fifth Meditation* of his *Meditations* (1641).

He highlights that it is part of the essence of a triangle (for example) is that it has three angles that when added together equal two right angles added together. This doesn't mean that there are any triangles existing, just *if* there are any, they must have this essential property. But with God, however, we must say something different, something like

- The idea of God is of a perfect being
- Non-existence is an imperfection
- Therefore, God must exist. [23]

Additions to the ontological argument by Gottfried Liebniz:

Gottfried Leibniz, another mathematician and seventeenth century contemporary of Isaac Newton (both are credited with inventing calculus independently of each other), criticizes Anselm's *and* Descartes' versions of the ontological argument.

Both Anselm's and Descartes' versions of the ontological argument suggest that an existent being must be more perfect than a non-existent one and so if God is the most perfect being in the mind as an idea He must therefore exist outside the mind as well.

Leibniz' point is that there is a missing premise in the ontological argument of Anselm and Descartes.

If God *cannot* exist, if the idea of God, a perfect being, is of an entity who's existence is a logical impossibility (like, say, the existence of a square circle is a logical impossibility), then the ontological argument does not work. [24]

However, it does work, Leibniz thinks, because God *can* exist (unlike the existence of a round square). Therefore, adding a further premise to this effect can make the ontological argument work. Thus the ontological argument now becomes via Leibniz.

- God is a perfect being
- *It is possible that a perfect being can exist*

      −   Non-existence is an imperfection

      −   Therefore God must exist.

The question now is whether this is legitimate. Is it possible that a perfect being *can* exist? It was suggested several times in the previous chapter 'Can God Exist?' that it is impossible for God to have all the attributes he is traditionally viewed as possessing, so He *cannot* exist. Leibniz, however, argues that it is possible for a perfect being to exist.

How does Leibniz do this? He suggests that 'perfection' is not analyzable. Commentaries often jump over further explanation at this point but what Leibniz intends is perhaps not difficult to appreciate. To say something is 'red' is not analyzable; it is red not because of some other property. By contrast, for example, the term 'beneficial' *is* analyzable it terms of something else. X may be said to be 'beneficial' if it, say, increases happiness. But being red is not analyzable in terms of something else. It red because it is red.

So it is Leibniz thinks with God's 'perfection'. He is not perfect because of something else (as in the 'beneficial' case above), He is perfect because He is perfect (as in the case of 'being red' or not being 'red' above).

It follows that anyone who says God is perfect because of something else, like He knows all, or because He is all-powerful, and so forth, is mistaken.

As a consequence, any argument that these traditionally held attributes of God cannot exist together, becomes immaterial to whether God is perfect or not or to whether He exists or not. If God is perfect, He is perfect and that's it (like something being red, because it's red).

And so via this analysis Leibniz is able to retain the ontological argument by inserting the missing premise *It is possible that a perfect being can exist.*

      −   God is a perfect being

      −   *It is possible that a perfect being can exist*

      −   Non-existence is an imperfection

      −   Therefore God/perfect being must exist.

The problem of 'existence' as a predicate:

Anselm's and Descartes' and now Leibniz' versions of the ontological argument however, are still open to question. They all see the 'perfection' in a perfect being as necessarily including the attribute of existence.

In this way all three seem to mistakenly regard existence as a standard predicate. Existence, however, is not a standard predicate. In the sentence, 'God exists' *grammatically* 'God' is the subject and 'exists' is the predicate.

But in a logical sense, 'exists' is not a real predicate because it does not add or subtract anything, or in any way modify the subject.

This was pointed out by David Hume (1711-1776) in his *Treatise on Human Nature* (1739) [25]. Immanuel Kant (1724-1804), probably the greatest German philosopher (and there are many of this nationality to choose from) is the person best known for pressing home this type of attack on the ontological argument. He notes that if you take as the subject God and then refer to this subject by listing all the standard characteristics such as 'almighty' or 'omnipotent' or perfectly good etc. you do not add another characteristic by putting the word 'exists' [26]

Almightiness, omniscience etc. are the defining characteristics, or properties of God. We could produce a definition of God by exhaustively listing these attributes. We could say that God is omniscient, omnipotent, is everlasting, and so on through a list, until arrival at the complete concept of God. The ontological argument of Anselm, Descartes and Leibniz, attempts to establish the existence of God from the idea or concept of God by adding 'exists' to the list.

'Exists', though, as Hume and Kant expose, is not just another attribute, like almightiness, omniscience etc.

Norman Malcom: Saving the Ontological Argument?

The ontological argument is not quite finished yet. There are other versions, all well aware of the problem of 'existence' being mistaken for a standard predicate.

A different version has been put forward by American philosopher Norman Malcom, (student and friend of Ludwig Wittgenstein) in a 1960 paper published in the 'Philosophical Review' journal.

This takes as its starting point Anselm's rejection of the Gaunilo perfect island criticism of his ontological argument for the existence of God.

It may be remembered from the above, that Anselm points out that Gaunilo has the wrong concept of perfection.

The existence of a 'perfect' island would depend upon sea levels, say, and so may be regarded as 'contingent' - dependent on other things for its existence.

God, however, as a 'perfect' being does not depend for His existence on anything else, His existence is therefore 'necessary' and not 'contingent'.

It follows that if God a perfect being is possible (not self-contradictory like a round square) then He 'necessarily' exists (i.e. does not depend on anything else for His existence).

This is Malcom's starting point – that God's existence is 'necessary' not 'contingent' (as God, that which nothing greater can be conceived of, depends on nothing else for His existence).

- God's existence is either (logically) impossible (like a square circle is 'impossible'), or logically necessary (like squares *necessarily* cannot be circles).
- To say 'the perfect being does not exist' would be a logical contradiction (akin to the contradiction 'a round square').
- God's existence cannot be (logically) impossible since the concept is not self-contradictory: God exists, is not self-contradictory (like a round square is self-contradictory).

Therefore, God *necessarily* exists (as a matter of logic).

There is no problem with erroneously regarding existence as a predicate here as existence is shown to be logically necessary for a perfect being.

Hume and Kant do not appear to consider the point that the perfect being's existence, is a matter of logical necessity.

There may, however, be a good reason why Hume and Kant did not mention this point. It may be *logically* necessary that squares are not circular, but this does not tell us if any squares exist in reality, only that if there are any squares in existence, they necessarily are not circular.

Similarly, it may be *logically* necessary that God exists, but this does not tell us if God exists in reality, only that if there is God is in existence, He necessarily exists (as if squares exist, then necessarily they are not round).

Therefore, Malcom does not, in the end, show us that God does exist in reality.

Notwithstanding, showing that God does exist in reality may not have not been Malcom's intention. Like Anselm above, Malcom's version of the ontological argument can serve to help those *already* with faith seek greater understanding. Serve, that is, to help those who *already* believe in the existence of God.

It reveals why their belief may be so strong as it exposes why God, the perfect being, exists not 'contingently' (i.e. not because of anything else), but *necessarily* (as squares necessarily cannot be round).

2. The Cosmological Argument for the existence of God:-

Anselm's ontological argument was dismissed by St Thomas Aquinas, a13th century monk from the Italian county of Aquino, and a man of huge influence in the development of Christian theology.

Both Aquinas and Anselm believed in the existence of God, of course, but Aquinas rejects Anselm's ontological argument in his great work *Summa Theologica* on the grounds that we as mere humans cannot possibly presume to fully understand what God is (whatever words we use to describe Him).

As a consequence, we are not to be able to conclude from our limited human understanding that He (therefore) exists. Starting out from our limited understanding of God is not the place to begin to construct an argument for His existence.

The stature of Aquinas appears to have taken Anselm's ontological argument off the intellectual agenda for several hundred years. Up until Descartes' 16th century version of the ontological argument (just described) it seems.

Aquinas uses several other arguments (five) for the existence of God, three of which will be described shortly.

Anselm's ontological argument, set down in the 11th century, was based on the thinking of Plato. Aquinas' arguments for the existence of God set down in the later 13th century are, as we shall see, are based on the thinking of Plato's pupil, Aristotle.

Aristotle's works had not been available in Europe since the fall of the Roman Empire in the 5th century (and so were not available to Anselm in the 11th century).

Aristotle's works, however, had been retained and translated into Arabic in the Islamic Empire. European contact with Islam in the 13th century made available Aristotelian texts for translation into Latin.

Plato, a founder of rationalism, had held that we must reason our way to knowledge (as will be shown in Part III of this book). For later thinkers this must, therefore, include the knowledge of the existence of God. This is what Anselm attempts to do with his ontological argument; to reason his way to knowledge of the existence of God.

Aristotle, as a founder of empiricism, starts from the point that the route to knowledge begins with what is experienced. This is where Aquinas starts his cosmological argument for the existence of God; from what lies in experience.

The cosmological argument for the existence of God employs Aristotle's arguments for, in particular, a 'Prime Mover'. It starts from what exists in experience in the cosmos and attempts to draw the conclusion that God must (therefore) exist.

The starting point of a cosmological argument can be, for instance, that the *idea* of God exists in the cosmos, and this raises the question of where this idea might have come from. (Could it only have come from God?).

Another empiricist line of argument may also be to note that certain physical things are experienced as existing in the cosmos, and the experience of the existence of these things can only accounted or if it is allowed that God exists.

One issue, then, is establishing how the *idea* of God in could have arisen since there appears to be nothing like God (the perfect being) in experience.

One possibility is that the idea of God is placed in humans (by God) and so it is innate. Something we are born with; since it is nothing that is experienced after birth.

The idea of God as innate:

René Descartes argues that the idea of God is innate. We have met Descartes several times before, particularly in Part 1 Epistemology, and in this chapter with regard to his ontological argument for the existence of God.

It should be remembered from Part 1 Epistemology how Descartes establishes that even if a deceiving evil demon exists he himself must exist, and he must be a thing that thinks. Such he is certain of because to doubt it seems only to confirm it.

To doubt he exists, he argues, demonstrates he exists (to do the doubting) and to doubt that he thinks, is to demonstrate he thinks.

Among his thoughts Descartes also finds the idea of a perfect being. How, he asks, could such an idea arise? Descartes argues that his idea of God does not come from any experience because he has not ever experienced an infinite being. It cannot be constructed by putting together other ideas either. This is because, in particular, the idea of God is the idea of an infinite being and no amount of addition of lesser ideas could ever reach infinity. [27]

Descartes argues, therefore, that we, as humans could not construct the idea of God for ourselves. It follows that since we cannot generate such an idea of an infinite being from our own limited experience, it must, he concludes, be from the Infinite Being Himself, and planted in us before birth (because it is not something we can experience after birth). We arrive in the world with this idea - although it may take time to access it.

John Locke's rejection of the idea of God as innate:

John Locke (1632-1704), as one of the 'British Empiricist triumvirate' (Locke, Berkeley, Hume) points out that evidence for the idea of the infinite being as innate is weak, not least because it is not known by all. Writing in the late seventeenth century he makes it clear that the idea of God is not universally known. Suggesting that (at that time) it is not known in Brazil, or the 'Caribee' islands. [28]

The fact that it is not universally known, however, does not mean that it is not an innate idea in all humans. It may still be innate but humans in different parts of the world take a different time to access it, which could explain why it does not appear to be universally known.

Locke is aware of this but notes further that even if the idea of God were universally known, this would *still* not establish that the idea of God is innate - no more than universal knowledge of, say, fire around the world establishes that it is an innate idea.

On the other hand, the lack of universal knowledge of God does not then mean there is no God, no more than lack of universal knowledge of fire means there is no fire. It just suggests, as the fire case, that in some places humans may not have figured things out properly.

Applying the human mind 'properly' we can discover that fire exists. Similarly, for Locke, if we apply our minds 'properly' we can establish that God exists (although not all humans, of course, may get around to this).

Argument from First Cause:

Locke, then, is suggesting that the idea of God is not innate. His position is that the idea of God existing can be established by 'proper' reasoning. [29]

The proper reasoning here is sometimes called the 'argument from first cause'. The argument from first cause can be traced back to Ancient Greece and Plato's pupil, Aristotle.

It may be put formally as follows:

- Something cannot come from nothing.
- There is something
- Therefore, something has always existed to produce what has not always existed
- That which as always existed and is the cause/creator of what has not always existed is known as 'God'.

This is also the Aristotelian argument used by Aquinas in the 13th century as one of his five ways to demonstrate the existence of God. It is a *cosmological* argument because it starts from what exists in the cosmos and attempts to deduce that God must therefore exist because of what is experienced as existing in the cosmos.

Another of Aquinas' five ways described in his *Summa Theologica* draws on another argument given by Aristotle, the argument for a 'Prime Mover'. This is described next.

Argument from motion/change:

- Our senses reveal that there is motion/change
- Things move when potential motion becomes actual motion
- Only an actual motion can convert a potential motion into an actual motion
- Nothing can be at once in both actuality and potentiality in the same respect.
- (For example, if a particular thing is actually in motion it cannot then be potentially in motion in the same respect, and something potentially in motion is not yet actually in motion).

- Therefore, nothing can move itself.
- Therefore, each thing in (actually in) motion is moved by something else.
- The sequence of putting in motion cannot extend back *ad infinitum.*
- Therefore, it is necessary to arrive at a Prime Mover, put in motion by no other that starts everything off.
- It is this Aquinas holds 'everyone understands to be God'.

Aquinas' 'Second Way'. Argument from First Cause:

Aquinas' version of the First Cause argument for God is similar the Argument from motion just mentioned. It starts from the experience we have that each event or thing in the cosmos has a cause.

- Everything that is caused is caused by something else.
- An infinite regress of causation is impossible.
- Therefore, there must be an uncaused (First) cause of all to start the chain of causes and effects.
- This uncaused causer of everything, this 'Prime Mover' we may know as God.

Some problems for the Cosmological Argument:

Like the ontological argument, the cosmological argument is to be found in Christianity and in Islam. It does have its problems in that it seems God, as traditionally understood, still may not be required to satisfy its premises.

That something must be the uncaused cause, the 'Prime Mover', need not mean such as something must be God; God with the usual divine attributes of omnipotence, omniscience, supreme goodness etc.

This is point was forcefully made by David Hume (1711-1776). It may be still be any being that the most whimsical imagination can conceive of. [30]

Locke's and Aquinas' (Aristotelian) cosmological arguments only allow that there be something that creates everything (causes motion, etc.). This something that creates everything may therefore be regarded as the 'creator'. Beyond this however, it does not allow us to produce the idea of God as, say, an infinite or perfect being. Hume goes so far as to suggest is could be could even be a *team* of creators.

As an argument for the existence of God the cosmological argument is thus deficient; deficient in that the first cause or Prime Mover need not be God with His traditional divine attributes. Furthermore, the question as to what caused God here might always be put, as Richard Dawkins sometimes mentions. (It will be possible to return to this point and reject it in just a moment).

Aquinas' 'Third Way':

Aquinas' 'Third Way' of demonstrating the existence of God avoids some of the above problems

- Many things in the universe may either exist or not exist and all are finite. Such things are 'contingent' as opposed to being 'necessary'.
- It is impossible for everything in the Universe to be *contingent* (dependent on something else for its existence), for then there would

be a time when nothing existed, and so nothing would exist now, since there would be nothing to bring anything into existence.

—   Therefore, there must be a *necessary* being, a being whose existence is not contingent, not dependent on any other being or beings or state of affairs.

—   This necessary being need not be God with traditional attributes, but because it is *necessary* (not dependent on anything else), the question as to what caused it becomes an absurd question, since (not being contingent – not dependent on anything else), it cannot have a cause.

This need for a necessary being, to account for the existence of the contingent, can counter the 'what caused God?' challenge mentioned above.

The Kalām Cosmological Argument:

It has so far been described under the broad heading of 'The Cosmological Argument' how Descartes argues that the idea of God is planted in us by God and is innate. We have also seen and how Locke rejects this innateness theory and argues that the idea of God can be established by 'proper' reasoning. This is done he thinks by, in particular, referring to the first cause argument. This effectively is the same approach as Aquinas' 'Second Way' and both versions are borrowed from Aristotle.

It has also been shown how David Hume forcefully rejects the assertion that the first cause argument establishes the existence of God with all the traditional divine attributes of, omnipotence, omniscience etc.

Hume's own view about the origin of the idea of God is that it is simply a product of human psychology. This question will be returned to after description of a powerful Islamic version of the cosmological argument, sometimes termed the 'Kalām' cosmological argument'.

It was remarked above how, after the fall of the Roman Empire in the early 5th century, texts by Aristotle were still available in the Islamic Empire and translated into Arabic. Access to the philosophy of Aristotle by Islamic scholars led them to adopt and adapt the cosmological argument for the existence of God.

They were able to do this several centuries before the works of Aristotle became available again in Europe in the 13th century where the cosmological argument was then given fresh impetus by Aquinas in a Christian context.

Before Aquinas it may be remembered it was Anselm's ontological argument (based on the work of Plato) which had influence in the Christian world. At the time of Anselm, though, Islamic scholars were then drawing upon the 'Prime Mover' argument of Aristotle.

The Kalām version of the cosmological argument seems to overcome many of the problems exposed by David Hume and others. Most significantly, it is able to face up to the challenge that the cosmological argument does not appear to establish that the 'Prime Mover' or 'first cause' or 'creator' need be God as traditionally understood (with all His divine attributes).

The Islamic cosmological argument tradition was publicized by Willaim Craig in his (1979) book 'The Kalām Cosmological Argument'. The name arises from 'Ilm al Kalām' a term essentially for 'theology' in Islam.

Craig states the Kalām cosmological argument, runs like the argument from first cause.

- Everything that begins to exist has a cause
- The universe began to exist

Therefore

The universe has a cause.

From the conclusion of this initial syllogism that the universe has a cause, a further consideration of what this cause must be ensues. What sort of thing must it be to cause the universe?

It cannot be something that is *natural* because something natural cannot be used to explain the cause what is natural (since the natural cannot exist until it is created by something else).

What is in the natural world is space-time and its material contents.

It follows that the first cause must therefore lie 'outside' space and time, in order to create it and to create its contents.

So we now know the first cause must exist 'outside' of time and space, it cannot be physical, and it must be powerful to bring space-time and material reality into existence.

We also know the Prime Mover or first cause, cannot be caused by something else (of course.) so it must have its own volition. It must act from its own volition and not act because it is acted upon.

This Kalām cosmological argument, therefore, brings us very close to the traditional idea of God. The universe must have a first cause (to avoid an infinite regress of causes causing causes). That cause must act from its own volition. It cannot be material. It must exist 'outside' of space and time, and it must be extremely powerful.

Between the 9th and 12th centuries, then, the cosmological argument based on the thinking of Aristotle, developed as a concept within Islamic theology. This Aristotelian approach reached Christian theology in the 13th century and was, as has been described, adopted by Aquinas among others (displacing prior ontological arguments, such as that of Anselm, based on the rationalist approach of Plato)

3. Argument from design:-

At the start of this chapter the ontological argument for the existence of God was examined, and was followed by consideration of the cosmological argument.

The 'argument from design' for the existence of God, like the cosmological argument, takes as its starting point what exists in the world (or universe). In brief the argument holds that because the world/universe exhibits design, it must have had a designer, namely, God. It was mentioned in the introduction to this book how Isaac Newton, perhaps the greatest of all scientists, said as much when commenting in his world-changing book *Principia* "This most elegant system of the sun, planets, and comets could not have arisen without the design and dominion of an intelligent and powerful being."

The argument from design is sometimes known as the 'teleological' argument. This is from the Greek word *telos*, which can be translated as 'purpose' or 'design'.

Perhaps the most famous statement of the argument from design is provided by the former Archdeacon of Carlisle, William Paley (1743-1805). He proposes a 'watch analogy' in his book *Natural Theology*, published in 1802, (57 years prior to the book 'Origin of Species', by Charles Darwin). Here Paley notes that if he found a watch on the on crossing the heath he would have to suppose, from its complexity, that it had an intelligent designer. Similarly, the complexity of the eye and other features nature suggest that it also must have had an 'intelligent designer'. [31]

Thus we have today in popular culture borrowing from Paley the 'Intelligent Design' Argument for the existent of God.

Paley is saying that the complexity and subtlety of the eye – how it seems perfectly suited to its task - demands that we conclude, as with a watch, that it was designed by an intelligent creator. And even if the eye alone existed, it would *still* be necessary to conclude that an intelligent creator must have designed it.

The Argument from Design runs, then, as follows:

- Watches (houses, ships etc.) exhibit design
- Therefore, they must be planned and produced by an intelligent designer
- The universe exhibits design

— Therefore, the universe must be planned and produced by an intelligent designer.

Darwinism and the Argument from Design:

It seems clear that biology can, post Darwin, now explain the complexity of something like the eye via evolution; via a long and progressive sequence of natural causes and effects. There is no need for us to conclude from the complexity of the eye, as Paley does, that an intelligent creator *must* have made it. Such is publicized by Richard Dawkins in his book, *The Blind Watchmaker* (1986), the title clearly echoing the words of William Paley.

While the explanatory power of the theory of evolution seems clearly to damage William Paley's argument from design, it does not mean, however, that the argument from design is completely defeated. This is because, in particular, the theory of evolution only offers an account for the complexity of the *biological* universe.

The *physical* universe, as a whole, is not accounted for simply by the theory of (biological) evolution. Furthermore, the laws of nature as part of the universe (like Newton's law of universal gravitation) also seem perfectly suited to their particular purposes. These cannot be explained by the Darwin's theory of (biological) evolution, so their existence appears to require us to conclude that they were designed and created by an intelligent being, as Newton himself surmised.

In addition, it may also be asked where the force of evolution itself comes from, a force which also seems perfectly designed for its purpose of allowing life to adapt and survive.

The existence of evolution is cannot be explained by the theory of evolution either. It still seems a *possibility*, therefore, that God could use (and continues to use) the force of evolution to bring about his purposes as regards the biological universe. This approach is sometimes termed 'theistic evolution'.

Richard Dawkins was reported above as attempting to challenge religious belief with a 'What causes God?' question. We also saw above how this challenge is avoided by noting that God, the greatest being, must be a 'necessary' rather than a 'contingent' entity (i.e. not dependent for existence something else). Now it seems we might respond to a 'what causes God?' question in another way as well by asking 'What causes Evolution?'

David Hume's objections to the Argument from Design:

David Hume (1711-1776), as with much else, has insightful comments to make about the argument from design. These are to be found in his in his *Dialogues Concerning Natural Religion* first published in 1802 and in his *Enquiry Concerning Human Understanding*, first published in 1748. Hume, of course is writing more than 50 years before the publication of Paley's *Natural Theology* (1779). His arguments, however, are not only effective against Paley's statement of the argument from design but also against other versions that attempt to conclude that God must have been the creator.

One of Hume's key points in all of this is that there is no need to postulate God as the creator from the apparent 'intelligent 'design' of the world. In his *Dialogues Concerning Natural Religion* (1779) he points out that the faults and imperfections of the world suggest a pretty hopeless workman, not a perfect being like God. [32]

Hume is arguing then that, even accepting the thrust of the argument from design, the imperfection of the world could not possibly justify the conclusion that that designer must be an omniscient, omnipotent supremely good, everlasting God. Rather, if at all, it points towards the effort of some fairly hopeless designer.

Hume's This line of attack here also poses a challenge to all the cosmological arguments for the existence of God described previously including the powerful Kalām cosmological argument.

David Hume also has criticisms to make of the use of the 'causation' in the argument from design and its positing of an intelligent designer.

In the design argument we have only one effect to go on, namely, a designed feature of the universe. A particular cause, God, is inferred from this *one* effect.

But Hume points out that we cannot infer the cause of something if we have only *one* instance of an effect to go on.

Suppose I hear a strange sound in the house. I am new to the country and so I can't say anything about its cause, except perhaps what it was *not* made by (since I know what sounds animals make in my own country). I need multiple cases to be able to establish cause and effect in this new country, to establish that the cause of the strange sound was a something called a 'gecko'.

Hume's point is that a cause cannot be inferred from experience of just one effect.

This, then, not only challenges the design argument for the existence of God. It also challenges the scientific explanation of the origin of the universe as science too has only one effect to infer cause from.

If, therefore, God as creator of the universe is ruled out by this argument, so is any alternative scientific explanation of the cause of the *one* effect i.e., the universe– the 'Big Bang' as a cause say.

In both religious and scientific approaches, Hume exposes that the experience of multiple cases is needed for humans to be able to establish a cause and effect relation.

God as a product of Human Psychology:-

David Hume regards the idea of God as a product of human psychology. There have been several thinkers besides Hume who very much agree. One of these, and perhaps the most referred to, is Sigmund Freud (1856-1939). Hume's observations are described here first.

David Hume's psychological explanation for the origin of the idea of God:

In his book 'A Natural History of Religion' (1777) David Hume suggests an explanation for the belief in the existence of God based on human psychology. [33]

Hume's view here is that humans by nature (with a passion!) fear death and pain, and desire security and pleasure. But various events (bad weather, illness, wars, etc.) lead to misery and are unpredictable. We don't understand the causes of these damaging events. In these circumstances Hume thinks the unknown causes are conceived of as depending on invisible, intelligent agents. The sufferers hope, as with appealing to ordinary mortals, they may influence such (causal) 'gods' by means gifts (e.g., sacrifices), entreaties (e.g., prayers), and oaths of allegiance. By such means, humans hope to control what they do not understand and are afraid of because it threatens them.

It is as a result of a combination of fear and ignorance, therefore, that the world becomes populated with (human-like) invisible, intelligent powers that are objects of worship.

Attributing greater and greater powers and perfections to a particular god (a God of gods) means that appeals are made to that which has *greatest* influence in the world (and so most potential benefit to humankind). At last a point is reached where God is represented as infinite and entirely perfect.

Sigmund Freud's psychological explanation for the origin of the idea of God:

Like Hume, Freud (1856-1939) suggests that people are more receptive to religious belief when in difficulty in life. At such times, he argues, there is a tendency to *regress*; to in one's mind return to a safe childhood time where all felt comfortable and such difficulties did not exist.

At such a childhood time according to Freud, especially in boys, there is a fear of the father's power and a fear of losing the love of the father. This complex of childhood thoughts and feelings remains in the unconscious but in times of difficulty regression may 'activate' it all again.

Comfort and safety then is to be found when surrounded by a father or father figure. The child regards their father as supremely powerful and all knowing. The child is dependent on his father, grateful for his mercy and fearful of his power. This (safe) relationship to an all-knowing, all-powerful father figure is projected on to a supernatural being, in times of distress via, in particular, regression. [34]

Such, of course, may well be the psychological attraction of a strong political leader in times of difficulty – a 'father' of the nation.

Problems with psychological explanations for the belief in God:

Psychological explanations like those of Hume and Freud tell us *how* some beliefs (e.g. in God) come to be held.

They don't, however, deal with the epistemology. They do not necessarily show that these beliefs (e.g., in God) are false or true.

Evolutionary psychology may, for example, provide a good evolutionary explanation for why I tend hold the belief that those outside my family group are a threat. But this has no bearing on whether they *are* actually a threat or not - they may be, they may not be. Believing they are a threat, though, may be a useful strategy for ensuring the survival of my family, just as a belief in the existence of an all-powerful God might be a useful survival strategy.

The *usefulness* of a belief, moreover, may actually reduce any incentive to test it and see if it is actually true. It requires a disturber of the peace (a 'lover of wisdom' in fact) rather than someone who employs that which tends to bring success or progress as so regarded.

It could still be *possible*, then, even with a psychological explanation of how we come to have the idea of God, that God does in fact exist.

A psychological explanation for the idea, does not rule this out. It does not rule out, for instance, that God exists and has planted in us a psychological mechanism enabling us to have the idea of Him.

On the other hand, if the idea of God can be fully accounted for without reference to any to anything supernatural, there would appear no role for God to play in establishing such an idea, and God falls out of the picture as being an unnecessary explanatory tool; unnecessary to explain how the idea of God arises.

Psychological explanations for the origin of the idea of God can thus give us a plausible account for the belief in God, and may indeed thereby leave no role for God to play in establishing such an idea. Nevertheless, a particular psychological explanation for the idea of God may not be the 'right' account.

This is at least suggested by the large number of different possible psychological explanations on offer. In addition to Hume and Freud we have, for instance, and the competing theories of Carl Jung (1875-1961), Alfred Adler (1870-1937) and in more recent times evolutionary psychology, to name but three.

It might be useful to a scientist or group of scientists in attempting to remove what they regard as an irrational belief in God to have a plausible psychological explanation for why humans have such an irrational belief in God.

A belief lacking evidence perhaps, and so advocates of science like Richard Dawkins are able to place the belief in God as a 'delusion' (arising from human psychology) rather than scientific investigation.

It is perhaps unfortunate for the advocates of science in this context, then, that psychological explanations themselves often do not reach the standards of scientific knowledge themselves.

If this is so, such (unscientific) psychological explanations for belief in the existence of God appear to carry no more weight than (unscientific) religious explanations for the belief in the existence of God.

Therefore, psychological explanations cannot be relied on by science to reject religious explanations for God as *both* do not satisfy the internal criteria for being science.

To establish whether or not a particular psychological explanation for the origin of the idea of God is true, it would seem that we need, in science, to be able to test it. Many psychological explanations however, do not seem to be capable, in principle, of being tested.

For example, Alfred Adler's psychological theory presumes that humans act on the basis of an 'inferiority complex'. If they do believe in God it is due to the inferiority complex and if they don't believe in God it too must be due to the inferiority complex. No fact then, belief or non-belief in God, (no result of any test) could ever refute such a theory.

Similarly, with Freud: If a person believes in God they may be said to have regressed to a child-like state. If not, they may be said not to have so regressed. Like Adler's 'inferiority complex', the theory seems, in principle, incapable of ever being proved wrong. Whatever the results of any tests, no result could ever challenge either theory. Both, theories, in other words are, in principle, 'unfalsifiable'.

This concept of 'falsifiablity' will come up again in the following chapter on religious language. For now, though, it may be said that which is unfalsifiable is generally regarded as unscientific.

Therefore, unfalsifiable psychological reasons for the belief in God can carry no more scientific weight than unfalsifiable religious reasons for believing in God.

This mention of falisfiablity leads on to consideration of the language of religious discourse. Might all religious language actually have no real meaning? Questions such as this form the subject matter of the next chapter.

3

RELIGIOUS LANGUAGE

(Is it meaningless?)

Logical Positivism & the Religious Language Debate:-

The 'Vienna Circle' consisted of a selection of eminent philosophers, mathematicians and scientists, who formed a critical group on the world stage in the 1920s. A central tenet of their intellectual position was what has become known as the 'verification principle', and their greatest influence was Ludwig Wittgenstein's 75 page book 'Tractatus Logico Philosophicus' first published in 1921. In the Tractatus Wittgenstein, among other things, asserted that propositions with sense concern only facts about what is the case. Anything that does not concern facts about the world cannot be (really) be spoken about. This led on to one of his famous maxims, 'whereof we do not know, thereof we cannot speak'. The Vienna Circle later became known as' logical positivists', concerned with what can be logically posited in propositions *that* something is the case.

Religious language and the verification principle:

Under the logical positivist's 'verification principle' a statement is meaningful if and only if it is in principle capable of being verified. It is possible to verify the proposition that it is raining by going outside. It is not *practically* possible to verify the proposition that Pluto is actually a planet, however, because we do not yet have a spacecraft able to make the journey. We can, in principle, verify it though and may well do so in the future. Thus it is, in principle, a verifiable proposition.

149

It turns out under the 'verification principle', however, that religious statements are rendered meaningless. This is because they do not seem capable, even in principle, of being verified. Take a statement such as 'God is Love'. Unlike 'Pluto is a planet', it does not seem possible, even in principle, that this can be checked to verify if it is true.

A.J. Ayer's attack on religious language:

Verification then is a criterion of *meaning* as well as a criterion of truth (judging if the proposition that it is raining is true etc.). If a proposition is not capable in principle of being verified, it cannot, in principle, be shown to be true or cannot be shown to be false and it has no meaning, because it says nothing true and nothing false; it says nothing, in other words.

British Philosopher Alfred Ayer (1910-1989) pressed this point home in his 'Language, Truth and Logic' (1936), a book much influenced by Ayer's experiences with the Vienna Circle. His key argument here is that a proposition which seems to be, but is not, really about anything, and which cannot, in principle be verified via experience, is not a genuine proposition.

The apparent proposition that 'God is Love' is not really a proposition that something is the case at all. Such *non*-propositions are logically meaningless because they cannot, in principle, be either true or false, and religious language is meaningless in this sense.

Ayer goes further in saying this does not support atheism, and nor does it support agnosticism. This is because *all* religious statements cannot, in principle, be either true or false. Verificationism does not lend any support to the atheist because the atheist's claim that 'there is no God' is, under the verification principle as meaningless as the theist's claim that 'there is a God' because neither claim can, in principle, ever be shown to be true or shown to be false.

Prominent atheists like Richard Dawkins may sometimes be open to this verificationist challenge. There can be no verification, even in principle, of the claim that 'God does not exist', therefore under logical positivism

'God does not exist' is also a non-proposition, a statement without real meaning because it cannot, as a matter of principle be shown to be true and it cannot, as matter of principle be shown to be false.

The agnostic position fares no better under verificationism. Agnosticism is the position that it is not certain whether the claim that 'God exists' is true or not. Ayer's point is that the claim that 'God exists' is a non-proposition empty of meaning, and as such it is not simply *uncertain* if it is true, as the agnostic holds.

There is *no uncertainty* about it. It is a non-proposition because, in principle, it cannot ever be shown to be true or ever shown be false. [35]

Ayer, then, is arguing that to say 'God exists' is to make a metaphysical claim which cannot be either true or false and so has no meaning. It follows that any statement describing the attributes of such a being (almightiness, ominipotence etc.) cannot be true or false either. [36]

Antony Flew and Falsification:

Antony Flew (1923-2010), another British philosopher active in the first half of the twentieth century, produced a theory in the same vein as verification. Although subtly different, his 'falsification' theory can be said to complement verification by producing the other side of the argument.

Flew argues in an academic paper 'Theology and Falsification' (1945) that in asserting that something is the case, if it is meaningful, what is also being said is that there are facts/evidence that may count *against* the assertion –facts that would 'falsify' the assertion.

There are, for example, possible facts that could render false the claim that, say, 'all swans are white'. Conceivably there is a sense experience that would count against the claim, e.g. seeing a black swan. This is why, for Flew, the proposition that 'all swans are white' has meaning. It is possible, in, principle, for such to be shown to be false.

Religious utterances, Flew thinks, do not have a conceivable sense experience that would count against them – and so they are without meaning. For example, take 'the statements 'God has a plan' or 'God loves us as a father loves his children'. There is, in principle, no evidence that could ever 'falsify' either assertion.

R M Hare and 'bliks':

Anthony Flew sees propositions that are not falsifiable as having no meaning, and religious language is thus empty of real meaning. A 'Symposium on Theology and Falsification' (proceedings published in1951) now well-known in academic circles, attracted contributions from then other Oxford philosophers R.M, Hare (1919-2002) and Basil Mitchell (1917-2011), as responders to Flew.

R. M. Hare attempts to show there are many propositional beliefs that are not falsifiable but still have meaning. If these (unfalsifiable) beliefs are central to our lives and how we live, then to argue, like Flew, they are all meaningless, would make it impossible to function; impossible, for instance, to function to construct a theory to challenge religious beliefs.

Hare makes his point via a parable. He describes someone suffering from paranoia who believes that all university professors want to kill him. No amount of evidence of gentle professors will dissuade him from this view. Hare labels this kind of unfalsifiable conviction as a 'blik'. He proposes that all people – religious *and* non-religious – hold 'bliks' (beliefs that cannot be verified or falsified).

Hare argues along the following lines. I could develop the blik (unfalsifiable belief) about the strength of the metal in my car. I might even develop a belief that metal in my car was not strong enough to support the steering at low speed, No amount of safe arrivals or bench-tests would remove my blik and restore a normal one because my blik is compatible with any number of such tests.

It is likely as well that even Flew has an unfalsifiable belief about the strength of the metal of his car, and many more besides. If religious beliefs are meaningless because they are unfalsifiable, then so Hare points out are these normal bliks of life.

Basil Mitchell and meaningful unfalsifiable beliefs:

Another Oxford academic, Basil Mitchell (1917-2011) also comes up with an unfalsifiable belief that is not meaningless, and he also uses a parable to do so.

Here, a member of a resistance movement is met one day by a man claiming to be the leader of that movement. The member of the resistance is suitably impressed with the stranger, and pledges to keep faith in him as leader. As time goes on, the member of the resistance sees the 'leader' fighting for the resistance, but at other times, he is apparently fighting for the enemy (!)

The member of the resistance nevertheless carries on with his belief that the stranger is in fact the leader of the resistance movement.

Whatever side the man fights for it does not *falsify* the belief he is the leader of the resistance. However, this lack of falsifiablity does not render the belief meaningless (as Flew would have it).

In addition, there are still reasons to hold the belief he is the leader of the resistance movement *and* there are reasons that can count against the belief he is the leader of the resistance movement. Mitchell's parable thus reveals that, although evidence can challenge a religious belief (or belief that the man in the parable is a resistance leader), a believer can still have reason to hold their beliefs.

John Hick and Eschatological Verification:

John Hick (1922-2012) contributes to the debate by showing that, although it may appear that religious statements are not verifiable (and so meaningless as they cannot be true or false), an 'eschatological' verification may still be possible.

In his 'Faith and Knowledge' (1957). Hick uses a parable of a theist and an atheist travelling along a road together. The theist believes that there is a Celestial City at the end of the road; the atheist believes that there is no such city. These beliefs will be verified or otherwise when the end of the road is reached.

This, of course, is an allegory of the Christian belief in an afterlife. The belief Hick is arguing can be verified after death. (He uses the term 'eschcatologcial' verification). Therefore, the belief in the Celestial City (i.e. the proposition that there is life after death) is not meaningless religious language.

Hick's position does, though, seem to suggest that religious belief should be provisional (wait until death?). Notwithstanding, it still does not render religious beliefs and religious language meaningless (as it can be verified later).

It therefore, challenges the logical positivist view that religious language is meaningless because it cannot be verified as true or established as false.

Falsification, Karl Popper, and Science:

Anthony Flew's falsification angle on the meaningfulness of religious language seems to be following a an earlier work published in 1934 in Vienna by Karl Popper (1902-1994), 'Logik der Forschung' (translated as The Logic of Scientific Investigation). Popper is an Austrian-British citizen (like Ludwig Wittgenstein). He was to become a central figure in the analysis of science and scientific method.

Popper, writing before Ayer and Flew, is not interested in working out if something is a proposition or not or has *meaning* or not (unlike Ayer and Flew). He describes how focus on meaning leads to infinite regress.

Defining what a term means, for example, requires that a new term or terms be introduced into the definition, otherwise all that is being said is 'X is X'. A definition (i.e. what a term *means*) requires 'X is Y'. The problem then arises that the new term or terms Y need to be defined as well, which also involves the introduction of a new term/s. In saying 'Y is Z', for instance, and Z here also requires definition, and so on *ad infinitum*. To focus on clarifying meaning of terms will result infinite regress. The Vienna Circle's focus on the meaning of religious language, therefore, Popper regards as a mistake.

Popper makes clear that he is drawing upon the work of David Hume when he also reveals that, although application of the verification principle may operate to dismiss religious language as meaningless, the very same verification principle if applied to science, will dismiss all of science as meaningless as well (!).

This is because any causal relations 'discovered' (any laws of nature) cannot be empirically verified. Hume has shown us that no number of repeated experimental results will ever give evidence of what will happen in the future, not even evidence of what will probably happen in the future whatever our psychological make up encourages use to believe. (See the introduction to this book for one version of this exposure and Part I Epistemology for another).

Popper, then, against the verificationists, is making the same point as Hume (which he acknowledges) in that scientific laws are *not* empirically verifiable because of the 'problem of induction'.

As a consequence the verfication principle, strictly applied, rejects religious language a meaningless *and* the verification principle, strictly applied, also rejects all scientific laws as well (because they cannot, in principle, be verified)

Therefore, if the absence of evidence for verification dismisses all religion, it also dismisses all of science as well.

Popper moves away from reliance on '*in*duction' toward '*de*duction' and holds that for a theory to be scientific, it must be 'falsifiable'.

If a theory, when tested, can, in principle, be falsified by results that conflict with it, it can be regarded as 'science'. 'All swans are white' can never be verified because of the problem of *induction* – all future swans can never been seen. 'All swans are white' can nevertheless be falsified - it can be *deduced* as being false by the discovery of one black swan. The theory that All swans are white, then, is capable of being a 'scientific' one.

If a claim cannot, in principle, ever be *deduced* as being false (i.e. is not, in principle 'falsifiable'), it cannot count as a scientific proposition.

Popper's targets here are what he regards as pseudo-science. Freud's psychoanalytic theories, for example, mentioned very briefly at the end of the previous chapter. Psychological theories of behavior such as that of Freud, Adler and, more recently, Evolutionary Psychology, seem to be able to account for any and every type of behavior. No behavior could ever falsify any of the theories of behavior. And so they cannot in principle ever be deduced as being false.

He regards Marxism as falsifiable, incidentally, and so occupying the status of science. He complains, however, that there was a refusal to recognize it had been falsified by the evidence.

Popper also mounts an extensive attack on quantum physics on the same 'falsification' grounds. As regards religion he is as well able to state it is not science (because its propositions are not falsifiable).

This is all Popper says about religion, however, and all he can say based on his Falsification criterion. He does not condemn religion for being such.

Is Popper's falsification too strict?

Popper's falsification criterion to judge if something can count as science may be too strict. Where the application of verificationism, results in all science having to be rejected as meaningless since laws of nature cannot, in principle, be verified, it may still be that too much of science is lost via the application of falsifictionism, because too much science seems to fail the test of falsifiability.

The theory of evolution perhaps (like Freudian psychodynamics) seems capable of being *adjusted* to account for any and every biological development or behavior, and so may be incapable, in principle of ever being falsified.

If, for example, male humans desire to become leaders ('alpha' males) with several women attached to them, evolution can 'explain' it. If male humans do not want to be leaders and prefer to be 'house husbands', evolution can also explain it. (Freudian psychodynamics could 'explain' both as well, and is regarded by Popper as not science because of this lack of falsifiability.).

Another difficulty for Popper's falsification criterion for science is that scientific progress in history has often not taken place because of its application. When facts seem to conflict with a theory, the theory is often *not* rejected as falsified.

One example of this is the case of Uranus. It was known for a long time that the observed orbit of the planet Uranus was in conflict with Newton's theory of gravity. Rather than throw out the theory of gravity (which explained the orbits of the other known planets) the existence of a hidden planet that was affecting the motion of Uranus was relied upon - a convenient 'explanation' that could not in principle be falsified (because the planet was hidden). It turned out just such a planet was later discovered (Neptune). The existence of 'Dark Matter' today may fall into this same usefully 'hidden' category.

Thomas Kuhn (1922-1996) in his (1962) book 'The Structure of Scientific Revolutions' sees science historically as passing from one 'paradigm', one understood set of theories and ways of doing science to another. In a paradigm certain evidence may conflict with certain important theories but, for practicality and convenience, the conflict is allowed. Later, a new theory or 'grand' theory may be created that accounts for these conflicts *plus* everything else that had been previously explained as well.

At this point a 'scientific revolution' eventually takes place with a new paradigm developing and replacing the old. The move from Newtonian physics to Einstein and General Relativity can be viewed as one such paradigm-shift and the move from general relativity to quantum mechanics might be regarded as another, with each paradigm containing within it evidence which seems it ought to falsify *some* important theories, but does not.

Psychology, incidentally, is perhaps best regarded at this stage as in a 'pre-paradigm' state as there is no clear agreement on method. Sometimes Freudian factors appear to explain a behavior 'best' sometimes its rival behaviorism explains it, sometimes, biological factors, sometimes cognitive factors and so on – with no one agreed approach.

The 'Later' Wittgenstein and religious language:-

We have seen above how religious language appears unable to satisfy the verification criteria of meaning and because of this should perhaps be regarded as meaningless, since it can never, even in principle, be established as true or established as false.

It was shown how Hare, Mitchell and Hick gave arguments against this approach via the construction of several respective parables. A more fundamental challenge to verificationism comes from its chief source, Ludwig Wittgenstein.

In the post war period, drawing on ideas put forward what has become known as the 'Later' Wittgenstein, came to call into question his early work in the 'Tractatus Philosophicus Logicus', the short book which provided a foundation for of the logical positivist movement and the verification principle as a criterion of meaning.

Wittgenstein's later thinking on meaning was based on drawing an analogy with the use of language and playing rule governed games; 'language games' as compared, say, with 'ball games' such as football.

Wittgenstein observed that just like games such as football and rugby, language operates according to rules. Just as soccer players understand the term 'off-side' in the context of the game, someone not familiar with the rules of the game might think it means, say, players standing off to the side of the field. (It does not). Similarly in American football, those who play the game understand the term 'clipping'. Those not familiar with the game might think this even has something to do with producing newspaper cuttings. The key role of the 'hooker' in rugby probably leads to misinterpretation as well.

Terms like these have meaning within the context of a game, together with rules for the right and wrong way of using these terms in the context of the game – when to call 'clipping' or 'off-side' and when not to, for example. And the terms have different meanings outside that game; different meanings in different language games with different respective rules to establish right and wrong uses.

This Later Wittgenstein view, then, is based on the idea of rule-governed language 'games'. As the above examples suggest, terms in a language have meaning according to their use in a particular game (a language game), and the same terms can have different meanings in different language games.

Armed with this 'Later' Wittgenstein 'language game' idea, religious language can perhaps be seen as meaningful, and not meaningless as verificationists would have it, when relying on the thinking of the 'early' Wittgenstein as did Ayer, Flew and others.

The religious expression such as 'God is love' need not be interpreted as a description of anything that may be true or false about what is the case. The claim can be viewed (if not quite understood) by an 'outsider' as something like an expression of 'reassurance' - the rules of the religious language game permitting this kind of use of the expression for such a purpose.

To take a more extreme case, suppose someone from secular society who knows nothing of religion visits a monastery. Monks are seen chanting at times and sometimes all being silent, at others being intensely concerned with what appears to be triviality, and performing other strange coordinated rituals. The secular visitor would likely not understand what was going on and why it was going on.

Such is similar to a case where many 'outsiders' do not understand what is going on in a community of cricketers and the strange language they use; bowling a 'chinaman', fielding at 'silly point' pausing the game for 'tea'(?) and so forth. A community of cricketers and the language they use can only be understood from 'inside' this form of life as perhaps a community of monks or religious believers and the language they use can only be understood from the 'inside' their particular form of life.

If the Later Wittgenstein is right, the activity of science is itself can be regarded a language game as well. The 'presentation of evidence' in science, for example and what that term means in this community, could be one which only makes sense within a scientific language game where it is understood that there is a distinction between appearance and reality.

The 'presentation of evidence' in science is not, for example, the same as the 'presentation of evidence' in a legal community (or language game.) In a religious community with a different language game 'God is love' can be meaningful in this religious form of life, but perhaps as meaningless from within the scientific or verificationist form of life.

Is it rational to hold religious beliefs?

Many religious beliefs appear to be about factual states of affairs. For example, a religious believer may comfortably claim that he believes that God exists and intervenes in the world, and he may even go so far as to claim that God's existence and intervention are absolute facts. The trouble with this kind of religious belief in facts is that it is open to non-believers to, for example, deny that God's existence is a fact on the grounds that there is no objective evidence for the belief, evidence which could be used to verify it, or be used to show the belief is false. We saw above how the verificationists would regard non verifiable claims like this (e.g., 'God exists and intervenes in the world') as meaningless because they cannot, in principle, be shown to be true or shown to be false.

It is useful at this point to distinguish between two types of belief: Belief-*that* (or factual belief), and belief-*in* (or attitudinal belief).

Belief-*in* can be contrasted with belief-that by saying that belief-in implies an attitude of evaluation, assessment, trust, or loyalty, on the part of the believer. I may, for example, believe *that* there is a Republican Party, without believing *in* the Republican Party to bring about desirable political ends. I can believe *that* someone promised to do something without believing *in* them to carry out their promise.

It may be that 'belief-*in*' best describes religious belief. To say that religious beliefs are beliefs-*in* contrasts with views of religious belief as factual, or based on evidence - evidence which is objective and so available to believer and non-believer alike.

The reason for this emphasis on religious belief as 'belief-*in*' is to try to avoid the objection that in order for religious belief to be rational, there must be a way of establishing what counts as evidence for the belief, and what does not count as evidence for the belief.

Many believers would agree that religious belief is not a matter of evidence and rational deduction, but at matter of faith and commitment. It is, in other words, a matter belief-*in*.

We saw earlier in chapter 2 how Soren Kierkegaard vents his anger at those who think otherwise. Religion he notes is about a 'leap of faith', a believing *in*.

A Believing *that*, for Kierkegaard, is not being religious at all. And so to complain that religious beliefs lack evidence (as some in the scientific community do) is absurd, and for Kierkegaard at least extremely annoying, since this is not what religious beliefs and being religious is about, something that perhaps cannot be understood from within a purely scientific form of life.

PART IIB

METAPHYSICS AND PHILOSOPHY OF MIND

(Exposing Mind)

INTRODUCTION

Metaphysics is concerned with what does exist in reality, what can exist and what must exist (if anything). A standard natural science view of the universe is that whatever it may *appear* to look like, in *reality* what exists is made of atoms and these behave according to certain laws of nature. It has been mentioned more than once (e.g. in Part I Epistemology) that one deep problem still faced by science is the 'problem of induction' (exposed by David Hume), and so belief in the continued operation of laws of nature could be construed as a matter of faith because it cannot be supported by evidence. What is not supported by evidence is, by definition, 'unscientific' (and regarded with some contempt by advocates for science such as Richard Dawkins currently). It was mentioned as well in Part I Epistemology how the results of the main scientific tool, controlled experiments, cannot on considered reflection count as evidence either because causal relations are not something that are actually experienced (a point also exposed by the work of David Hume).

These troubles may be further added to also by asking, for instance, if the natural science conception of reality as purely physical is too simplistic. Strong arguments will be described in this Part IIb that support the view that mental substance must exist in reality in addition to physical substance; a 'dualism' position. Such a proposal will raise problems of how, if mental substance must exist, it can possibility interact with the physical without breaking numerous physical laws of nature. The physical seems to occupy space and the mental not, and self-generating mental energy affecting the physical would (at the very least) violate the law of conservation of energy.

One way of removing this interaction of the mental and the physical problem is to deny there is any physical at all; by holding that only the mental exists. Such can make sense if it is considered that all we are aware of ultimately are our ideas and thoughts about what there is. We occupy a world of ideas and thoughts. This was the position of George Berkeley also considered in chapter Part I Epistemology.

Another way of removing the interaction problem, on the other hand, is to deny there is any mental for the physical to interact with. This is an accepted position of the natural sciences today and thus much effort has been put into rejecting the existence of the mental. Some of these attempts are examined in this Part IIb Metaphysics and Philosophy of Mind, but, as will be shown, it is probably fair to say at this point in time that it not (yet?) certain that dualism is wrong.

In this Part IIb Chapters 1, 2 and 3 have a focus on whether mental and physical substances can, must or do exist. Chapters 4, 5 and 6 concern different (but sometimes related) questions as regards 'mind'.

Chapter 1 asks the question, must mental substance exist? (Are there facts about the world that can only be accounted for by the existence of if mental substance?) Chapter 2 looks at some difficulties in attempting to hold that both mental and physical can exist together; perhaps mental and physical existing together is an impossibility (perhaps a soul existing 'in' a body is thus an impossibility). Chapter 3 considers attempts to reject the mental completely. One of these, 'logical behaviorism', suggests that talk of mental is a problem created by failing to understand how language works. A second attempt to reject the mental is to suggest that the mind is the brain, and a third attempt questions that the mind need not be a brain at all. Could mind be a sophisticated computer? Is any project that attempts to do build such a computer doomed from the start because it is impossible that mind be a physical machine?

The remaining chapters of this IIb focus on three other metaphysical problems related to 'mind'. In chapter 4 is described the problem of the existence minds other than one's own. Those high on the autistic spectrum seem to have problems in appreciating that minds other than their own exist. Why do I (unlike the autistic) believe other bodies have mental states different from mine? Can I have *knowledge* that in reality there are mental states besides my own?

Chapter 5 concerns the existence, or otherwise, of free will. I think I have just chosen to write this but if, in reality, I consist entirely of atoms governed by laws of nature, then what appears to be free choice must be an illusion. And if it wasn't an illusion, then reality would contain self-acting elements and so violate several fundamental laws of nature such as the conservation of energy.

Chapter 6 concerns the existence of personal identity. You change over time mentally (you have new experiences and forget experiences), and you change physically (your cells die and renew). How, if all is changing, can you continue to be you through all this changing? How can you continue, that is, to retain the same personal identity? And there are others around you who also seem to you, to remain the same identifiable person through their constant changing.

CONTENTS PART IIB

1

DUALISM

(Must mental substance exist?)

It was described in Part IIa Metaphysics and Philosophy of Religion, how the Kalām cosmological argument' suggests with some force that God must exist and how He must be a non- physical substance. There are strong arguments and good evidence to suggest that humans cannot be purely physical beings as well. All these will need to be to be countered if the possibility of a non-physical substance existing in the universe is to be rejected, rejected in favor of a (scientific) purely physical reality (whatever its *appearance* might be).

Most of the arguments and evidence for the existence of non-physical substance are based upon the imbuing of humans with mental substances as well as physical. This is known as a 'dualist' conception of what it is to be human. We might wonder as well if those non-human animals that can recognize themselves in a mirror also create a problem for a purely physical conception of the universe. This is because these non-human animals appear (as least) to have consciousness of themselves as a distinct entity in the world. This mirror test has been passed by a variety of creatures including, for example, gorillas, chimpanzees, bonobos, orangutan, orca whales, bottle-nosed dolphins and elephants.

Plato has some strong arguments for the position that we are not purely physical substance, but, for now, we take for a starting point the 17th century where the idea that humans are both mental and physical, both mind and body, was considered with some intensity by various great intellectuals of that time.

There are many such intellectuals to choose from in this age of Isaac Newton. René Descartes (1596-1650) was one of this group. He has a 'conceivability' and an 'indivisibility' argument for the existence of mental substance. These two arguments are considered now.

Descartes' two arguments for substance dualism:

One of Descartes' arguments relies on being able to *conceive* the mind as existing without the body. The other argument relies on the apparent fact that while the body, like all physical substances, can be divided up into smaller units, the mind cannot so be divided; it is *indivisible*. Both these two arguments thus seek to establish that mind and body must be different - they cannot both be the same thing as they have different properties

Descartes two arguemnts influence the agenda for what follows historically on the mind and body (mental and physical) distinction. This agenda-setting dimension is an important reason for understanding the Cartesian approach, even if his arguments turn out not quite to work. This is because the Cartesian 'start' gives direction to the subsequent debate. Like a large cruise ship on the open sea, it may difficult to change the direction of a debate, once started in a certain direction.

Understanding how a problem was constructed in the past, can help with understanding why it is problem today. This is true of academic endeavor and progress in many different areas as has been described already in Part I Epistemology, particularly with regard to the exposure of how misunderstanding of how language functions can be a cause of problems in relation to meaning and knowledge.

This theme concerning the need to understand how a problem was constructed will be demonstrated several more times in this Part IIb Metaphysics and Philosophy of Mind and in the final Part III of the book on Plato', the chief architect of many of the intellectual problems, questions and their possible solutions that that have shaped intellectual endeavor ever since.

In his 'Meditation II', as was mentioned in Part I Epistemology, Descartes thinks he establishes that he knows he exists ('I think, therefore I am'). He goes on to suggest he knows he is 'a thing which thinks', as he cannot doubt he thinks; since to doubt he thinks is to think. On the other hand, he *can* doubt whether he has a body - an evil demon could be deceiving him about this. Descartes moves on from this point to say he can *conceive* of himself as existing without a body. If he ceased to have a body he could still exist. [37]

The failure of conceiving the mind as existing without the body:

Descartes (like many others) thinks he can conceive of his mind existing without his body. However, this does not necessarily mean that his mind in reality *can* exist without his body – and think without that body.

The idea that the mind can live on without the body has, rightly or wrongly has had considerable acceptance throughout history in many different cultures with different religions. This belief will be considered again in the chapter on 'personal identity' at the end of this Part IIb Metaphysics and Philosophy of Mind. We may wonder here in anticipation, though, how many words could retain their meanings; 'up', 'down', left' 'right' and so forth, if we could exist without our bodies. Would too much language lose its meaning?.

We can also here bring in some telling facts, facts arising from modern medicine, which suggest (contrary to Descartes) that the mental cannot, in reality, exist without the physical.

Modern medicine seems is able to make use of the apparent close link between the brain and thinking by administering chemicals to the brain that alters that thinking. Antipsychotics such as fluphenazine that control the levels of the neurotransmitter dopamine are able 'correct' distorted perceptions of reality in some schizophrenics. Antidepressants such as fluoxetine which boost the levels of the neurotransmitter serotonin can alter an attitude to a perceived reality, perhaps making it more positive than otherwise; a patient may think there is no point to carrying on living before taking fluoxetine, for example, and think there *is* a reason to go on living after taking it.

This evidence and more from modern medicine points to a state of affairs where thinking (some of it, or even all of it) is closely connected with neurochemical processes in the brain. It raises the prospect that such thinking cannot, in reality, take place without the brain and these neurochemical processes. As a consequence, just because a thinking mind can be *conceived* to exist without a body or brain, as Descartes (and others) do, this does not mean a thinking mind *can* exist in reality without a body/brain.

Descartes' second argument for the mind-body or mental-physical distinction surrounds the apparent *indivisibility* of mind and the divisibility of body. He can remove a piece of his body, a leg say, but he cannot remove part of his mind. The mind seems indivisible and physical body divisible. They have different properties, so they are not the same thing. They are different things. [38]

The Failure of the 'indivisibility of mind' thesis:

Freudian psychology, contrary to Descartes, *does* hold the mind has parts, in particular a conscious thought part and an unconscious thought part. It might also be noted that the conscious- unconscious division also incorporates, for Freud, a tripartite division between an id, ego and superego.

The mind may not be indivisible in an obvious sense then. At least Freud seems to think so. It is thus *conceivable* under this psychodynamic approach that we could, say, lose the unconscious part of our minds (or part of it…) and carry on without problem. It is even something that might lead to much relief in many cases. Indeed, psychoanalysis often aims precisely at stopping a person being directed by forces from the unconscious part of their mind, unconscious forces patients have no conscious access to and so no conscious awareness of.

Further support about minds being not being indivisible (despite Descartes' view minds *are* indivisible) comes from split-brain operations. In experiments with split-brains (e.g. Sperry, 1968), communication between hemispheres can be prevented via cutting the corpus callosum, a procedure to be mentioned again and in more detail in chapter 6 of this Part IIb on personal identity.

These split-brain experiments reveal that one hemisphere of the brain can know things the other hemisphere does not (until it communicates with it).

Therefore, either the mind consists of parts (as some parts can know what other parts do not) or each brain perhaps comprises *two* minds, one in each hemisphere; each brain might even be described as consisting of two people or two 'souls' even.

The latter, of course, asks significant questions of a religious view that we have or are our (one) soul. The split brain evidence makes it difficult to continue with such a view, as we shall see again in chapter 6 of this Part IIb.

We are, then, pushed to accept that, although Descartes thinks the mind can be thought of as 'indivisible' but a physical body can be thought of as 'divisible', this may be in error. Mind may be thought of as divisible as well as body. In addition, we may be forced by evidence and logic to accept that being able to *conceive* the thinking mind as separate and able to exist without the body does not establish it *can* actually exist without the body or that it is distinct from the body.

The discussion above seems to establish clearly that Descartes' two arguments for the Mind being distinct from body, the evidence of being able to be *conceived* as existing without body and the evidence of being *indivisible*, are not conclusive in establishing there are mental as well as physical substances in reality. In particular because this evidence is not quite there; the mind, contrary to Descartes observations, may not in fact be possible without the body and it may not be indivisible either.

There still exist however, a number of key characteristics of mental states very difficult to account for in terms of a purely physical explanation of the universe. If these cannot be all be accounted for, if they are impossible to explain in terms of a purely physical description of the universe, it may be that we *must* accept that the universe contains non-physical as well as physical substances. One such key characteristic is the fact of the subjective quality of experience or, as it is termed 'qualia'

Qualia:-

Experiences appear to be *private* to the subject that has them. It may be possible in the future to understand the brain in such detail as to identify the exact experience you are having. It is already possible to identify from brain scanning if someone is having pain sensations. However accurate this identification of pain sensations is, though, an observer of them would not be having *your* experience of pain. He may know what feeling pain is like, but he will not know from observing the neurological events what it is like for you to feel *your* pain.

Even if brain states linked to experiences can be observed 'objectively' and in great detail, there is still a 'subjective' element that remains out of reach. This suggests that it will *never* be possible to explain mental events by reducing them to physical events – mental events can never be just physical events because of the existence of 'qualia'; the existence of 'what it is like' to experience something.

This may not only apply to humans. As has just been mentioned, experiments with reflections in mirrors have shown that some animals appear to be conscious of themselves as objects in the world. They seem, therefore, to have mental states. No matter how much we study the physical activity of the brains of these animals we will not get at the subjective element to their experience, the 'what it is like' for them to experience something (such as seeing their reflection). Thomas Nagel and more recently Frank Jackson have argued in support of mental being fundamentally different from physical using the existence of 'qualia'.

What is it like to be a bat and what Mary didn't know?

American philosophy professor Thomas Nagel (b. 1937) describes this seemingly impossible problem for the physical sciences – accounting for the subjective element of experience (qualia) - by attempting to consider what it is like to be a bat in his influential paper 'What Is It Like to Be a Bat?' (1974).

We might be able to learn all there is to learn about the physical processes of a bat, but we will still not know what it is like to be a bat.

Similarly, we may be as bats to sophisticated aliens. Aliens might capture you and find out all there is to know about your physiology and physical processes, but they would still not have knowledge of the fact what it is like to be you. Only you can know this.

This approach of Thomas Nagel was taken up in a slightly different way by Frank Jackson in a 1982 paper entitled Epiphenomenal Qualia' and in a follow up paper What Mary didn't know' (1986).

Jackson's thought experiment is set in the far future where all physical facts and their causal relations have been discovered. Mary is a super neuroscientist at this future time and she knows all of the physical facts and their causal relations including, for a neuroscientist in particular, the physical facts about color experiences. Mary, however, has had no direct color experiences herself. For some reason she has spent her whole life in a black and white room and she researches and learns via monitors that only display in black and white. Mary, then, has had no direct color experiences but does have all knowledge of physical facts and their causal relations.

There comes a point when Mary leaves the room. She sees colors for the first time.

When she does this, it seems that she must learn something new, even though she knows everything physiological about experiencing color before she left the room. The new thing Mary learns is 'what it's like' to see colors (akin to what it is like to be a bat, above). That is to say, she learns about *qualia*, the properties that characterize 'what it's like'.

Her new knowledge of this phenomena ('what it is like' to see color) is knowledge of a fact about the world and so all facts about the world cannot explained in terms of physical entities and their causal relations, since Mary knew all these before she left the room.

This 'what it is like' to see colors argument has received much attention in academic circles. Such is perhaps no surprise since a lot is at stake. It places in danger the project of physical sciences to account for all that exists without postulating anything other than physical entities and the causal relations between them.

One way of helping the physical sciences here is to argue that what Mary learns is not a new *fact* about the universe, which then cannot be accounted for by explanation in physical terms.

What she learns could be an *ability*, or set of abilities – instead of a new fact about the world. If so, she does not learn something new that cannot be accounted for by her deep knowledge of physical processes.

She perhaps does not gain 'knowledge' *that* something is the case. That is to say, she perhaps does not gain 'propositional knowledge' (a term explained in Part I Epistemology). She perhaps does not gain something (a proposition) that can be true or false. Rather she gains a new 'ability', a knowledge *how* and a knowledge of *how* is not a knowledge *that* something is the case.

'What it is like' for Mary to see color for the first time could then be to have certain new practical abilities such as knowing *how* to imagine having the experience of seeing colour in Mary's case, *how* to remember color, *how* to recognize color etc.

There is much more to be report on the adventures of Mary such as the' blue banana' attempted defense of physicalism put forward by leading physicalist Daniel Dennett. The reader is thus invited to look into this significant controversy independently. Further elaboration of the Mary debate here would be a digression, and Frank Jackson, Mary's creator, has now retracted and moved to the physicalism camp.

Further digression into the Mary story also needs to be avoided because several other strong arguments exist to show that a purely physical view of the universe is unsustainable. One of these arguments involves zombies.

The attack of the zombies:

One purveyor of the zombies attack on a purely physical description of reality is Australian born philosopher David Chalmers (b. 1966)

In a 1996 book, 'The Conscious Mind' Chalmers asks us to imagine zombie world where, for instance, a zombie version of ourselves exists. A zombie here is an exact physical replica of you. He or she behaves in exactly the same way in response to stimuli, but he or she has no conscious experiences (as they are a zombie).

It is clear that because the zombie is made of exactly the same physical stuff as yourself, a physical state or behavior can occur in the zombie without the corresponding mental state that is in you; pain behavior, say. You are feeling the pain in response to a stimulus but the zombie with the same stimulus is not – it has no feelings. Therefore, there is more to you than an identical physical replica of yourself. Physicality is not enough to capture all that you are. It fails to capture what it is like to be you with your feelings of pain etc.

This zombie attack on the purely physical view of reality, however, may not quite yet be successful. Like Descartes' argument for the independence of mind mentioned above, being able to *conceive* the mind as separate from body, does not mean it can exist in reality independently of body.

Chalmers is relying on a *conception* of a zombie world. As with Descartes, however, conceiving of something, does not mean is it able to exist in reality. If it cannot, the zombie conception is no argument against a purely physical explanation of mental events. A zombie physical replica of yourself (as something that does not have mental states, but it identical with you in every physical respect) needs to be possible in reality, for the purely physicalist position to be challenged on these grounds (i.e. on grounds that an exact physical duplicate is not you with your mental states and with 'what it is like' to be you).

Other Properties of Mental States:-

We saw above that the qualia of mental states, a fact about the universe, seems impossible to reduce to a purely physical explanation, so providing support for insisting that the mental *must* be different from the physical. There are still other characteristics of mental states that support the view that mental states cannot just be physical states. These are addressed now and include what is called, 'intentionality', 'propositional attitudes', 'privileged access,' 'lack of spatiality', and 'free will'.

Each of these (in addition to qualia) will need to be explicable in purely physical terms, at least in principle, if the existence of a purely physical universe is to be retained. The first of these characteristics of mental states to be considered is 'intentionality'

Intentionality:

'Intentionality' concerns the fact that thinking always seems to be *about* something.

The position is that mental states are distinct from physical states because of this 'intentionality'. This thesis is attributed to Austrian philosopher, Franz Brentano (1838-1917). His work gave rise to a significant intellectual movement termed 'Phenomenology', the study of consciousness-and-its-objects; the study of mental *phenomena*. Phenomenology has been highly influential particularly in Europe. In his book 'Psychology from and Empirical Standpoint' (1874) Brentano notes how no physical phenomena exhibits intentionality but every mental phenomenon does. [39]

Thinking seems more than a physical process because thinking is always *about* something. You might think about what you did last summer, or about an imaginary white rabbit who keeps looking at his watch, or whatever. You desire something. You believe something.

Thoughts point to something beyond themselves; they are 'intentional'. Nowhere in physical nature does this *aboutness* occur. A molecule or an electrical process are not about anything. They do not direct their attention to any object. They have no attention.

Therefore, if intentionality is a fact about what exists in the universe (and this is part of the data received by our experience) it cannot be accounted for if it is regarded as purely physical, since the physical has no such quality.

Propositional Attitudes:

My thoughts about what I did last summer contain a number of propositions. These are matters which can be true or false like, I went to Scotland, I did some climbing, I ate haggis. Such thoughts, are 'propositional attitudes', because they can be true or false.

It is difficult to see how a purely physical system can have propositional attitudes like this. The mind is sometimes regarded as just a sophisticated computer, a gooey computer. A computer can cause sentences to be flashed on a video screen in response to electric signals sent into it, a computer can even speak to us these days. Inside the computer, however, all that is going on is electrical processes of one sort or another. The propositions, 'I went to Scotland', 'I did some climbing' can become true or false propositions to *me*. This is a fact about the world. However, they cannot be true or false to the computer – the electrical processes of a computer do not have 'propositional attitudes' so we cannot simply be (purely physical) sophisticated computers.

The existence of propositional attitudes, therefore, further suggests that mental activity cannot be reduced in explanation to just physical activity.

Privileged Access:

If private experiences were just physical brain states then it would be possible, in principle, for observers to speak authoritatively about what you were experiencing by observing those brain states, using whatever scanning device is available for such.

However, you know better than any scientific observer (scanning your brain, say) that you are feeling pain or feeling stressed and the extent of each.

Research in psychology by Johansson (1978) showed that physiological data (levels of adrenaline) on the amount of stress in a work environment matched self-report data on levels of stress. That is to say, workers who said they were stressed had higher physiological readings of stress. [40]

A work-based study, however, by Evans (2008) revealed via physiological data (levels of adrenaline) that women working in a noisy office were more stressed than those working in a quiet office. However, the self-report data from the women reporting how they felt revealed those in the noisy office were actually less stressed than those in the quiet office. A person would seem to know better what they are feeling than any physiological data because they have 'privileged access' to what they feel. [41].

This privileged access to mental states by the holder of those states does not seem to be explicable if all is regarded as physical. Privileged access is a fact about what exists in the universe and it does not seem not reducible to a purely physical explanation about what exists in the universe.

Mental states not known via observation but by introspection:

I do not come to have knowledge of my mental states by observing them, like one observes physical states or data. We come to know our mental states in a *different* way, by 'looking' within ourselves. We come to know by 'introspection'.

This difference between coming to know physical states and coming to know mental states is a fact about reality. It suggests a distinction between the mental and the physical since we know the former in a different way than we know the latter. They are not both known via observation so they cannot be the same thing – physical processes are not known via introspection, so mental processes cannot simply be physical processes since they *are* known via introspection.

Mental states do not exist in physical space:

If you rub your eyes, soon you will see spots. Where is this mental image? Where is this experience located? Could we say the experience is *in* your brain or *in* your spine (the central nervous system comprises brain and spinal cord). Aristotle thought that mental activities were located *in* the heart. Is Aristotle wrong because he's got the wrong place or is it, rather, that 'location' is not a concept that can be applied to mental experiences?

When we see something light waves hit the retina of the eye. An upside down image of the object is created at the back of the retina (although this is not what we *see*). Next our optic nerve is stimulated and an electrochemical impulse moves along it. Then the occipital lobe of the brain is stimulated. Finally a visual *sensation* of seeing something occurs. All the stages leading up to the *sensation* have a physical location in the brain. The actual sensation, however, doesn't seem to be anywhere, doesn't seem to have a place.

No explanation of brain activity like this reveals 'where' a visual experience is located. The question, 'Where is this visual experience?' doesn't really make any sense, nor does an answer like 'three inches behind the eyes'

It *would* make sense, though, to ask where a physical neural process is going on, and the answer might then well be three inches behind the eyes.

The concept of 'space' or 'location' doesn't seem to apply to mental activity, so this amounts to a further reason supporting the view that mental activity must be distinct from physical activity which, unlike mental activity, does have a location and occupies space.

The existence of free will?

This issue was touched on in the previous Part IIa Metaphysics and Philosophy of Religion. Here it was suggested that if God is regarded as existing outside of time and God knows all, He can see the movie of your life and you cannot change it – you do not have free will. You can no more change your actions than an actor can change the actions of a character after a movie has been shot.

The purely physical conception of reality also leaves no room for free will. If we are purely physical, like all other physical things, our behavior is determined by prior causes governed by the laws of nature. If all our behavior is determined by prior causes, then we have no free will (although we may still *feel* we have free will). We are not then really responsible for our behavior.

If we are not in reality responsible for our behavior we cannot be blamed for our bad behavior. Indeed the concept of 'blame' seems irrelevant. It would be a little bit like trying to blame a dog for its urge to chase cats or cats for their urge to chase mice.

Without responsibility for actions, though, there is no room for a moral system, for right and wrong acts. Physical activity isn't right or wrong, it just *is*.

There are further characteristics of mental states that do not seem to be explicable in purely physical terms. It should already be clear, though, that a substantial case can be made against the physical science presumption that all in the universe is physical. Those who want to insist on a universe that is purely physical governed by laws of nature, need somehow to account for mental activity with is set of properties that physical activity seems unable to possess. Some responses from the advocates of the purely physical on how to account for the strange properties of the mental, without invoking a non-physical substance, will be considered soon. First, though, attention needs to be be given to the further metaphysical question of 'Can, if at all, mental and physical substances exist together?' If they cannot exist together, then the universe perhaps must be entirely physical or entirely mental, or neither. This is the subject matter of the next chapter.

2

SOME CHALLENGES FOR DUALISM

(The impossibility of mental interacting with physical?)

This forms part of the 17th century debate on attempting to demonstrate the possibility of humans consisting of both mental and physical, and most essentially mind rather than body. We can they observed and surmised exist without parts of the body and conceivably without it altogether. We can doubt we have a body, Descartes says, but we cannot doubt we are thinking and have mental activity, since to doubt is to think.

If a Cartesian-style dualist standpoint is accepted, if it is held that we are both mental and physical (we think our physical bodies contain non-physical souls, say), a new problem is created. How can the mind and the body possibly interact as one is mental and the other physical?

This question has now been given a title 'the mind-body problem'. Some of the great names of the 17th century addressing this' mind-body problem' in addition to Descartes include Malbranche (1638-1715), Spinoza (1632-1677), Leibniz (1646-17-16) and la Mettre (in the early18th century). The views of each will be touched on in what follows.

The Mind-Body Problem:-

It seems clear we are made of physical stuff, flesh and blood. It seems clear also that we perceive feel and think; we can be *conscious* of ourselves and of our surroundings. The philosophy of mind issue here is whether there must also be some non-physical stuff to account for this 'consciousness' or can seeing, feeling, and thinking be explained in purely physical terms?

We have just seen in the previous chapter how difficult it is to account for all mental activity in purely physical terms because mental activity appears to contain characteristics not reducible to purely physical description; features such as qualia, intentionality, propositional attitudes, privileged access and lack of spatiality.

On the other hand, if it is accepted that there *must* be dual substances, one physical and the other non-physical/mental, we then have the problem of explaining how the physical can interact with the non-physical/mental. How, for example, can it be that my *will* can cause a physical event, like waving my arm? How indeed can 'will' be accounted for at all in a physical universe of matter in motion governed by the laws of nature? The issue of explaining how the 'mind' or mental processes, is related to the 'body', or physical processes is, as has been mentioned, now known as the 'the mind-body problem'.

The Problem of Interaction:

'Dualism' is the view that there exist two substances, physical and non-physical/mental. If we see ourselves as being made of observable physical stuff ('body') and unobservable mental stuff having private experiences ('mind'), these seem too different to be able to interact. Yet they appear to do so. Furthermore, this interaction seems to be in both directions. Explaining it requires explanation of how the mind can affect body, how mental affects physical, *and* how physical can affect mental.

One specific issue is feeling pain: If someone pinches you on the arm or you cut yourself, basic physiology has it that signals are sent through the central nervous system into the complex neurophysiology of the brain. At some point, though, you feel pain. This *feeling* still remains to be explained (it seems) after *all* the physical events have been described. Moreover, signals can be, say, slow or fast, but pain *hurts*. Signals don't *hurt*. How is this to be explained?

Contemporary psychological and medical research suggests the situation is even more complicated than this with regard to pain. It has been established that mental activity (thinking/cognition) can affect whether pain from given damage to the body is felt as pain or not. This is called the 'Gate Control Theory'. According to this theory if we *expect* bodily damage to hurt, it will hurt and if we don't it won't (or at least not as much). This is why we distract children into thinking about something else just before they are, say, given an inoculation. If they expect the injection will hurt it will hurt more than if they do not expect it to hurt.

It is established, then, that *feeling* pain can be a matter of damage to the body affecting the mental and the mental converting this tissue damage, which may be trivial into pain, or not converting it into pain, even if tissue damage is substantial. The latter is perhaps the case with many rugby players who play though all the hits and bodily damage during a game but generally feel no great pain until after the game has finished.

Thus it seems there can be no pain even though there is substantial bodily damage. In addition, severe pain can be felt even though there is no bodily damage at all, and even if there is no body at all. This is the case with feeling severe pain where an amputated leg used to be, as in the case of 'phantom limb' pain. There is significant pain in the 'leg' but no physical leg, damaged or otherwise, to cause it.

These strange cases of pain add to the standard problems of interaction. I can clearly *will* to move my arm and then move my arm. I can *intend* to open the door and then open the door. My mental activity seems to cause physical activity every day. We can either say these are two different substances interacting, or all is just physical or all is just mental or mental and physical events are always separate but their occurrence is precisely coordinated.

Casting a long shadow over this, of course, is the prominence give in modern times (in contrast with, say, the 17th century) to the explanations of the universe in terms of the purely physical. The physical sciences today have no room for non-physical events causing physical events. For the physical sciences the universe is purely physical and acts according to laws of nature and never according to any supposed ('free') mental willing.

Are mind and matter too different to interact?

It was highlighted in the previous chapter how the mental and physical appear to be very different in several ways. Unlike physical events, for instance, mental events, like willing to do something, do not seem to occur in any observable space - they lack 'spatiality'. Unlike objectively observable physical events mental events are also 'private' to the individual, and there is something it is like to have them (they possess 'qualia'). Unlike physical events, mental events are *about* things. I see *something*. I will *something*. Physical activity is not about anything, it does not direct any sort of attention - it has no 'intentionality'. Mental events cannot be observed by others, unlike physical activity which in principle can be observed by anyone. An individual has 'privileged access' to their own mental states as well. My thoughts about things e.g., 'that there is a computer screen in front of me', can be true or false to me but such a proposition is not true or false to the computer, even if something to the effect is written on the screen; physical processes unlike mental activity cannot have 'propositional attitudes'.

Must the mind and body interact?

In spite the above difficulties and more, there appears clearly to be *some* kind of connection between mental activity and physical activity, a connection between what I might call my mind and my body. I *will* my arm to go up and it goes up. I cut my finger and I *feel* pain.

We cannot simply conclude because of the above difficulties and more that there is *no* connection between mind and body since it appears to run contrary to the facts of experience. What is needed, it seems, is to find a way of resolving the difficulties in explanation. A solution needs to be found to the mind-body problem. There must be some way of accounting for the *fact* of the clear connection between mind and body (such as thinking and acting). Or somehow it must be denied there is a connection and such interaction is merely *appearance* rather than *reality*.

This problem occupied Descartes and his 17th century partners. Could these great intellectuals and more come up with a way of explaining what seems to be the obvious; explaining how the mental and physical can interact?

Possible Solutions to the Mind-Body Problem:-

René Descartes *(1596-1650)*
'Interactionism' as a solution to the mind-body problem:

In Meditation Six Descartes' offers as a solution to the problem of explaining mind-body interaction that he observes he is lodged in his body as a pilot in a vessel, a ghost in a machine we might say. He also observes, however, that he is not like a pilot in a vessel, because he is very closely united to his body. He does not, for example, simply perceive damage to his body as a sailor perceives damage to his vessel. He instead *feels* pain from damage to his body. Such modes of thought are produced by this clear interaction between of mind and body.[42]

Where does this union or intermingling of mind and body take place? Descartes answer was in the pineal gland at the center of the brain. He apparently thought that the pineal gland was a likely candidate for this role because it appeared to be the only component in the brain that is not duplicated. While still a little mysterious the pineal gland has now been found to play a key role in regulating sleep.

Nicolas de Malebranche *(1638-1715)*
'Occasionalism' as a solution to the mind-body problem:

It seems impossible that mind and matter causally interact. The apparently clear connection/correlation between them, however, creates a need for an explanation. (How is it that when I will to move my arm it moves? How is it when I cut my finger I feel pain). How can the mind-body problem be solved?

Descartes' solution to the mind-body problem above ('interactionism') was to suggest that the mental and physical interact in the pineal gland in the brain. This hardly counts as a 'solution', of course, since it only moves the question one step further back. The question now just becomes, *how* do mind and matter interact in the pineal gland?

Descartes interactionism solution, is not really a solution at all, His writings on this were published in the 1640s. A little later another French thinker, Nicolas de Malebranche (1638-1715), offered 'occasionalism' as a solution to the mind-body problem.

How can the connectedness between mental and physical events be explained? It cannot be, Malebranche thought, because each *causes* the other, because they are too different. Yet they still seem connected. (I will my arm to go up and it goes up. I cut my finger and I feel pain). This connectedness, this perfect correlation between mental and physical events, must be explainable somehow.

One way out of this (and there seems perhaps to be no other option) is to suggest, as Malbranche does, that something else is making *both* mental and physical activities happen at the same time –feeling pain and cutting a finger occurring together. There needs then to be no causal interaction explanation to explain their strong correlation. God (or something with god-like the power) could be acting as an intermediary and cause both to occur at the same time. This is the Malebranche's 'occasionalism' position.

When I will to move my arm this could be the occasion for God (or whatever) to make my arm move. When I cut my finger this could be the occasion for God (or whatever) to produce a sensation of pain. When an object is in my visual field this could be the occasion for God (or whatever) to produce a visual experience in my mind. And so on. There seems perhaps to be no other means of accounting for the clear correlation between mental and physical events, since they are too different to actually interact with each other.

Occasionalism and Idealism:

It is a small step from 'occasionalism' to 'idealism', the approach of George Berkeley (1658-1753) described in Part I Epistemology. If, as Malbranche suggests, the mind-body problem can only be accounted for by positing God as producing mental events which precisely correlate with physical events, then why have the physical events at all?

If God plants these ideas in us then maybe ideas are all there is, ideas of being cut and ideas of feeling pain. We saw how Berkeley holds that there is no need for physical substance to explain our experiences, just God and minds.

Occasionalism and Empiricism:

It is also a small step from occasionalism to the empiricist conclusions of David Hume (1711-1776) as regards causation. If God is removed from the occasionalist picture, we end up with the position of only experiencing regular occurrences of mental events with physical events.

Hume points out, however, that this experience of regularity provides no evidence that a particular physical event is *necessarily* connected to a particular mental event. There no evidence in experience that when I cut my finger it will *always* hurt, no evidence in experience to suggest that one *causes* the other as. This is because in experience, there is only 'regularity' and 'repetition', not 'causation'.

Hume suggests that what we call 'causality' is in fact nothing more than the regular occurrence of one thing with another, and there is nothing in experience to count as evidence these things will continue to regularly occur together in the future. There is only our *habit* of expectation that they will, due to our human psychological make-up.

Hume, of course, exposes this as a problem for all supposed *causal* connection; all so called purely physical causal connections, as well as any presumed *causal* connections between mental and physical substances.

Gottfried Leibniz (1646-1716)
'Parallelism' as a solution to the mind-body problem:

Under occasionalism, God (or something like God) must be *constantly* intervening to produce mental events that occur at the same time as physical events. This seems a cumbersome explanation. It is perhaps improved upon via Gottfried Leibniz with his idea of 'parallelism'.

Gottfried Leibniz (1646-1716) proposed the possibility of a 'pre-established harmony', according to which bodily and physical states have been preordained by God to correspond at every point in time with the appropriate mental states. This removes the need for God (or something like God) to be *constantly* intervening to produce mental events when physical events take place. God could have just set up the whole thing in the beginning, like setting up two clocks to tick at the same time.

It might be easier to think of this as akin to sitting in a cinema watching a movie. Here the visual images on the screen and the sound track is operating in *parallel*, but they are not causally connected. The person on the screen appears to be causing the sounds you are hearing. But in reality these sounds are produced separately. They are synchronized at the start to occur with the appropriate movement of the lips.

'Epiphenomenalism as a solution to the mind-body problem:

Occasionalism and Parallelism ask us to accept not only the existence of God but also a particular role for God in ensuring that the appropriate mental events are precisely correlated with their respective physical events. Even if we accept that God exists *and* could have this role, we still may want a perhaps more plausible explanation of what appears to be a *direct* causal relation between mind and body.

'Epiphenomenalism' offers itself as an explanation of the apparently clear connection between mental and physical events, and without recourse to God. It does so by saying that physical events can cause mental events but mental events do not causally affect physical events.

Probably the most well known advocate of the 'epiphenomenalism' solution to the mind-body problem was the American philosopher and psychologist William James (1842-1910). His epiphenomenalism theory suggests that the causal connection between the mental and the physical goes in only one direction, from body to mind.

Epiphenomenalism does not deny dualism, that mental and physical are very different things, with different properties, but it does claim to remove the problem of interaction arising from attempting to maintain a dualist position.

One of the chief problems facing someone wanting to hold on to a dualist position is the scientific view that the universe can be explained in terms of physical events conforming to the laws of nature. There is no room here for any mysterious mental *will* to affect physical events.

Science could not continue to operate if it did. Predictions of physical events occurring according to the laws of nature would no longer be possible since any prediction could be upset via the impact of an unpredictable *will*.

This problem can be avoided, however, if it is denied that the *will* can cause physical events, if it is denied that the mental can affect the physical; only physical states can cause change in other physical states.

Without the problem of the mental affecting the physical, science can continue to make its steady progress in providing explanations of how physical events cause other physical events according to the laws of nature.

What is the place of mental events in Epiphenomenalism?

Consider a car. As is the engine is running, various dials and numerical displays indicate how fast the vehicle is moving, the oil pressure, the temperature and so forth. The car, however, will continue to function if some or all these numerical displays and dials are damaged. Epiphenomenalism views the mental in relation to the physical a little like the relationship between the functioning of the car and the various dials. The mental and numerical displays and dial movements are just a by-product, an 'epiphenomenon' – something that is caused but *itself* causes nothing.

The mental here could also be likened to the smoke coming out of a steam train. The smoke is caused by the operations of the physical engine according to the laws of physics, but the smoke itself causes nothing. A change in the direction in which the smoke is blowing does not cause the train to change direction. It is a consequence of the train changing direction. This is how we are to view mental events under epiphenomenalism. They do not cause physical events they, like the smoke, are just a by-product.

Furthermore, if the steam train here used smokeless fuel, so there is no smoke at all, the train would still continue to run. Taking this analogy further, it follows that it is possible under epiphenomenalism for there to be no mental events at all and still the physical body still continue to operate – continue to run.

Many animals with a simple biology continue to run, continue to survive effectively, but we would hesitate to attribute to them mental states. Animals with a more complex biology like us could operate with the same principle. Animals with a more complex biology may have some mental states but these mental states are not essential to their operation/survival, just by-products.

Some Problems with Epiphenomenalism:

It seems that *prior* to willing my arm to go up, my arm to goes up. The mental event often seems to occur *before* the physical behavior and seems to play a causal role in *causing* such behavior. Epiphenomenalism has it the other way around, the physical occurs before the mental (or at least at the same time) so it doesn't quite seem to fit the all facts here.

It is perhaps interesting to note that Frank Jackson, referred to in the previous chapter, was a supporter of epiphenomenalism when he proposed the Mary thought experiment. He considered that Mary's new mental state of the experience of seeing color for the first time was caused by a new physical state on seeing color for the first time.

However, Mary might also say "wow" on seeing color for the first time. Thus, in concord with epiphenomenalism, we have the physical state causing the mental state (seeing color), but this mental state *then* leading to a physical behavior, uttering "wow". Mental states like this then causing physical states (like uttering "wow") runs contrary to the epiphenomenalism position as causality is supposed only to be from physical to mental.

Epiphenomenalism also asks us to accept that we could carry on in the same way even if we had no conscious experiences at all (the train could continue without emitting 'smoke'). We also saw in the previous chapter how zombie versions of ourselves could behave in exactly the same way as our supposedly conscious selves.

If a zombie world like this is possible, if epiphenomenalism is possible, it is not, as David Chalmers notes *our* world. We are not just zombies.

Dual Aspect Theory as a solution to the mind-body problem:

The name most often associated with this theory is that of the Dutch philosopher Benedict Spinoza (1632-1677).

A reminder of the 'mind-body problem' maybe needed at this point: Mental and physical events seem to be connected; mental events and physical events appear to *cause* each other. However, because the mental and physical are so different, it is hard to see how this apparent *causal* interaction can be explained.

The 'dual aspect theory' (like the occasionalism and parallelism approaches) attempts to explain the precise correlation of mental and physical events without trying to say how one can *cause* the other.

The 'dual aspect' solution to the mind-body problem (and remember there *must* be some way of explaining what appears to be a clear correlation between mental and physical events) is to suggest that mind and body are different aspects of the same *one* substance. Mental events and physical events need not interact. They can be different aspects of the one underlying reality.

Water, for example, can be both wet and cold. Coldness and wetness are clearly connected in some way since they occur together, but they do not *cause* the other. Similarly, it may that although physical and mental events occur together, the mental need not cause the physical nor vice versa. The physical and mental could both be aspects of one underlying thing, like coldness and wetness can be aspects of water.

Some problems with Dual Aspect Theory:

A difficulty with the dual aspect solution to the mind-body problem is that a mysterious new substance has been introduced. What could it be? Something that is not mental or physical, yet somehow has these aspects.

This seems, then, to replace one type of explanatory problem with another. Nevertheless, it does not immediately mean dual aspect theory is false. Peter Strawson (1919-2006) provides a way in which it might be understood

In his book, 'Individuals' published in 1959 Strawson argues that that the mental and physical can be aspects of what it is to be a 'person'. An answer to the question 'What is a 'person'?" is that "It is something that can think and act; something that has a mind and a body". [43]

This might be as far as explanation can go. "What is 'water'?" Is not the answer simply, something that can be cold and wet, and all its other attributes?

This is one way we go about answering a 'What is it?' question.

Notwithstanding, still the rather obvious problem with dual aspect theory is that it removes the mystery of explaining mental and physical interaction but at the cost of replacing it with another. What could be this third thing now, that the mental and physical are both aspects of – a thing that is neither mental nor physical?

3

REJECTING DUALISM

(Can talk of mental be abandoned?)

It was noted in in the previous chapter that the seeming impossibility of explaining how mental and physical events causally interact led some to propose much needed 'solutions' to this mind-body problem.

Much needed because mental and physical activity *do* seem to interact; their interaction looks like a fact about the world. In the 17th century, when the existence of God tended to be regarded a given, 'occasionalism', and 'parallelism', were offered by the some of the great intellectuals of that era. A little more recently, where received wisdom is that the universe can be explained purely in terms of physical activity and God is dead (as Nietzsche put it), 'dual aspect theory' and 'epiphenomenalism' have been put forward as solutions to the mind-body problem.

All of these ideas attempt to account for the apparently obvious connectedness/correlation of mental and physical events (when I will my arm to go up, it goes up – when I cut myself, I feel pain). They seek to explain the connectedness/correlation without resorting to the notion that mental events *cause* physical events, although epiphenomenalism does allow that physical events can cause mental events.

Accounting for the interaction of mental and physical events, even with all these attempted 'solutions', still seems to be an intractable problem. The conundrum that mental and physical events appear to cause each other but can't cause each other since they are too different remains, staring up at us from the metaphorical page.

Another way out of this predicament is to deny the existence of mental substance altogether. If there only existed one substance, physical substance, then the problem of explaining the interaction between mind and body disappears. As mentioned, we live at a time where natural science holds all should be explicable in terms of the purely physical. What then are we to make of mental activity? In what follows three ways of looking at providing a denial of the mental will be described. The names given to these are, 'logical behaviorism',' identity theory', and 'functionalism. All belong to our modern age.

a) 'Logical behaviorism' as a rejection of the mental:-

Any denial of mental substance in favor of the purely physical still has to account for mental activity which, as we have seen, has very some different properties from physical activity.

The view of logical behaviorism is that we may have become tangled up in language here. Logical Behaviorism is a mixture of analysis of the language of mental activity and the approach of the psychological theory of behaviorism.

Behaviourism and Logical Behaviorism:

Behaviorism is a psychological theory of why humans and other animals behave in the ways they do. It explains all behavior in terms of learning by means of 'conditioning', without reference to 'thinking'. In the 'operant conditioning' version of behaviorism, famously put forward by American psychologist B.F. Skinner (1904-1990), the important features of learning a behavior via conditioning are rewards and punishments. A behavior that is rewarded will be more likely to be repeated than a behavior that is ignored or punished; the rewarded behavior is said to be 'reinforced'.

To stop a puppy wetting the carpet, for example, one punishes it when it does it and one rewards it when it goes outside. Eventually the puppy will *learn* not to wet the carpet. No reference to internal mental states in the puppy is necessary for this *learning* to take place. So it may be with children. Giving a child praise or chocolate for a good behavior like, say, not running across the road is a positive reinforcement. Repeated reinforcements will eventually cause the behavior to be *learned* – the child will acquire the habit of not running across the road. Again, no reference to any unobservable mental states here is necessary to explain how the learning takes place.

This 'operant conditioning' seems to have great power. A guide dog for a blind person is trained by means of operant conditioning reinforcements and punishments. Thus, we are prepared to trust the life of a blind human to the psychological theory of behaviorism in its operant conditioning form.

The point here again for the mental–physical problem is that what the dog is thinking – if it is *thinking* at all – is not relevant in creating the extremely sophisticated behavior of being able to guide a blind person around a noisy, busy, dangerous world.

It follows then, from the guide dog example in particular, that it may well be that sophisticated human behavior and perhaps all human behavior follows this pattern. The resort to mental activity is not needed to explain the sophisticated behavior of the guide dog for the blind, so perhaps it is not needed to explain human behavior as well.

If this is so, the language of mental events is not needed to explain human behavior (or guide dog behavior). What, then, could this language of mental events referring to?

Under behaviorism, talk of mysterious internal mental states becomes irrelevant to explaining how behaviors are learned. The belief in inner mental states could perhaps be like the old belief in magic and superstition, but now, this belief in inner mental states may perform no explanatory role with regard to the explanation of behavior. British philosopher Gilbert Ryle (1900-1976), attempts to expose how the language of mental states is still used, and why it can lead us up blind alleys, with the 'mind body problem' accounting for how the mental and physical can 'interact', being one of these blind alleys.

Gilbert Ryle and the Misuse of Mental Language – The Source of the Mind-Body Problem:

Gilbert Ryle, in his book 'The Concept of Mind' (1949), makes use of behaviorist thinking in his *logical* behaviorism. His position, however, is based on the approach of Ludwig Wittgenstein (1889-1951) whom we have met previously in both Part I Epistemology and in Part IIa Metaphysics and Philosophy of Religion.

Ryle's thesis is that the mental-physical problem is not a real problem at all. It results from a misuse of language and concepts. Suppose you were asked "What color is the number 84?" This is to place color in the category of things that numbers have. It is to make let us say a 'category mistake'. It creates a problem that isn't real and therefore has no solution.

Imagine someone watching and being told about the game of cricket or baseball. He learns what the functions of those who bat, field, bowl or pitch but then wonders who performs the function of 'team-spirit'? This again is a *category mistake*. 'Team spirit' does not belong to the category of functions someone performs, like throwing the ball, or hitting the ball or catching the ball. It is more like how energetically all these functions are performed. 'Team spirit' is not a thing like batting or bowling or fielding that *clearly* exists in cricket or baseball but mysteriously cannot be found among any of the functions of the players. Not being able to find the person who performs the function of 'team spirit' is not a real problem.

Could it be that 'consciousness' is like 'team spirit'? It is only impossible to find and mysterious if we misuse the concept, or fail to understand the role it plays in language?

Might it even be that *all* human behavior can be explained without reference to 'consciousness' and mental concepts, akin to explaining the behavior of guide dogs for the blind without reference to mental concepts? If so, the problem of explaining how the mental interacting with the physical disappears; the mind-body problem disappears.

We could still talk about the sort of behavior that constitutes 'team spirit' in a cricket match without mentioning 'team spirit' – by only referring to the observable behavior of the players. It would take a lot of words to explain all these observable behaviors and would be very long winded. Ryle sees words like 'team spirit' as a way of making a point more quickly and conveniently, but with the danger of creating unreal problems if it is not understood how the language is being used (or misused) in this context.

This is also how Ryle sees the language referring to the mental. Like 'team spirit', it does not refer to anything mysterious, only to observable behavior. This means that mental terms (like 'team spirit') can, in principle, be translated into observable behaviors.

An example is needed to show how talk of the mental can be converted to talk about observable behavior (only). The key to this is to think about what Ryle calls 'dispositional explanations'. He describes dispositional explanations. We can say why a glass broke by citing the event that caused it to break. We can also say why the glass broke by saying it was brittle. Brittle here is a dispositional adjective it does not describe an event but an 'if…then' proposition; the glass can be described as brittle because *if* in a certain situation *then* it will shatter easily (not dissolve or twist etc.) [44]

How does the notion of a 'dispositional explanation' help to solve the mind-body problem?

It does so by converting terms that appear to refer to inner mental activity into 'dispositional hypotheses'. What is thought to be mental is really a disposition to behave in certain ways.

The statement "He boasted from vanity on meeting the stranger" on the mental *causing* physical behavior approach can be construed as saying that "He boasted and the cause of his boasting was the 'feeling' *in* him of vanity."

On the '*dispositional* explanation', though, there is no *inner* activity. His 'vanity' is to be regarded as something like, '*if* there is a chance of securing the admiration and envy of others, *then* he behaves in a way that attempts to produce this admiration and envy.'

It is quicker to say "He acted out of vanity". But this economical use of language may tempt us to think that 'vanity' refers to a mysterious inner mental activity, when it doesn't.

This analysis can also be extended to relations between mental states such as beliefs and desires. I might say I run away from the tiger because I *believe* it will eat me and I *desire* not to be eaten.

Under operant conditioning behaviorism, when we say a dog *desires* not to be eaten by a tiger, we do not have to attribute to the animal an inner mental state; we just have to consider its outward behavior. For example, you might say in answer to the question "Why does the dog run away?" "The dog *believes* a tiger is approaching and runs away because it does not *desire* to be eaten".

You do not have to attribute mysterious inner mental states of 'believing' and 'desiring' to the dog if you say this. You know that, in principle at least, the dog's behavior is capable of being converted into language that does not require attributing inner mental states, such as *beliefs* or *desires*, to the dog. You do not have to hold that the dog has inner mental states just that if X happens then you know the dog will do Y.

By such dispositional means Ryle hopes to have eliminated the position there are two worlds - one with inner mental phenomena, and the other with outer behavioral activity. He hopes, via his logical behaviorism, to have provided the means for us to abandon the notion of a mysterious spirit in a material world or 'ghost' in the machine.

This sort of elimination of inner mental phenomena (by the materialists) is sometimes known as 'eliminative materialism' and its target is called 'folk psychology', a pejorative term used by William James to describe what is normally thought about the existence of inner mental states such as beliefs and desires etc. There are, however, some problems with logical behaviorism.

Two problems for Logical Behaviorism:

i) Can, in principle, all mental language be converted to the language of observable behavior?

It seems a tall order to suggest that *all* uses of mental words can be replaced by words referring to observable behavior. This is what needs to be possible if the logical behaviorist position is to be maintained. If there are mental concepts in principle not replaceable by words referring to observable behavior, then they would appear to *have* refer to the unobservable mental – and we would be back with the mental-physical gap.

Logical behaviorism suggests that the use of 'mental' language is a short hand way of communicating, and is useful because of this. Translating mental words into the long form of observable behaviors is bound almost by definition to be impractical, but still may be possible in principle, and so its impracticality is no challenge to it in principle.

ii) Ruling out logical behaviorism in principle?

To say that someone is in pain under logical behaviorism is to say that they will behave in a certain way if stimulated. If they are sitting silently and still, however, we can't know if they are in pain, like we cannot know if salt is soluble in water just by looking at it.

We have to put the salt in the water to see if it the dissolves, to see if it has a soluble *disposition*. Similarly, we have to provoke a person's behavior to see if someone has the behavioral propensities that constitute pain. This is how we come to know that someone is in pain, we infer it from their behavior – we cannot know if they are in pain if they're just sitting silently and still.

Contrary to logical behaviorism American philosopher, Hilary Putnam (b.1926) argues that it is perfectly possible a person exhibit no pain behavior and still be feeling pain. Careful training might create a race of Super Spartans or stoics, who never show pain. For the logical behaviorists, these have no pain behaviors, dispositional or otherwise, and so cannot really be feeling pain. However, they do, of course, *feel* pain (just do not show they are feeling it).

If it is possible to feel pain but have no pain behaviors that this can be translated into, logical behaviorism must wrong. Putnam thinks it *is* wrong, since logical behaviorism argues that, in principle, *all* mental states (including feeling pain) can be converted to observable behaviors and his Super Spartans have no observable pain behaviors.

In addition to this Super Spartan point, it may be said that we infer that someone is in pain from their observable behaviors. This does not appear, however, to be how I know *I* am in pain. You do not *infer* from your behaviour (active or passive) that you are in pain. You feel your pain.

I infer that a team is has 'team spirit' from their behaviors so 'team spirit' can be converted to language of observable behaviors.

However, I do not say that "I am in pain" because I infer it from my observable behaviors. Therefore, unlike the 'team spirit' case used by Ryle, it appears I cannot, in principle, convert "I am in pain" into the language of observable behaviors.

Wittgenstein's private language argument:

Logical behaviorism has a problem in the above two examples because of the apparent disconnect between feeling pain and observable pain behavior (feeling pain without any observable pain behavior). It may be possible to save logical behaviorism, however, by making use of what has become known as the 'private language argument' put forward by Ludwig Wittgenstein.

Wittgenstein exposes the fact is that we cannot construct a language on our own, a *private* language. We need a language community to provide rules on how to use words.

I learn how to use a word like 'pain' in a community. Using the sentence "I am in pain" needs the learning of when it is appropriate and inappropriate to use this expression – the various situations of its use.

If this is true, when I talk about my own mental states (as above), like saying, "I am in pain", I *must* learn how to do so on the basis of my observations of when others use the word 'pain', and on the basis of the observations of myself.

I could not come to learn how to use the word 'pain' in any other way – I see how others behave and use it (re. their observable behaviors) and use it myself. My use of the word 'pain' is appropriate when I follow the rules of the community of language users when I am in the 'right' situation for its use.

It is no attack on logical behaviorism to say then, as Putnam does, that someone may be in pain without having the observable behaviors and so the language of pain cannot be translated into observable states.

Wittgenstein points out in his 'private language argument' here that there would be no language of 'pain' unless the word could be learned using observable behaviors of when it is appropriate to do so.

There will be more on Wittgenstein's private language argument in chapter 4 of this Part IIb Metaphysics and Philosophy of Mind. For now though we consider the modern view that the mind is the brain.

b) Identity Theory as a rejection of dualism:-

Dualism is the view that there are both mental and physical substances and these are connected (when I will my arm to go up, it goes up – when I cut my finger, I feel pain). The mind-body problem amounts to finding a way of to explaining this mind-body connection. Occasionalism, parallelism, epiphenomenalism, and dual-aspect theory are all attempts to do this while preserving the distinction between the mental and the physical. Logical behaviorism above, asks us to reject the mental altogether, leaving only the (observable) physical.

Logical Behaviorism aims to demonstrate that the mind-body problem is not actually a real problem by showing that it arises from a failure to appreciate the precise role of mental terms in our language – the mind-body problem arises from a category mistake. Mental terms do not refer to any particular (mysterious) thing, as 'team spirit' doesn't refer to any particular (mysterious) thing in cricket or baseball. They are just a quick way of making a point. And such terms can be replaced by other terms (perhaps a long list) that refer only to objectively observable behavior.

Here, another attempt to eliminate the mental called 'Identity Theory' is described. Like Logical Behaviorism, Identity Theory 'solves' the problem of explaining the mind-body connection by rejecting the mental in favor of the physical.

Unlike Logical Behaviorism, though, it does *not* do this by suggesting that mental terms do not actually refer to any particular thing (like 'team spirit' does not refer to a particular thing). In Identity Theory mental terms *do* refer to something, but they are identical with physical brain states. The mind, in other words, *is* the brain.

We saw just recently in chapter 1 of this Part IIb how there appear to be characteristics of mental states that physical states do not have, such as qualia, intentionality, propositional attitudes, privileged access and lack of spatiality. It seemed, therefore, the mental and the physical could not, therefore, be the same thing.

With this information, one might be tempted to say right at the outset that Identity Theory is bound to fail. Surely it must be mistaken in simply saying the mental is identical with physical brain states, since all the property differences problems between mental and physical remain in place.

Identity Theory, however, is well aware of the different properties of mental states as contrasted with physical states. It attempts to find a way around what appear to be these fundamental difficulties. Much hinges on the term 'identical' here.

What is meant by the term 'identity' in the Identity Theory?

When I say this football is the 'same' as that football over there in the field, I mean they have the same qualities – color, shape, weight etc. But there are *two* balls.

When I say this football is the 'same' ball I played with yesterday, I am not saying there are two balls. Today's ball does not just have the same qualities as yesterday's ball, it is not just the same type of ball, it *is* the same ball – there is only *one* ball in question.

It is in the latter sense that mental states are to be considered the same/identical to brain states. There are not two things with the same qualities – mental states and brain states are one and the same.

The 'Evening Star', appears in the eastern sky before dawn and the 'Morning Star', appears in the western sky after sunset. The ancient Egyptians and Ancient Greeks thought these must be two stars. The Greek the names for them were Phosphoros (the morning star) and Hesperos (the evenings star). Considered investigation later revealed that these stars are 'identical', in the second sense of 'identical' above. Hesperos and Phosphoros are the same star.

Both are the planet Venus. The Evening Star *is* the Morning Star – they both refer to one and the same thing. Similarly, the UK 'Prime Minister' and the 'First Lord of the Treasury' may appear to those without knowledge of UK political offices to be different positions. In fact both currently refer to David Cameron. He is the PM *and* First Lord of the Treasury, as Venus is the Evening Star *and* the Morning Star.

How to account for the specific characteristics of mental states which seem to make them different from physical states?

Identity Theory is saying the mind is 'identical' with the brain, in the sense that they are one and the same thing. How does Identity Theory deal with the characteristics of mental states which seem fundamentally different from physical states – characteristics which would appear to make it impossible that the mind *is* the brain in the same way that the Evening Star *is* the Morning Star or the Prime Minister *is* the First Lord of the Treasury?

Let us take one of these 'fundamentally different' characteristics of mental states, the fact that they can be learned by 'introspection' and not by 'observation' as with physical objects. Suppose I have the mental state 'feeling pain'. I can know something about how much it hurts via introspection. How much it hurts, though, cannot be known by examining objective brain states. This property difference seems to ensure that (physical) brain states cannot be identical to mental states. There may, however, be way around it.

I might, for example, know a lot about what the UK Prime Minster does while, at the same time, not know that he is also First Lord of the Treasury. Further investigation would reveal this knowledge.

It certainly isn't the case, though, that it is *impossible* that the PM cannot also be the First Lord of the Treasury, simply because I don't (yet) know it.

Similarly, I may know quite a bit about water, its 'wetness' and so forth, but still not (yet) know that water *is* the same as two hydrogen molecules and one oxygen molecule.

Thus, I may know as well quite a bit about pain, how much it hurts and so forth, but not (yet) know that pain is identical with neurophysiological activity in the brain.

The expressions above are taken by the identity theory to refer to what is physical. 'Wetness' of water and the 'hydrogen' and 'oxygen' of water both refer to what is physical. 'Intensity' of pain and 'neurological activity' of pain may therefore both refer to what is physical as well. It is not on these grounds *impossible* that this be so at least.

In all these cases further investigation and learning can reveal how things that may appear to be completely different can actually turn out to be identical in the sense of being exactly the same thing. It certainly doesn't mean that because things *seem* to have completely different qualities that it is *impossible* they be the same. The Evening Star appearing in the east and the Morning Star appearing in the west can turn out with more knowledge to be one and the same - as pain and neurological activity may, with more knowledge, turn out to be the same.

The Plausibility of Identity Theory:

The plausibility of identity theory relies on the fact that not knowing how something can be identical with something else doesn't necessarily mean that it cannot turn out to be identical with that something else after more knowledge is gained, just as the Evening Star turned out to be identical with the Morning Star. Water a liquid, with its liquid characteristics, turned to be identical with hydrogen and oxygen (two 'gases'); so mental states could, in the end, all turn out to be identical with brain states – even if we're not sure exactly how just yet. Not being sure how they are identical now, does not rule out that they will turn out to be understood as identical later

There is also empirical evidence in support of the Identity Theory. It has been mentioned how, for instance, changing the physical state of the brain via say, anti-depressant drugs which boost the activity of the neurochemical serotonin, or antipsychotic drugs (given to schizophrenics) which reduce the activity neurochemical dopamine, can change mental states. The same may be said for alcohol consumption, nerve tissue degeneration with old age and so forth.

The simplest explanation for these changes in mental states is that there are not *two* different entities one physical and one non-physical occurring at the same time and (somehow?) interacting with each other, but just *one* thing.

The 'best' hypothesis seems to be that physical brain states *are* mental states. Change one and you must change the other (as if you change the evening star and you must change the morning star).

Suggesting that there are characteristics of mental states that we do not appear explicable in physical terms, as was done in the opening sections of this Part

IIa Metaphysics and Philosophy of Mind, is no fundamental rejection of the principle of the mental being identical to the physical.

It was not easy to see how the 'wetness' of water could be accounted for by hydrogen and oxygen molecules - "Molecules can't be wet!" we might have said before we knew more. But this should not have ruled out in principle that they are identical since it has turned out to be the case.

Objections to Identity Theory:

For Identity Theory to stand up it must be the case that there can be no mental states without brain states since they are one and the same. Identity theory would be disproved if it could be established that in a case where there was *no* brain activity (a dead person maybe) there were still mental events – thoughts and experiences taking place. If it were possible for someone to exist (thinking and feeling) outside their bodies, identity theory would also be disproved.

Identity Theory is threatened more immediately, though, by the fact that there remain certain properties of mental events which seem always destined to defeat *any* attempt to reduce them to purely physical events. In particular, the characteristics of the lack of a location and the existence of qualia.

i) Lack of Location and Identity Theory:

Two different things can turn out to be one and the same only if they have the same location. The Evening Star is really in the same location as the Morning Star – if you find the planet Venus you've found 'both' (If you find David Cameron, you will have found the UK PM *and* the UK First Lord of the Treasury).

Mental events, though, do not seem to have a location – it makes no sense to say that experience is located five centimeters behind the eyes or some such. Thus, it cannot be the case that thoughts and neural events are identical because of the lack of any location for mental events.

ii) Qualia and Identity Theory:

'The Morning Star is the Evening Star.'

'Water is hydrogen and oxygen.'

'Heat is molecules in motion.'

'Mental states are brain states.'

The first three statements above are analogies to the mental-physical case.

However, it may be that the mental-physical case is very different from these three claims and so cannot be analogous to them.

If there is a God who created the world, then in order to create heat, He would only need to create molecular motion – as they are identical. But in order to create minds, would it be enough for God just to create brains?

For the Identity Theory to be true creating brains has to be enough to create minds at the same time. But having created brains and the neurological activity that, say, pain is supposed to be identical with, it seems God as a creator still would have to create something else, the *felt* experience we call 'pain'.

A stimulation would have to be felt as pain and not as, say, a sweet taste. It seems it would be within God's power to make the brain state occur without the pain (or indeed without any feeling at all). The connection between the brain state and a pain, therefore, is not a *necessary* connection – it is possible in principle to have one (brain state) without the other mental state (feeling of pain).

This used to be a strong argument against Identity theory. It is weakened now, however, by the psychological phenomena of 'Synesthesia'. Patients, suffering from this condition have the 'wrong' mental states associated with a given physical stimulation.

Some experience different names as different tastes, or different numbers as different colors or sounds as smells and so forth. This can be because their physical brains are operating differently than 'normal' people. Associated brain scans seem to indicate this, so further suggesting that mental states are brain states in support of Identity Theory

Notwithstanding, how it feels to the person experiencing numbers as colors or whatever, this qualia, this 'what is it like' to experience this, still seems to be more than a brain state description. Such was Thomas Nagel's point in his 'What is it Like to be a Bat?' paper and the experience of 'Mary' in seeing color for the first time in Frank Jackson's paper 'What Mary Didn't Know?' (Both described in chapter 3 of this IIb Metaphysics and Philosophy of Mind).

In addition, we may also want to note that, if identity theory is true (the mind *is* the brain), then we may have to conclude that only those creatures with *human* brains can have the sort of mental states and feelings that we do, since mental states are identical with human brain states. Perhaps only humans can feel the pain that humans feel.

Identity Theory might also suggest that it is impossible to build a machine that can think and feel like humans, as only human brains can do this. This question of whether machines can think is also addressed below under another challenge to the view that mental substance must exist, 'Functionalism'. This is considered now.

c) Functionalism as a rejection of dualism:-

Logical Behaviorism, as a form of 'eliminative materialism', argues that all terms appearing to refer to that which is mental can in principle be *eliminated* from the language, and be replace by words referring to what is observable (as 'team spirit' refers to what is observable).

Identity Theory does not claim that talk of mental events can in principle be eliminated from the language and be replaced by words referring to what is observable. It does claim, however, that mental events are identical with neurophysiological events in the brain. The mind *is* the brain) – there is no mental substance.

A possible problem for Identity Theory noted above, a problem sometimes called 'chauvinism', is that creatures that don't have a human brain become viewed as unlikely to feel and think as humans do because minds are human brains. And it also becomes impossible to build a machine that can think and feel as we do – only human minds/brains can to this.

The importance of structure:

The Functionalism, approach, like Identity Theory (and Logical Behaiviorism) aims to dismiss the existence of mental Substance. Functionalism, however, can do this by avoiding the Identity Theory problem of 'chauvinism' and also allow for the possibility of building a machine which can think as humans do.

The latter is a project that is being attempted currently in various parts of the world. If it is ever successful, Identity Theory will have been rejected.

Functionalism is the view that mind is not produced by a particular *sort* of material like human brain matter (or electronic circuits, or whatever). Minds are rather the product of the relations between different parts, its *structure* – how the stuff is put together, not what it is made of.

Humans and octopuses and parrots all have very different sorts of brains and nervous systems. But if they are all put together in a specific way, then functionalism allows that they can all, for example, feel pain, or engage in thinking, not just humans.

Analogies with computer software and computer hardware can also be used to explain Functionalism. Different makes of computer, different types of hardware, can all run the same software. Different hardwares can run Microsoft Word, for instance, as long as the relations between the parts are 'right' – as long as its *structure* is 'right'.

Can machines think?

If mental is to do with relations between parts, to do with structure, what that structure is made of becomes irrelevant. Functionalism holds that the structure could be made of brains, or electric circuits, or some other material if they are arranged in a sophisticated enough way. Functionalism allows, then, that machines put together in the 'right' way can think.

Under functionalism the relations between the parts of brain is what gives it the capacity to think and feel. If, then, the relations between electronic circuits on a circuit board or the equivalent are the same as the relations between the parts in the brain, a computer constructed in this way could think and feel as we do. Alternatively, we could say that the brain might better be described as a complex organic computer – a gooey computer.

'Hardware' is the actual computer with its circuits. In the case of human minds, the hardware might be the brain and its neurological circuits. 'Software' is the program that gives the computer specific instructions. In humans, we might say that some specific instructions can be 'hard wired', as in the case of instincts. The general functionalist point, however, is that the mind is nothing other than an complex program.

How would we know if a machine/computer could think?

The British scientist, Alan Turing, is widely regarded to be the inventor of the computer (such were initially called 'Turing Machines'). He seems to have considered the question of establishing whether machines can think at some length. In his paper 'Computing, Machinery and Intelligence' (1950) published in the primary British philosophy journal, 'Mind' he explicitly considers the question 'Can machines think?'. He does this by proposing the idea of an 'imitation game'. Here the machine is to be asked any questions and a human is to be asked any questions. Both are out of sight and questions can be printed and sent 'in' with answers being printed and sent back. If by such means it is impossible to tell which is the machine and which is the human, then Turing holds we would have to conclude that the machine thinks. [45]

Turing's key point here, then, is that if a computer were interrogated along with a human, and it was impossible to distinguish between the human and the machine, the conclusion that he computer could think would be forced upon us.

A case against machines being able to think:

The functionalist position consists of three basic points:

1. The view that what a machine is made of is irrelevant to whether it can think or not. What is important is not the materials, but how they are put together.
2. Mind is like a computer program or software, capable of working on different types of hardware, as long as they have the 'right' set up.
3. Passing the Turing test would be evidence of thinking: How would you conclude a human was thinking? By conversing with him/her. If you conversed with a machine and were convinced by such conversations that it was human, then you must conclude (as you would in the human case) that the machine could think.

The American philosopher John Searle (b.1932) argues strongly in his paper 'The Myth of the Computer' (1982) that it is not possible, in principle, to build a machine that can think. He rejects the functionalist view that only structure is important together with its view that what the brain is made of is irrelevant. He also rejects the claim that passing the Turing test is evidence that a machine/computer could think.

a) John Searle's rejection of functionalism:

Searle first points out that it would not even be possible to build a machine that could feel thirsty, let alone think. This is because, he thinks, feeling thirsty and desiring to drink depend upon our biology. [46]

Searle's point is that a computer program and hardware might simulate the physical behavior associated with thirst, but it does not produce the feeling of thirst and the desire to drink. It could simulate such a thing but this would not be the actuality. – such depends upon biology. As Searle notes further the materials are often fundamental. A computer program and hardware could also simulate lactation but it would not produce milk. A computer program and hardware could also simulate photosynthesis but it would not produce sugar – this depends upon the materials involved. Similarly, it could simulate thirst and simulate thought, but it would only be a simulation.

b) Rejecting the view that mind is a program and that passing the Turing test counts as evidence for thinking:

Searle creates a thought experiment about communicating in Chinese to reject the notion that passing the Turning 'imitation game' is evidence that a machine can think. He knows no Chinese and is locked in a room full of Chinese symbols in boxes. He has a book of rules in English telling him which symbols should follow another symbol. Chinese symbols are fed into the room and by looking at the rules Searle is able to send out the 'right' response symbols. And he may become really quick at this and so be able to pass the imitation game for being a Chinese speaker. The problem is that he still would not understand a word of Chinese, even though he passed the test. A computer program could enable him to pass the imitation game test as described by Turing by getting the right responses to questions and convince all that it was thinking. However it still need not then understand any of the questions or any of the answers. [47]

Searle, then is saying that the project of attempting to build a machine that can think may well be doomed from the start (and, presumably, potential investors in such a project perhaps need to put their money in something else.)

4

THE EXISTENCE OF OTHER MINDS

(How can we know them?)

This issue may be approached by consideration of the plight of those suffering from autism.

Simon Baron Cohen Professor of Developmental Psychophathology at Cambridge University has devised a face recognition test for his work with autistics. The eye regions of a number of faces are presented to adults on the autistic spectrum and non-autistic adults. The task is to match particular facial (eye region) expressions with given target words such as, 'desiring' (a feeling word) and 'convinced' (a thinking word) and so forth.

Those high on the autistic spectrum are generally unable to do this successfully compared with non-autistics. That is to say, they are unable to read from a face what another is feeling or thinking. It is as if they are surrounded in life by what would be to non autistics faceless beings, and so the behavior of such beings cannot be understood or predicted – a frightening world.

I can feel my pain when I hammer my finger. I know in a direct way that I am in pain. I do not *infer* it from my behavior. It is not possible, however, for me to feel the pains of others. Thus, the question arises, how can I know others feel pain as I do? How can I know other bodies and faces are having mental experiences?

All I can do is *infer* from the behavior or expressions of others that they are in pain or have mental states – I cannot feel their pain or have their mental states, I have no access to such. It would seem that the severe autistic is unable precisely to make such inferences, unable to know that there are minds other than his own.

The epistemological problem here is that I could be mistaken in thinking as I normally do that others have mental experiences, that others are feeling pain or pleasure or have sensations or thoughts or feelings, so I cannot really be said that I have *knowledge* there are other minds. Can this skeptical challenge be answered? Can we have 'knowledge' other minds exist?

We could build a machine to make the appropriate responses to certain questions about whether it was really in pain, but it would not really be feeling and pain – it would not really be having this mental state.

How, though, would we attempt to find out if the machine was or was not feeling pain? All we could do is observe its behavior.

We can ask the same question of humans. How could we be certain that other humans are or are not feeling pain? By asking them? This, however, would be no better than asking the machine if it was in pain. All we can do, as with machines, is observe others' behavior. Why, then, are we not like those high on the autistic spectrum unable to identify other minds, since, like the autistic, we have no access to the mental states (if any) of other entities?

Attempts to solve the problem of other minds:-

1. *'Argument from Analogy' as a solution to the problem of other minds:*

One argument used to confirm other minds exist is called the 'argument from analogy'. It is set down with clarity by the English philosopher John Stuart Mill (1806-73) in his book *An Examination of Sir William Hamilton's Philosophy and of The Principal Philosophical Questions Discussed in his Writings* (1865), then generally an attack on the views of an esteemed Scottish philosopher and writer on human psychology. [48]

The 'argument from analogy' here consists of a number of stages:

- I know that I have thoughts, feelings, beliefs, desires, intentions etc.
- I know that certain external causes on my body (like hammering my finger) produce internal feelings (e.g., of pain) and produce physical behavior (e.g., wincing and hopping about).
- I observe how certain external causes regularly produce certain physical behaviors in others and that this is the same behavior as I exhibit when acted on by the same external cause. (Others wince and cry out when they hit their finger as I do).
- I know in my own case that the first link, certain external causes, produces the last link, the internal sensation (e.g., the pain from hitting my finger).
- I observe that other human beings are composed of the same materials as I am; skin, bones, nerves, blood vessels etc.
- I conclude that they therefore must be having the same mental experiences and I do (e.g., feeling of pain) when acted on by a certain external cause (e.g., hitting their finger) and exhibiting the very same external behavior as I do (e.g., wincing and hopping about) when acted on by that particular cause.

The failure of the argument from analogy:

The 'argument from analogy' seems like a fancy title for our 'common sense' view of why we think others have mental states similar to ourselves. Others are physically like us and they exhibit the same reactions when they, say, hammer their finger. I feel pain when this happens, so they probably feel pain too. Unfortunately, however, this argument fails completely.

The argument from analogy starts from the position that behavior alone cannot be completely relied upon as evidence for mental activity causing that behavior.

This is why I can wonder in the first if others have minds with mental states similar to my own.

If behavior alone could be relied upon as evidence for other minds, the argument from analogy would not be needed. I would not need to examine my own case and consider it analogous to others if I could tell from their behavior what they were feeling.

I would not need any argument from analogy to establish there are others with other minds like mine, since it would already be clear from their behavior.

The argument from analogy is needed because behavior alone is *not* evidence of mental activity taking place in others (I cannot be sure if others have minds just from their behavior).

I notice there is a link between behavior and mental activity taking place in my own case. The 'commonsense' (argument from analogy) view is that I conclude by drawing an analogy from my own case that behavior alone in others *is* evidence of mental activity taking place in those others (others have minds similar to mine).

This, though, is from examination of just one single case, my own. The problem remains firmly in place. How can I have knowledge there is a mind behind the faces of other beings like there is in me?

A fish could in some ways be considered analogous to me. If I had hook stuck my mouth it would hurt and I would move vigorously to get it out. A fish behaves in ways similar to the ways I would, if 'hooked' in my lip (i.e. strain to get unhooked)

This does not make it certain that the fish has a mind like mine, or feels pain like me. I cannot from the argument from analogy, the common sense view, be certain I have knowledge that there are other minds in other bodies, no more that I can be certain in saying that a fish has a mind because it behaves like I would if I had a hook stuck in my mouth.

My conclusion is still based on the evidence of my own single case and the question of whether there can be knowledge of the existence of other minds and their mental contents in other bodies remains unanswered.

The mistake of starting with solipsism?

The situation where all you can be certain of is the existence of your own mind is known as 'solipsism'.

The argument from analogy above, the common sense view, starts from this solipsism position and tries to overcome it by employing analogy.

The behavior-mind connection in you (that you know about) is regarded as the same in others as you can see that are like you physically and when provoked in a certain way behave like you when you are provoked in a similar way.

But the question remains open, nevertheless, whether other bodies have minds analogous to your own, since behavior of other bodies is no indication that there is another mind. (If it was, the argument from analogy to establish the existence of other minds in other bodies would not be needed).

In much of twentieth century Anglo-American philosophy the view has been that the argument from analogy starts in the wrong place, starts with 'solipsism' and tries to overcome a problem that does not exist - which it cannot do. The mistake it is argued is to assume that solipsism (the certainty of your own case) is a tenable starting position.

This starting position, this intellectual framework, appears (for better or for worse) to have been heavily influenced by the thinking of René Descartes in the 17th century, in regarding what he is certain about – that he cannot doubt he exists, or doubt he is a thinking thing, but he can doubt there are other thinking things.

If solipsism is not a tenable position, then such will dismiss this well-known Cartesian claim that all you have certain knowledge of is that you exist and are a thinking thing (since to doubt this is to exist and it is to think).

The mistake in the argument from analogy, the common sense view, is to start off with the presumption that you can start from you own case; from, say, your knowledge that you feel pain, to wondering if others feel pain.

This starting with solipsism creates the problem that you cannot conclude with certainty that others feel pain as you do. And thus, in the end, it leaves you only with the certainty of your own case – with solipsism.

The rejection of solipsism as a tenable position, the starting point for the argument from analogy, is given by Ludwig Wittgenstein's private language argument – outlined just previously in chapter 3 of this Part IIb Metaphysics and Philosophy of Mind

2. _The 'Private Language Argument' as a solution to the problem of other minds:_

Wittgenstein aims to reveal in this context that starting from the certainty of my own case, I know I feel pain when (say) I hit my finger, to then wondering if others feel pain, or have minds at all like me is to start in the wrong place.

Wittgenstein performs this exposure by using his private language argument. It seems we learn the meaning of, say, 'chair' by someone, perhaps a parent, pointing at a chair and saying, "chair". We could then start to use the word 'chair'.

Sometimes, no doubt, we would get its use wrong. We may call a small table 'chair'. We would be corrected, perhaps again by parents, and the differences between 'table' and 'chair' pointed out. As time goes on, we learn how to use the word 'chair' properly, learn how to follow the rules for using the word 'chair'.

How, then, do we learn to use words like 'pain' that refer to inner mental states?

The situation is not the same as the chair case. The private feeling of pain, cannot be pointed to, unlike the publicly observable chair. So, how did 'pain' become part of a public language like the word 'chair' can become part of a public language?

The key Wittgenstein point is that words which refer to private inner mental states like 'pain' cannot be given a meaning in language by _one_ person.

If I give a name to a special inner feeling using the word, 'zog', I cannot communicate anything to others. Saying "I feel zog" would communicate nothing because it means nothing to them. I cannot give public meaning to 'zog' by myself.

The creation of a public language including the use of words like 'pain' (or 'zog') needs a community of language users - other people – to agree (tacitly or otherwise) on how the word/sound is to be used.

'Pain' and words referring to other *inner* mental states are part of a public language. Thus, since they cannot be given meaning privately (by yourself alone), you can only learn them by observing *outer* behavior.

This is how we *must* have learned how to use the word 'pain'. By seeing when others (e.g., parents) used it, and what their behavior was when they used it.

The problem the argument from analogy seeks to rectify is a mistake; solipsism is not a tenable position. Solipsism attempts to hold that 'I am certain I have mental states; certain (for instance), certain that I am in 'pain, but I am not certain that there are others with mental states'.

The private language argument point is that there *must* be others for us to be able to use the word 'pain', to be able to use pain language in the first place

We cannot start from the certainty of our own case and then ask if there are others like us. We need others like us to use language (including the language of asking questions) *before* we can ask if there are others like us.

Wittgenstein's 'Philosophical Investigations' published after his death in 1951 contains a famous discussion by him about something in a small box, perhaps a beetle. It would not be possible to name this something privately with a word and then communicate to others about it [49]

The point here is that if mental states like feeling pain were like private little beetles in boxes that no one could get at except the owner of the box, then we could not talk to each other about what was in the boxes. We might all mean different things by a word like 'beetle' or there may be no beetle at all.

It is important to note that this is a matter of 'logical' possibility not 'practical' possibility. The problem is not that it is *practically* impossible for one person to give meaning in a language entirely private to them. The problem is that it is not *logically* possible that words ('pain' for example) have meaning in a language where there is only one person and that person creates the sounds in that language.

The notion of 'possible worlds' created by 17th century thinker Liebniz is helpful here. If the problem were *practicality* alone, there could be a possible world, a set of circumstances, where it was possible for a single individual to create a language.

If the problem is *logical*, there is no possible world in which it could be the case that a single individual could create a language by themselves (and use it to wonder if there are other people with other minds). This is as logically impossible as there being a world with round squares in it.

Could you be mistaken in thinking you are in pain?

It is also possible, under the private language argument (logically *and* practically possible) that you could be mistaken in thinking that you are in pain.

This contradicts the starting point of the argument from analogy, the Cartesian solipsistic position that that you are *certain* you know your own mental states, *certain* that you know you are in pain for instance.

It may be by watching the behavior of others you have grown up using the expression "I am in pain" when, for instance, you only feel sick. It may not be until much later that a situation arises whereby this mistake is pointed out to you and you realize 'pain' should not be used in these circumstances.

You have not always been using the word 'pain' correctly, You haven't fully understood its use.

Such a (correcting) situation may never arise, of course. you may just continue to be unaware that you are mistaken when you say "I feel pain" where in fact you should be saying "I feel sick."

3. *'Ascription' as a solution to the problem of other minds:*

British philosopher Peter Strawson (1919-2006) also rejects solipsism by appeal to how language works. He argues a mental concept like 'pain' is a concept that pain is something that someone *has*; and that this concept (that pain is something someone *has*) requires the behavior of others to be established. Therefore solipsism, (the view that I can only know for sure that I exist) is an untenable position.

Strawson's argument runs like this:

A child may learn as a replacement for simply crying out to more sophisticated expressions like saying "It hurts me" when he bangs his his knee. When standing with his parents he sees his brother John bang his knee in the same way he is asked the question "Does it hurt?" He may say at this time, "No"

In this case, although he understands how to use the expression 'It hurts me', he does not understand how to use the expression "It hurts John".

To be able to *ascribe* pain the boy needs to learn when to say "It hurts John" as well as when to say "It hurts me". To learn how to *ascribe* pain like this he needs the behavior of others and the verbal rules of a language community. Only when he has grasped these rules will he be able to say in the appropriate circumstances "It hurts me" *and/or* "It hurts John". [50]

To summarize: I cannot ascribe pain to *myself* unless I learn the concept of *ascribed* pain, and do this I need the behavior of others and the verbal rules of a language community.

I can only apply 'mental' words to my *own* thoughts and feelings if I can I apply them to *others*. In rejection of the solipsist again, I cannot have knowledge of myself unless I have knowledge of others first.

Chapter 4 Conclusions:

In this chapter it has been shown that the argument from analogy although close to commonsense, appears not to be strong enough to reject solipsism and so does not solve the problem of other minds. The argument from analogy it could still not avoid the skeptical challenge that certain *knowledge* there are minds other than my own is not possible.

Nevertheless, the private language argument by Wittgenstein, seemed to reject the solipsist position as untenable and so provide a solution to the problem of the existence of other minds.

It does so by suggesting that it is not a 'real' problem. It shows that the argument from analogy attempts to solve a problem that cannot exist, because it begins from a mistaken 'Cartesian' intellectual framework; the certainty of knowledge of my own case and my doubts about knowledge of the case of others. Descartes seems in the 17th century to have started out heading in the wrong direction and also shaped subsequent debates about the issue

5

THE EXISTENCE OF FREE WILL

(Is it an illusion?)

Physical determinism:-

This is the (scientific) view that every event in the universe has a cause, and there are rules governing these causal relations, the laws of nature. What causes what can, in principle, therefore be discovered.

Such a situaion makes it difficult to see how human free will can exist. This is because human acts are events in the universe. Therefore, every human act must have a cause. There does not seem to be any place for the existence of free will, then, in this 'hard determinism' picture.

The problem, though, is that we *also* want to hold people responsible for their (free) actions.

If all actions have a cause, however, they cannot be a product of free will, no one can be responsible for their behavior.

Furthermore, if there is no free will, there can be no morality since we cannot be praised or blamed for actions we have no control over. Free will is a pre-condition for morality.

The problem, then, is that we appear not to be able to hold a (scientific) deterministic view of the universe *and* hold that people are responsible for their 'freely chosen' actions (including 'choosing' to pursue a career in science.)

227

Determinism is not 'Fatalism':

Fatalism is the view that, whatever you try and do, the end is inevitable. Determinism posits that *if* certain prior conditions are satisfied, *then* certain outcomes will happen. *If,* for example, water is heated in the 'right' conditions to 100 degrees Celsius, *then* it will boil. An end is not inevitable. It will only occur *if* the prior causes take place.

Determinism is not Predestination:

Pre-destination belongs to theology. This is the (theological) view every event in the universe is known to God.

The doctrine of pre-destination again makes it difficult for free will to exist because God knows the future and so it is true now what you will do, and your power to choose a different outcome is just an illusion.

The 'Pelagian Controversy' in Christianity, mentioned in Part IIa Metaphysics and Philosophy of Religion, was concerned with exactly this problem and it led to the excommunication of British born monk Pelagius (390-418) for attacking the tenets of Christianity by advocating that that humans did have free will and could choose the right course of action without God's help. Pelagius had to reject predestination to make room for the existence of free will.

Unlike determinism, under predestination whatever you try and do, the end is inevitable. It does not depend on any prior conditions (as in the determinism case).

The Incompatibility of Determinism and Free Will:

The source of the incompatibility between physical determinism and free will may be said to have its origin in the discovery in the 17th century by Isaac Newton that the universe is matter in motion determined according to laws of motion and gravity. 17th century mathematician Pierre Simon La Place

(1749-1827) famously claimed that, in principle, if the location and motion of every material object in the universe could be known, the future location and motion of every material object in the universe could be predicted.

As humans are part of the material universe, this includes predicting anything we would ever do, so any notion that we can freely choose to act becomes absurd. This is now known as 'hard determinism'. Although we might still *feel* we choose to act, the hard determinism of La Place under Newtonian physics tells us we cannot be free in reality.

Indeterminism and Quantum Physics:

There are today other kinds of physics besides Newtonian, and some allow for 'indeterminism'.

Indeterminism is the view that not everything is determined. This, then, creates the possibility that human behavior is one of those things not determined and so free will is perhaps possible.

Discoveries about the behavior of atoms at the quantum level suggest determinism does not exist at this subatomic level. The 'Heisenberg Uncertainty Principle' was discovered by Werner Heisenberg (1901-1976) in the early 20th century. It says that we cannot know both the location *and* the momentum of a subatomic particle. Coming to know one of them makes it impossible to know the other at the same time. Events at the subatomic level are not, then, capable of prediction. They cannot, therefore, be regarded as determined and so cannot be presumed as being caused.

Does this indeterminism leave a space in the universe for human free will? It would appear that it might because humans, like everything else, are held as made of atoms. And at the heart of atoms, the subatomic level, determinism breaks down. There are, however, at least two problems with the view that indeterminism makes the existence of free will possible.

One problem with the view that indeterminism at the quantum level allows for free will is that quantum physics applies to the micro level, the very small. At the macro level Newtonian physics seems still to hold and human behavior is obviously at the macro level. At the macro level, then, for explanatory purposes, it still seems that the universe consists of matter in motion governed by natural laws of motion and gravity.

At the very large Newtonian physics also breaks down of course. This level is now explained by Einstein's General Relativity. (The Search for a Grand Theory to account for all levels now amounts to the quest for the holy grail of physics).

A second problem with the view that indeterminism at the quantum level allows for free will is that indeterminism is not the same as free will. If various neurological processes in the brain were not explicable in terms of cause and effect, i.e. they were 'indeterminate', it could mean that what we do was determined randomly.

We might, say, suddenly find ourselves acting in a certain way, like someone afflicted with Tourette's Syndrome finds themselves acting in certain (often undesirable) ways. This type of behavior is not regarded as free will. Acting from free will is deciding what to do and then trying to do it.

Indeterminism at the quantum level, then, does not seem to make the existence of free will possible and, of course, determinism at the macro level also rules out the existence of free will.

Or does it?

Could Determinism and Free Will be Compatible?

The 'compatibilist' view accepts a determinist position that any decisions, we make on a course of action are in principle predictable if one knows enough about prior causes such as upbringing, character, current environmental influences and brain states.

David Hume, however, argues that free action cannot mean action that is undetermined, uncaused, a matter of chance. We could not hold a person responsible for actions on this basis.

We have seen above how determinism seems to rule out free will as it makes all actions caused, but indeterminism at the sub atomic level does not make free will possible either, because it just allows for sudden uncontrollable behaviors. Hume has a similar view regarding such acts but he also exposes the point that determinism, far from ruling out free will, actually makes free will possible. This is because free acts, acts one can be held responsible for, must proceed from some *cause* in character and attitude.

Freedom of choice and responsibility for action, he points out, can make no sense outside a framework of determinism. I could not be blamed for hitting you in the face because of some uncontrollable muscle spasm. This would make no sense. But I can be blamed for hitting you in the face because I dislike you; because of my attitude toward you. [51]

We are free then, Hume points out, if we can do what we want to do *and* what we want to do proceeds from a *cause* in character and attitude. If what we want to do does not proceed from some *cause* in character or attitude, it is absurd to hold us responsible for such. Indeed, in his famous 'I have a dream' speech Martin Luther King looks forward to the day people are judged by the content of their character (rather than the color of their skin).

Hume may be right in exposing here how we normally think of free will and responsibility for actions. Many times it has been mentioned how terrorists with an evil character are responsible for (freely) carrying out acts of terror.

There may be problem with this way of holding people responsible, however. If I am not in control of my character formation, then the cause of the behavior that results from this character is perhaps not a free one. The blame for the Boston Marathon bomber was held by some to lie in his older brother who made him hate enough to go along with the plan. Modern psychology might suggest that character and attitude is caused by some combination of genetic inheritance and environmental conditioning, both of which are out of a person's control —as is thought to be the indoctrination of the young by terrorist groups.

David Hume's 'soft determinism' approach (as described pejoratively by William James) may have its problems then. Hume, however, is able to go further by rejecting hard determinism. If hard determinism is rejected, hard deterministic arguments against the existence of free will must fail.

Rejecting Hard Determinism:

It seems impossible, to find room for freedom of the will in a universe where every single event has a prior cause, in a deterministic universe of which we are all a part.

An alternative to trying to find room for free willing in a deterministic universe is to dismiss determinism. This can be done by calling into question the (scientific) view that every event has a cause?

We have seen in Part I Epistemology and elsewhere, how Hume exposes the fact that there is no evidence for what causes what. It is only a psychological habit of expectation that we think one thing *causes* another.

This he explains is because all we observe or experience, at best, is regular occurrences of event B after event A. We never observe actual causation, only regularity, and there is no evidence that this regularity will continue into the future. We must assume or have faith that the future will be like the past – the very thing we need evidence for.

The Compatibilism of Immanuel Kant:-

Immanuel Kant argues that hard determinism and free will are compatible, but not in David Hume's sense. Kant would regard being caused to behave by character or attitudes as not free will at all.

Free will for Kant means the power to be independent of natural (psychological, physiological, environmental) causes or laws.

We have seen in Part I Epistemology how Kant says he was awakened from his 'dogmatic slumbers' by David Hume's revelations. Kant holds that the principle every event has a cause (universal causation) is how we *must* see the world. Causation is not 'out there' it is how we construct our experience. It is like looking through blue tinted spectacles- where everything is seen as blue.

Looking through our universal causation spectacles - everything is seen as causally related. And we cannot take our spectacles off, since then we could not 'see' (i.e. experience) anything at all.

Kant's point then, is that human actions must be seen (by humans) as determined by prior causes, like everything else, and so all are in principle predictable if one knows enough about prior causes; precisely the La Place formulation of hard determinism above.

We cannot know anything of reality as it is in itself (the noumena as Kant calls it), outside experience. We can only know the world as we experience it through conceptual categories such as cause and effect, and these categories make any experience possible, as spectacles make it possible to see.

Free will enters into Kant's picture via our ability to consider what *ought* to be and what *ought* not to be, whether we ought to follow an impulse or not. This he calls 'practical reason'.

We can only think like this, we can only reason *practically*, if we hold that we have free will, Free will is a postulate of our 'practical reason'. We cannot help postulating that we have free will when we consider what we ought to do.

This 'cannot help' is just like not being able to help thinking in terms of cause and effect when we consider what exists in reality.

As we cannot be certain that cause and effect relations exist outside our experience in the noumenal world, so we cannot be sure that free will exists outside of our having to postulate it when we reason practically about how we or others ought to behave.

In this way Kant is able to reveal how free will and determinism can be compatible. They just belong in different standpoints we take towards the world.

When we want to *know* something, we must adopt the standpoint of hard determinism. From within that standpoint, every event, including human actions has a cause, and so is determined. Free will here cannot exist.

From a practical reason standpoint, however, when deciding what we 'ought' to do, must consider we have free will and so can make decisions (about what we ought to do). We *cannot* think in any other way about ourselves except as acting freely when engaging in practical reasoning.

The answer to the question whether the postulate every event has a cause exists in the realm of noumena or whether the postulate that free will exists in the realm of noumena lies beyond what we can know.

6

THE EXISTENCE OF PERSONAL IDENTITY

(What makes you the same person through time?)

The Problem:

What makes Person A at time 1 (t1) the same person at the later time 2 (t2)?

Looking back we might also say to ourselves "I've changed a lot since I was young". We don't mean by this, though, that we have changed into someone else. We think it is us that has undergone the change. The difficult question of personal identity is uncovering just what guarantees the continuity of each of us in amongst all these alterations. This will also mean facing up to the possible answer that we are still the same person today as we were previously, because we have the same non-physical soul.

Two candidates for personal identity:

Two possible responses available as 'solutions' to this personal identity problem are the *body* theory of personal identity and the *memory and character* theory.

The *body* theory may be given as

Person A at t1 is the same person at t2 if A has the same body throughout t1....t2.

The obvious problem with this body theory of personal identity is that part of the body can be lost or replaced and still a person A remains the person A. For example, someone may undergo a heart transplant or a liver transplant, or they may lose an arm or a leg, but they still remain the same person. It does not seem (at least) that *all* the body needs to remain the same to maintain person A as person A over time.

On the other hand, if the brain of person A were removed from his body and transplanted into the skull of another body, say person B's body, and the brain from person B was removed and then transplanted into the empty skull of person A (i.e., if brains were interchanged), we would have serious doubt whether person A (or person B) had the same body. We would probably think that the person A (and/or person B) went where his brain went; person A at first had one body, and then, after the transplant, a different body.

The reason why we might think this is that the body in which the brain of, say, person A was housed would have the character, beliefs, and attitudes of person A. If it did not, if it possessed different character, beliefs, and attitudes, then we would inclined to say that it was not same person as person A.

This further suggests that continuity of character, beliefs and attitudes are perhaps what is essential here – not continuity of any particular stuff like brain matter which may (or may not) house such character, beliefs and attitudes. This leads us to the *memory and character* theory of personal identity:

The *memory and character* theory may be given as

Person A at t1 is the same person at t2 if A has the same memory and character throughout t1....t2.

Empiricist John Locke (1632-1704) argued for a version of the memory theory of personal identity in his book 'Essay Concerning Human Understanding'.

Here he notes that as long as he can remember that it was himself seeing the ark and Noah's flood and it was him seeing the Thames overflow and that it is himself that is writing then he has the same self and it does not matter at all if he is composed of the same matter or brain or the same non material soul. What is important is the connections in memory not what we are made of in securing our identity over time.

Memory and Character Theory and Forgetting:

According to Locke above then, memory (or 'consciousness' as he often calls it) constitutes personal identity not what we are made of soul, brain whatever. There is, however, a problem with the memory theory. This surrounds the fact that we forget. We can forget completely, we can distort a recollection and we can even 'remember' what did not actually happen to us. In short, memory is not reliable.

In 1957 the hippocampi of Mr Henry Molaison (HM), was removed in an operation. He was 31 at the time. He became an object of research as the operation left him with an inability to form new memories. Every time a researcher met him each day, it would be as the first time they met. Even if there was simply a lunch break which kept them apart for 'long enough' he would forget who the researcher was again. If Henry was his memories, then, there would be very little of him as it were.

For most of us, in fact, there are long stretches of our past that are completely forgotten. It is not clear therefore, on the memory theory of identity that we existed during those stretches. A further problem is that we sometimes remember things we haven't really done. Some people might even remember things they haven't done in very great detail via confabulation.

In psychology much work done on memory reveals clearly that memory is not reliable. This is essentially because recollection is a matter of *reconstructing* what happened in the past not simply playing back a recording of what happened in the past and various factors including expectations, leading questions and more can affect recall. A prominent figure in this field is Elizabeth Loftus. In one of her many pieces of research (1995) she shows how it is possible to plant the memory of being lost in a shopping mall as a child amongst the memories of an adult. [53]

Incidentally, this not only calls into question that it is memory that can secure personal identity over time (rather than any particular substance like brain) it also challenges any legal process that relies on evidence of witnesses using memory in recalling crime. If it is time to reject the idea that personal identity is secured by memory because memory is inherently unreliable, then it may also be time to change how the memories of witnesses are used in our courtrooms because memory is unreliable.

Brain Theory and Duplication:

We might still be tempted to say that what is most important is some bodily continuity like that of the *brain*. No matter what the person/persons above remembers, or claims to remember, what really makes them the same person through time is if they retain the same *brain*.

Person A at t1 is the same person at t2 if A has the same brain throughout t1....t2.

One difficulty with this *brain* theory of personal identity is that it is faced with a duplication problem.

Suppose person A's left hemisphere is transplanted into some other skull. Medical science can already remove one hemisphere of a person's brain and that person can carry on living more or less normally – walking, talking etc. This in effect is what happens if one hemisphere of the brain ceases to function because of a stroke.

An experiment in 1968 by Roger Sperry in involved looking at patients who had their corpus callosum cut. This lies at the join of the two hemispheres of the brain.

Subsequent testing on these patients revealed that one hemisphere of the brain could come to know things the other hemisphere could not. A normal brain can thus be viewed as two people as the hemispheres know and perceive different things,. Stop them communicating (via cutting the corpus callosum say) and hostility between right and left sides of the body can even break out, as each hemisphere controls one respective side of the body.

Suppose now person A's Suppose, then, person A's right hemisphere is also transplanted into another skull and the transplant takes. Brain continuity theory suggests that *both* half brains/bodies are person A since there is continuity of brain matter. But both cannot be identical with person A since both lead different lives, and form new memories.

Having the same brain over time does not then seem to guarantee personal identity over time because of this possibility of 'duplication': putting different brain hemispheres in different bodies and creating two people from 'one'.

Identity as a matter of degree?

We might be inclined to say in response to the problems of duplication mentioned above that personal identity is just a matter of *degree*. In the brain duplication case above, we might suggest that in this case person A survives *in part*. Each of the two latter half brains/bodies constitute A's later selves but neither are identical with person A – A partly survives as one and partly survives as the other.

Sounds reasonable. However, suppose that an alien surgeon captures you and announces that he is going to transplant your left cerebral hemisphere into one body, and your right hemisphere into another body. The alien informs you as well that he is going to torture one of the resulting persons and free the other. You can choose which person is going to be tortured and which to be rewarded. Which do you choose?

If you survive in part (if both subsequent persons are in part you) you should have reason for both joyous expectation and terrified anticipation. But none of the two future people (both to some degree you) are going to suffer a *combined* fate of torture and reward.

The possibility of this scenario suggests the idea that we survive in part (survive to some degree) in each body (because part of our brain remains the same) is not the correct analysis of what constitutes our personal identity.

Dualism and Personal Identity:-

You may remember how Descartes in his 'Meditation VI' notes that he essentially is a thinking thing and his body is not essential as he can lose part of it and still be the same person. And body is material and divisible and but his mind is not so divisible – so making his mind and his body distinct – the latter material the former non material. He goes on to suggest that because he is distinct from his body he can conceive himself as existing without it [54]

Descartes theory of personal identity may therefore be summarized as

Person A at t1 is the same person at t2 if A has the same *soul* throughout t1....t2.

Personal Identity as Soul and Duplication:

Continuity of the *soul* as a guarantee of personal identity avoids the duplication of brain problem (the potential for creating two people from 'one'). This is because it is 'unextended' in space. It is because matter (including brain matter) is extended in space that it possible, in principle, that it may be divided. An immaterial soul, however, is not extended – it does not take up space. Therefore it cannot be divided. It is indivisible, and so cannot be duplicated by division.

Can a person exist without a body?

Descartes says he can conceive himself existing without his body – his soul could continue to exist outside his body.

It may be doubted that he can actually do this. This is because our body seems to be involved in every activity we try to describe in language. We 'see' but no body means there are no eyes to see with. No body means no way of looking in a particular direction. There is no head to turn, no hands to touch, no touching at all.

Expressions like 'seeing' 'moving' 'touching' 'being in a place' and much, much more seem to lose all meaning if we have no body. Too much of language may lose its meaning if soul existing outside a body is allowed. Thinking at least in language then perhaps becomes impossible, and so existence essentially as a thinking thing, as Descartes has it, also becomes impossible.

The apparent impossibility of existing outside our bodies as thinking beings suggests it is impossible for us to exist as anything without our bodies.

It still allows, however, that it is your immaterial soul that guarantees your personal identity over time although such a soul must cease to exist (as a thinking thing) when the body dies.

The existence of immaterial souls in the universe, however, does not fit with the (scientific) view that reality consists entirely of atoms governed by laws of nature.

Could this understanding of reality (atoms governed by laws of nature) be mistaken? It might be interesting to discover that this (atomic theory) view of what exists in reality has its origin in the work of thinkers before Plato.

It might be interesting as well to find that Plato following on from this still holds that we can exist outside our bodies, and indeed existed before we had bodies.

It is to all this and more we now turn.

PART III

INVITATION TO PLATO

(Getting back to the start? Plato's Epistemology and Metaphysics)

INTRODUCTION

If Alfred North Whitehead is right in suggesting that all that comes after Plato in the Western intellectual tradition amounts to no more than 'footnotes' to Plato, even if he is only partly right, then an understanding of the history of Western thought requires some understanding of the conceptual framework together with the questions and problems considered by and bequeathed to later generations by Plato.

Greater appreciation of Plato's work, new interpretations of his ideas, the uncovering of misinterpretations, may still offer new ways of thinking about old problems and so make possible changes in direction.

We have already seen how Descartes set the conceptual framework for the understanding of the self. The certain knowledge of oneself and ones existence as a thinking thing, led to generations of thinkers some trying to make certain what then is comparatively uncertain, the existence of other minds and thoughts; trying in short to solve the problem of other minds. Plato's range and range of influence is much greater than Descartes, and Descartes himself inherits the rationalist approach to knowledge from Plato, its key founding father.

Plato set the conceptual framework for epistemology and metaphysics and for scientific endeavor for the centuries of human intellectual development that followed him. It is also the case, as will soon be demonstrated, that he set the framework for development in many other fields. These include religious thinking and political theory. Thus, at the very least he at impacts on our science, our religion, our politics and our philosophy.

This part III outline of Plato will be divided into six chapters. These are simply designed to provide an overview. It would be more than possible, for instance to devote six chapters (or even a life's work) just to a particular aspect of Plato's thought.

CONTENTS PART III

1

SOCIAL AND INTELLECTUAL CONTEXT

Plato expressed his thinking through in a set of dialogues where he generally describes his teacher, Socrates, discussing via question and answer complex questions with significant contemporaries. Each answer is subjected to analysis and generates more questions and more answers and more discussion.

Plato's dialogues were composed over many years. Socrates, it seems, never wrote anything down himself. There is therefore an issue as to how much of the dialogues (especially those written later in Plato's life) represent Plato's own views and how much the views of Socrates. There also exists the problem of establishing via examination of the dialogues how, and in what way, Plato's views changed over time. Such matters are the business of scholars of Plato. They cannot be ignored here completely though. What follows will be drawn in the main from his well-known dialogue 'the *Republic*.'

The Social Context facing Plato:-

An appreciation of the social context facing Plato helps in understanding his intellectual context. In particular, it reveals why Plato may have been motivated to criticize the democracy of his time and why, in suggesting an alternative political system, he enters into an examination of what is knowledge and what can be known to exist; an examination of epistemology and metaphysics.

Consideration of the intellectual framework preceding Plato is as necessary for understanding Plato as consideration of Plato is needed for an understanding of all that comes after him. Alfred North Whitehead's comment may be recalled here once more; the view that all which comes after Plato can be described as 'footnotes to Plato'.

Appreciation of an intellectual background reveals why what comes after takes intellectual shape it does and the questions it attempts to address. It has been revealed that much of what follows René Descartes in epistemology and metaphysics begins with his conclusion that it is certain we have knowledge that we exist and that we are essentially thinking things.

Descartes is drawing heavily on the rationalist approach to knowledge handed down from Plato. Much the same may be said for many operating in the area of religion and theology as will soon be revealed.

Plato's motivation to challenge Democracy:

Plato was born in Athens in 427 BC into a wealthy family with a long tradition of political involvement in Athens. From 431-405 BC Athens was at war with Sparta. Plato probably fought in this war and thus experienced the defeat of Athens. Athens, unlike Sparta, was a democracy and Plato might well have attributed its defeat at least in part to its democratic decision-making procedures.

There are further reasons why Plato may have disapproved of democratic decision-making. The politics of a democracy encourages the skill of rhetoric in the winning of the votes of the majority. A group of teachers, 'the Sophists', taught the art of rhetoric to those with political ambitions. This art often amounted to how cultivate the support of the majority via speech making both in style and content.

We might call such a people today 'media advisors'. Media advisors are able to teach those with political ambitions how to look and sound 'right' (what to say and how to say it) in order to win support and persuade a majority.

The learning of the technique of rhetoric with the aim of winning majority support in a democratic context is not concerned with any search for knowledge, or the value of knowledge for its own sake. The Sophists held that a search for knowledge as at bottom pointless since they regarded everything as relative (there is no non-relative knowledge to be found). A well-known Sophist, Protagoras, famously claimed that 'man is the measure of all things': there are only the different opinions of different people. In our modern society such a view is expressed in the claim that *everyone* has a 'right' to their opinion.

To be able to make speeches effectively was also made important in Athens by the fact that a person had to defend himself in court if accused of a crime. One's guilt or innocence would again be democratically determined by the will of the majority in court situation.

In an adversarial legal system too (such as that of the USA and others around the world based on the British Common Law), lawyers use what rhetorical techniques they have to persuade a jury to support their client. I know of one lawyer who plays close attention to the ties the jurors are wearing, feeling it will tell him much about what sort of words and postures they are likely to respond to. Persuasion of a majority by whatever rhetorical means is the primary objective here and so, at best, *truth* is an accidental by product of a contest between legal representatives. The primary interest of each lies in 'winning'.

Plato was further motivated to dislike the democratic system of Athens due to the fact Socrates, his teacher, was condemned to death by one of its courts after being found guilty of a charge of corrupting the young. Plato describes this trial in the dialogue, the *Apology*. Socrates is here depicted as not making very much effort to use rhetoric to persuade the court that he is innocent of the charges, probably to illustrate the failure of rhetoric with respect to truth and wisdom.

The pejorative expression 'sophistry' owes its origin to this Platonic critique of the Sophists. It may be recalled from Part I Epistemology and other places in this book how David Hume regards claims to knowledge not supported by experience as 'sophistry and illusion', and then exposes how all so called knowledge based on scientific experimentation can only therefore be 'sophistry' and how so called religious knowledge can only be 'sophistry' as well.

Both are exposed by him not actually to have the support of experience and so such, he says, should be 'committed to the flames', no matter the strength of support in practice from, say, the vast majority of scientists (such as the widespread 'faith' that laws of nature will continue to operate as they have done in the past).

Plato and Socrates:

As has been mentioned, the greatest influence on Plato seems to have been his teacher Socrates. Socrates (470-399 BC) was forty-three years older than Plato. He too lived in the Athenian democratic world where man was viewed as the measure of all things, and where all was nothing more than conflicting opinion, (rendering any search for truth and knowledge pointless), and where rhetorical tricks ('spin' we might also call it today) was learned and valued by the ambitious to persuade a majority.

Against this social background Socrates, according to the dialogues, claiming to know only his own ignorance, is described as developing a technique of questioning a (usually important) person who might be regarded as likely to know most about the respective topic under scrutiny.

Socrates usually ends these discussions by trapping this person, by continued analysis of their answers, in their own confusion and hypocrisy. Accordingly, Socrates made many enemies, enemies who would get him in the end. His young students, however, including Plato, perhaps saw him as a martyr for the truth in a corrupted society.

Plato's criticisms of democracy?

We saw above how Plato was motivated to criticize the democratic system around him. His *motivation* is not, of course, relevant to whether criticisms of democracy are right or wrong, no more than the *motivation* of someone to impose democracy on others renders their views of democracy right or wrong.

Thinking by itself, however, cannot provide motivation, only analysis. David Hume would say 'reason is the 'slave of the passions' and Plato has it that humans are like a chariot pulled by the horses of passions and appetites.

Reason can hope to control these horses but without them there is no movement through life (a controller needs something to control).

Sigmund Freud was to adopt this chariot model to describe the human psyche many centuries later with the 'Id' as the driving force (the horses) and the Ego as the controller of the chariot. Complaints about Elvis Presley and rock and roll in the 1950s America generally owe their origin a worry about 'frightening the horses' and so rendering the chariot out of control.

Plato's main point against democracy is that it places power with those least equipped to use it, those who have no relevant knowledge. For instance, at the time of writing the UK is soon to have a referendum on whether Britain should remove itself from the European Union and stay out to the common European currency, the euro. Are the majority really equipped to decide this? To decide, say, whether removing the UK from the European Union and keeping it outside the common currency, the euro, is better for the UK economy? Shouldn't this decision be made by, at the very least, those who know about international currency markets?

Plato would have regarded this kind of democratic decision-making for such an important issue as absurd. Indeed, democracy was considered absurd for reasons such as this until the eighteenth century – a little like a communist system is regarded now, perhaps, after the collapse of the Soviet Union.

Democracy was thought to be absurd in the sense that not only does it not work, it is also creates many dangers for the people. A tyranny of a one or a few may not be as dangerous as a tyranny of the majority, a majority who cannot be trusted (surely) to get decisions 'right' and may persecute the minority in order to stay in power.

A large corporation run by majority decision-making may soon fail. The economic output and sales of a country is often viewed as something like the actions of a nation-state corporation and yet the latter (nation-state) corporation is required to value a democratic decision-making process it would not adopt itself for fear of failure.

The US Constitution recognizes the 18th century Platonic fear and distrust of democracy, the dangers of the acts of the majority in particular. A majority may elect the wrong person (as it did in the case of Hitler). This fear of democracy gave rise to the placing many checks and balances on the power of a US President elected by a majority – and, technically, by not actually having that President elected directly by the people at all. It was thought 'safer' by the founding fathers have a two-stage process where members of an electoral college are elected first and then to have these elect a President. All this distrust of democracy clearly written into the US constitution owes much to the thinking of Plato.

The modern attempts to generate democracy in formally undemocratic states Plato would likely have viewed with dismay. This seems often to be a goal of much US foreign policy, despite the mistrust and suspicion of democracy exposed for all to see (if we would but look) by the venerated founding fathers in the provisions of the US Constitution.

Plato uses several different parables in the *Republic* to illustrate the failure of politicians and politics in a democracy. One of these is the parable of the beast. This is described next.

The parable of the beast:

In this parable Plato draws an analogy between the people in a democracy and 'a large and powerful animal'. Like an animal, the public has certain tastes and desires, and is impulsive and irrational. The master of this beast is the one who has studied its moods and wants and has learned to predict its responses. Such an individual is able to employ this understanding to tame the animal and render it more compliant to his wishes. [55]

In the first instance, the master of the beast is identified with the Sophists, the teachers of the skills of public speaking and persuasion. But Plato goes on to explain that *anyone* who merely caters to the whims of public opinion is analogous to the keeper of this beast, 'whether he be painter, musician, or politician'

The 'effective' democratic politician, then, is likened to the Sophist. He studies the moods of the public and learns the likes and dislikes of the crowd, and this enables him to control public opinion and bend it to his will.

The Sophists, it may also be remembered, suggest that everything is relative as there are only the different opinions of different people (man is the measure of all things). Plato therefore needs to demonstrate that knowledge *is* possible, that there is more than mere opinion, and to explain what this knowledge is, if he is to meet the challenge of the Sophists and construct a challenge to the worth of democratic decision-making.

Three important themes have now been identified from consideration of the social context facing Plato.

1. What is wrong with democracy? (Decision-making power is placed with those least equipped to use it – those without knowledge.)
2. How should the state be organized, who should make decisions? (Those with knowledge.)
3. What is knowledge?

Intellectual Context facing Plato:-

The Pre-Socratics:

Thinkers before Plato and Socrates have come to be known as the 'Pre-Socratics'. Plato is therefore faced with the questions and problems left by the Pre-Socratic thinkers. Many of these very much remain questions and problems for us today.

The Problem of the One and the Many:

The Pre-Socratics wrestled with what may be called 'the problem of *change*'. It is clear that the world around us is always changing: babies grow into adults, acorns into oak trees, and so on. The question is how can *change* be explained?

If A changes into B it cannot be the case, it seems, that A becomes nothing and B is created from nothing as, in particular, something cannot come from nothing - as there is nothing to generate it. Many of the Pre-Socratics concluded, therefore, that although there *appear* to be many changing things around us, there must in *reality* be just one thing which persists through the changes and which everything is composed of. This one thing that everything is composed of can be termed 'the One'. Thus A changing into B is explained by stating that thing that A is composed of (the One) is re-arranged to become B.

It has proved difficult in the history of thought and investigation to find the one thing out of which all the many things are composed. The first Pre-Socratic candidate for the One was 'water'. This was the theory of Thales (c. 640-546 BC). Water in some form seems to be in everything – human beings (the readers of this book), for example, are now known to be 75% water. Democritus (460-370 BC) put forward the idea that the One consists of atoms. There *appear* to be many different things but in *reality* everything consists of atoms. Atomic theory is still with us of course, but it is an old idea.

Explaining the problem of change, then, led to the problem of finding the One that accounts for all the Many: 'the One and the Many' problem. The modern equivalent is the search beyond atoms to sub-atomic particles to a 'deeper' more fundamental One that all is ultimately composed of. In recent times, quarks and super strings to belong to the effort to find ever smaller candidates for the One that the Many is, in *reality*, composed of (whatever *appears* to be the case).

Sameness and Difference:

This explanation of change by invoking one underlying thing (water, atoms, quarks or whatever) to account for all the many different things faces an even greater difficulty than deciding which of the candidates is the 'correct' one thing of which everything consists.

The difficulty amounts to exposing a much more fundamental question of how the One can be the Many at all? If the One is supposed to remain the same throughout its change into something different, how can it then really *become* something different? And if it does not remain the same throughout the change, it cannot be said that it is the One that *persists* through the change.

In other words, how can the One be the *same* as the Many and be *different* from the Many? When a baby changes into an adult, for example, we want to say a persisting something has altered. The problem is that we are here saying that the adult is the *same* as the baby and of course not the same as the baby, i.e., *different*. Is this not a contradiction?

Does, then, explaining change by postulating a one thing of which everything is composed lead us into contradiction because of this sameness and difference difficulty? If so, then perhaps we must recognize that there can't be just a one thing of which everything is composed. Our thinking may have gone wrong somewhere and we should stop wasting our time chasing after a non-existent one thing of which all the many things are ultimately composed.

One as a Process:

What can be done if reason shows us there cannot logically be one thing (water, atoms or whatever) that can stay the *same* through change and become something *different* (since it leads to contradiction)? We are still left with the problem of how to account for change. There is an alternative approach available which involves keeping a One which persists through changes but not a one *thing*.

It could be said that all things are in constant change but there is still a 'oneness' in the order or process that things always conform to while they change. Acorns change, for instance, but they only change into oak trees, not into human beings, and they decay into humus not silver.

There is a principle governing this order or process of change. A similar principle must be at work governing the change of fertilized human eggs into adult humans and not, say, chickens. There is an order in the change around us.

This 'oneness in the process' was the view of Heraclitus (c. 535-475 BC). He substituted the One as a *thing* for the One as an ordered *process,* or 'change according to the measures'. One of his illustrations of this approach refers to the example that you cannot step into the same river twice because the river is constantly flowing (being different), but it nevertheless continues to be a river (remains the same); it changes 'according to the measures'. Heraclitus is thus able to explain change without recourse to positing a one *thing* of which everything consists, and so avoids the problem of how a one thing can stay the same through change and become something different.

The laws of nature in modern science governing change, of course, sound very similar to Heraclitus' 'measures', which govern change. The idea of laws of nature, which govern change giving change according to the measures is, like atomic theory, a very old one.

Is change an illusion?

It was noted above that to account for change a One thing that all is ultimately composed of is postulated. And much of the history of scientific endeavor has been, and still is, discovering what this 'One' actually is. All the time this adheres to the notion that, although there *appear* to be many things but in *reality* there is only one thing.

This distinction between a One and Many it may be remembered arises in order to account for change. The problem of finding the One to account for change (a problem still with us) disappears if change itself is not real.

Could it be that change is not real, just what appears to be the case? If so there will be no need to explain change by, say, positing a *reality* of atoms governed by laws of nature. Another of the Pre-Socratics did invoke this idea – although it has not been one followed by mainstream science thus far.

An alternative solution to the problem of change, then, is to say that there is no change – it is as appearance; although there *appears* to be change but in *reality* there is none. If this is true, the scientific project of accounting for change by a One thing which persists through change becomes a project heading in the wrong direction (perhaps because the 'wrong' set of Pre Socratic ideas have been adopted and worked on by succeeding generations).

The view of change as mere appearance was offered by Parmenides (c. 515-450 BC). Although we have the *appearance* of change via experience (via the senses), reason tells us that such change must, in *reality*, be an illusion. Parmenides' conclusions were supported by the work of his pupil Zeno (489-430 BC).

Zeno is the author of a large number of paradoxes to illustrate the point that change must just be appearance, not reality. We normally think, for instance, that when an arrow is shot from a bow it flies through the air. He argues that this (continuous change of place) must be impossible.

Zeno points out when an arrow occupies a place even for a bare instant it cannot be moving just at that instant. It must be at rest at some instant to 'occupy a place' at some instant. To *be* the arrow must be somewhere. For the arrow to exist, then, it must occupy a place (it must be somewhere).

As it always occupies a place to be (to continue to exist), and it must be at rest to occupy a place, it cannot then be moving. It follows, therefore, an arrow shot from a bow cannot be moving through the air as it always occupies some place (to continue to exist). Thus, although we sense arrows flying through the air (and the movements of other things), this is just *appearance*. Reason tells us that, in *reality*, this movement is impossible (as impossible as the existence of a round square).

Could the idea that *reality* consists of atoms in motion be an impossible one on the same grounds? Atoms cannot be in motion, because to *be* they need to be somewhere; and being somewhere is not moving. Such thinking throws into new relief the electrons of quantum physics which are sometimes described as 'moving' from(?) 'nowhere' and 'moving to 'nowhere'. Zeno's reasoning, that change is only appearance, seems more plausible and more comprehensible than this perhaps.

The ingredients for modern physical science, then, the questions it addresses and its conceptual framework, are thus revealed as bequeathed to us mainly by the Pre-Socratics; atomic theory, for instance, plus with the idea of, change as 'according to measures' or laws of nature.

The counter idea that change is just appearance from Parmenides and Zeno, was not followed unlike the theoretical constructs of Democritus (atoms) and Heraclitus (laws governing change). This view of change as just *appearance* is perhaps lying dormant somewhere waiting to be awakened again. The 'success' of quantum mechanics may yet breath life into it as the traditional ways of thinking are called into question.

Attempts at creating new directions have been tried before. For instance, in the early twentieth century, where physics was developing much through the activities of Einstein and the quantum theorists, Swiss thinker Carl Jung (1875-1961) was offering the position that there may, in reality, be other types of interaction, than physical interaction. These can be called, 'a-causal' interactions, as contrasted with just the 'causal' interactions of atoms.

You are thinking of someone, the telephone rings, and (surprisingly?) it is that person on the line. Many of us have experienced this sort of thing. You are thinking of a song and it comes on the radio. There are, for Jung, too many such 'coincidences' for them not to be connected in some a-causal way, a way different than causal connections between atoms.

There is a different realm, as it were, where a-causal connections can take place as contrasted with the realm of causal connections between atoms. Reality, Jung held, is not what science thinks it is, composed entirely of atoms whose interactions are governed by laws of nature.

Is knowledge possible?

We have considered theories which suggest there must be a one thing (such as atoms) to account for the changing many, Heraclitus' view that the One must be a 'process' rather than a *thing* to account for the changing many, and Parmenides' view that a changing many must be just appearance not reality.

The fact that the Pre-Socratics mentioned above and many others had come to such opposite conclusions perhaps gives further support to the Sophists' view that everything is relative. There are just individual opinions relative to particular individuals, individuals like Democritus, Parmenides, Heraclitus, and so on. These individual opinions derive from people's different points of view and these depend, in turn, upon such things as differences in age, upbringing and social and intellectual environment.

Man may be the measure of all things and therefore perhaps only majority opinion can decide what is acceptable, in 'democratic' manner.

If Plato wants to reject democratic decision-making, it may well be, then, that he needs to show that knowledge is possible. If it is, decisions need not only be made on the basis of majority *opinion*, but instead on the basis of *knowledge*.

This knowledge may well reside with a few, as it is only a few who understand the technicalities of navigation on a large ship containing many passengers. In earlier times a (few) navigators might have been regarded merely as 'star-gazers' by the majority.

2

THEORY OF FORMS

This chapter introduces Plato's influential theory of forms as a solution to the questions and issues raised by the Pre-Socratics and by the Sophists.

These questions and issues included the following.

1. The 'One and Many problem' arising from accounting for change. (Is *reality* One thing and the experience of Many things existing just *appearance*?)
2. The view of Heraclitus that all is constantly changing (in flux- 'according to the measures')
3. The view of Parmenides that there cannot in *reality* be any change at all (all change must only be an *appearance*).
4. The view of the Sophist's that everything is relative. There are, in the end, only the different subjective opinions of different people. At best (therefore), only majority support can be sought for a position in order to give it a justification.

Plato's way of addressing all these issues was to argue that *both* Heraclitus and Parmenides were right and that the Sophists were wrong.

He does this by suggesting that there must be two realms or worlds. There is a Heraclitean realm of *Many* in flux/changing (perhaps changing according to measures or laws) and another Parmenidean realm of an unchanging *One*.

The world of sense experience is the Heraclitean world of a changing *Many* and about this a world there can only be subjective opinion not objective knowledge, as the Sophists would accept.

There can, nevertheless, contrary to the Sophist view, also be objective knowledge. This knowledge, though, is of the other Parmenidean unchanging realm.

Knowledge of this particular realm, however, unlike in the Heraclitiean world of change, is not acquired through sense experience.

This is because the unchanging realm cannot be seen with the eyes, or heard with the ears or touched etc. The unchanging realm can only be known through *thought* – it is an 'intelligible' world rather than one learned about through the senses. Scientific experimentation cannot, therefore, get at this world, no more than science can get at a noumenal world postulated by Immanuel Kant (as described earlier in Part I Epistemology).

By invoking a two realm vision of this kind *both* Heraclitus and Parmenides could therefore be right to come up with the apparently contrary positions of 'continuous change' versus 'no change' as each could be referring to different realms.

Furthermore, in response to the Sophists, it may also be admitted that there can only be subjective opinion about the changing world established via the *senses*, but this still leaves open the possibility that there is objective knowledge about the other unchanging realm known by *thought*.

The changing realm here is the ever-changing world we live in our day-to-day activity, a world of which we can only have opinion. The unchanging realm of which we can have knowledge is, for Plato, a world of 'forms'. We cannot, however, see or touch or apprehend these forms through the senses. We only know them through thought – it is an 'intelligible' world not a 'sensible' world.

Arguments in support of the existence of forms:-

All this talk of an unchanging realm of forms only knowable through thought perhaps sounds strange. Things should become clearer as we examine Plato's thinking in this regard in a little more detail.

The characters in the *Republic* and the readers of the *Republic* are expected to possess an understanding of the theory of forms, probably from acquaintance with the content of Plato's other dialogues. In order to appreciate Plato's explanation of the theory of forms in the *Republic*, therefore, we must ourselves look at how that theory is presented in some of the other dialogues. In particular, we must look in these other dialogues at Plato's arguments for the existence of a world of forms. A number of these arguments will now be outlined including his argument demonstrating the soul must exist and must be immortal (a line of thought underpinning many religious doctrines).

1. Being and Becoming:

In the dialogue *Cratylus*, Cratylus is represented as a follower of Heraclitus holding that everything is in a state of flux or change. The character of Socrates is allowed to make the point that what is in a constant state of flux cannot be known because as soon as it is approached to be known, it has become something else. [55]

Plato concludes here, like Parmenides, that the true reality must be unchanging and objects of knowledge must be unchanging. He argues that in order to *be* something that something must be capable of remaining in a certain state. If there is a world of continuous change, things cannot *be* anything (since they are always becoming something else). A world of continuous change may thus be called a world of 'becoming' whereas a world of the unchanging where things can *be* may be termed a world of 'being'.

Plato is also making the significant point here that objects of knowledge must be unchanging. If in a world of constant change one attempts to refer to some thing via a proposition by the time this is done that thing will have become different from what it was, because nothing remains in the same state. Where there is continuous change, there cannot *be* anything to refer to as an object of knowledge and so without any objects of knowledge there can be no knowledge. And where there is no knowledge there is only opinion.

This has significant implications, of course, for the need for propositions to refer to some thing in order to have 'meaning' as held under the Verificationism movement described in Part IIa. There is nothing given to refer to if all is in flux, and so all propositions referring to that which is constantly changing perhaps cannot have meaning.

A world of constant change, then, a world of 'becoming', is only *appearance* and we can only have opinion about it. An unchanging world, on the other hand, a world of 'being', is *real* and can be the object of knowledge.

For any knowledge of 'what exists' to be possible, therefore, it must be that this, 'what exists', is not constantly changing. This world of sense experience, *our* world, *is* constantly changing, and so (because it is constantly changing) cannot be an object of knowledge.

2. One over Many Argument:

In the early dialogues Plato has Socrates usually represented as asking questions of his contemporaries of the type 'What is X?' where X is a general term. Socrates then proceeds to show that each attempted answer offered is unsatisfactory because it is too particular. This then generates further attempted answers that are again shown to be unsatisfactory in the same way. In the dialogue *Meno* Plato has Socrates debating with Meno a famous political an military figure. Plato demonstrates via Meno's responses to Socrates' qustions that we call many particular things such as bees 'bees' because we identify them as having something in common. The key question is, what exactly is it that we see each bee as having in common by means of which we call each a bee and not something else? More specifically: what is the 'bee-ness' we see all bees as possessing, what is, in other words, the one universal 'form' of bee-ness that we see shared by the many particular bees? [56]

The listing of particulars instead of the thing they have in common is characteristic of many of the responses Socrates receives in the dialogues in answer to his questions. Socrates' respondents always (and with little difficulty) are able to point to particulars in this world, but they can never show him what the general or universal element is that the particulars have in common and by which they are all given the same name; 'bees', etc. Yet these common forms, (such as what makes a group of bees all bees) *must* exist for bees and other particulars to exist and have something in common to make them all bees as distinct from something else.

We cannot identify and point to these 'forms' in this world in the same fashion as we can (easily) see and point to all the particulars around us that are distinguished from each other by them. Meno and other characters questioned by Socrates demonstrate this point by their failings.

But these 'forms' *must* exist for particulars to exist as different things. And because these forms do not appear to exist by themselves in this world, there must be another realm besides this sensed world of particulars: a realm where these universal forms exist.

It is only because of the existence of these forms and the partaking of the particulars in them (that it possible for us to identify a group together (a group of bees, say); and by which particular insects that partake of the same form are given a name, such as 'bees' or whatever.

The particulars in this world, because they have common elements which divide them up into bees and other different types of thing, must partake in forms to make them what they are (i.e. bees or other types of thing). Thus we see bees exhibit the form of bee-ness and this is why we call all the different particular bees, 'bees'.

However, although this universal form *must* exist for the particulars (like bees) to exist, it cannot be found in this world of particular bees.

This is illustrated many times by the fact that 'experts' who should know being questioned by Socrates are unable to point out such universal forms in this world, although they concede that such *must* exist for classes of particular things, (like bees or whatever) to exist and have something in common (which, say, makes them all bees or whatever).

3. The Argument from Recollection and the existence of the soul:

If forms must exist, and we must know what they are in order to identify particular things like bees or whatever, how is it we get to know them?

Forms don't exist in this world and yet somehow we, who do exist in this world, still know them because we can identify particular things as bees or whatever.

How, then, can we have got this knowledge? An explanation is provided in the dialogue, *Phaedo*:

There are two connected arguments in the *Phaedo* one for the existence of the forms and one for the immortality of the soul. The former may be put in this way:

i) Argument for the existence of forms

- Through the senses, we have the capacity to recognize that the equality (of pieces of wood or stones or whatever) in this world always falls short of absolutely perfect Equality.
- To be able to understand this, we must already have knowledge of perfect Equality in order to be able to *recall* it and recognize that things first thought of as equal in this world perfection always fall short of absolutely perfect Equality. (there is always some flaw, however tiny or microscopic).
- We could not have got such knowledge of perfection in Equality from *this* world (as we recognize that there is no absolutely perfect Equality in this world).
- Therefore, there must be another realm from which we acquired such knowledge of perfection, a world that contains the ideal form of Equality. [57]

Other examples may be used to make the same point: We have knowledge (somehow!) that there is no absolutely perfect circle in this world. We also know that there is none which can be drawn and none that has ever been drawn – there will always be some flaw however slight or miniscule in a drawn circle.

We can *only* recognize that all circles in this world have some kind of flaw (are not absolutely perfect) if we have *prior* knowledge of what a perfect circle is.

And this is knowledge that could not have been acquired in this world of flawed circles. It must therefore have been acquired from a different realm that contains the ideal form of Circle.

To this it may be added that if something is absolutely perfect, like a perfect circle, it doesn't change. If it did, it would change into something less than it was, less than perfect.

Since it is unchanging it can be an object of knowledge and so be known (unlike that which is always changing).

If you are thinking that Plato's other realm of ideals or perfections sounds something like heaven, you would be right. This conception of a world of perfections which we might, as disembodied souls, be able to get back to is one employed by many religions.

ii) Argument for the immortality of the soul:

The second argument from the *Phaedo* above, runs as follows:

- Through the senses, we have the capacity to recognize that the equality (of pieces of wood or stones) in this world falls short of absolutely perfect/ideal Equality
- To be able to sense this, we must *already* have knowledge of perfect/ideal Equality in order to be able to *recall* it and recognize that 'equals' in this world fall short of absolutely perfect/ideal Equality.
- So we *must* have acquired knowledge of perfect/ideal Equality before we were born,
- Since it cannot be acquired from this world, we must somehow 'arrive' with it.
- Therefore, we must have existed before we were born into this world in order to gain knowledge of the perfect/ideal form of Equality before we arrived.

The same argument runs for all the forms. We must have become acquainted with them before we were born, as we know them, and this knowledge could not have been acquired here as because these perfections do not exist here (there are no perfect circles in this world etc.).

It follows for Plato that as the soul exists before we were born it can therefore exist outside our bodies.

This also means the soul need not die when the body dies.

Indeed we can look forward to death as an escape from this world and a re-uniting with the world of perfections.

Those who are reminded here again of religious doctrine with respect to the soul hoping to get to heaven (the world of perfections) when the body dies would again be right, although it is worth keeping in mind as well that Plato is writing around 300BC. His ideas therefore serve as a foundation for religious belief in this regard.

3

THE SIMILE OF THE DIVIDED LINE

The *Republic* offers us more detail of the two realms distinguished by Plato as being necessary to account for the existence of particular things (like bees or whatever). It also gives more detail on the relationship between the content of these two realms and on the relationship between 'knowledge' and 'opinion'. This detail is provided by means of three famous similes: the Sun, the Divided Line and the Cave. Each of these will now be outlined beginning with the divided line. The influence on religious thinking as well as on epistemology and metaphysics should become more and more apparent as the similes are brought into focus.

As highlighted recently, the reader of the *Republic* and characters in the *Republic* are presumed to already understand the distinction between the world of change or 'becoming', of which we can only have opinion, and the unchanging realm of 'being' of which we can have knowledge. Plato describes a line with divisions on it to convey the structure of knowing and what can and cannot be known [58]

The Divided Line

KNOWLEDGE		OPINION	
A **Dialectic**	B **Reasoning**	C **Belief**	D **Illusion**
Intelligible Realm (Forms)		**Sensed Realm**	
ONE		**MANY**	

Let us focus on some of the divisions of the divided line, starting with the main epistemological distinction between opinion and knowledge.

Opinion - This is uncertain, always being replaced by new opinions; it is directed at the changing and is itself subject to change.

Knowledge - This is certain and secure; it is directed at the unchanging and is always so.

Opinion:-

This is divided into what may be translated as (1) 'illusion' and (2) 'belief'

1. *Illusion* - This is just at the level of sensations. Sensations are not yet brought to a whole to form a perception of, say, an object.
2. *Belief* - This results from the movement from sensation to perception. It involves the classification of images as of some particular object. We might have the sensation of seeing something in the distance. We are tempted to refer to it as a dog. We *believe* it's a dog.

But beliefs like this are not knowledge, only opinion. The proposition 'This is a dog' is subject to change. It may turn out not to be a dog. It is only opinion.

In the state of belief I perceive the object as a dog, but I have no understanding/ knowledge of what 'dog' is. I may recognize it as dog again but not be sure how I actually did this.

I need to find out the 'form' of Dog (that which all dogs have in common) to be able to make secure judgments that particular objects are dogs – to convert them to *knowledge*.

Therefore we can say that belief apprehends 'forms' (of, e.g., dog) in the ability to recognize particular instances (e.g. particular dogs).

It does not, though, apprehend it clearly; the form of dog is mixed up with sensations of particular dogs.

You need to find out what 'dog-ness' is, taken out or abstracted from all particular circumstances, if you are to make any judgments of recognition and inference about particular dogs certain and secure.

Knowledge:-

This is divided into (1) 'reasoning' and (2) 'dialectic'.

1. Reasoning

This is the method of <u>Mathematics</u> and of <u>Science</u>.

The objects of reason are not particulars but 'forms'. At this level, though, forms are only apprehended *indirectly*.

<u>Mathematics</u>:

The person doing geometry, for instance, might draw a circle and deduce various things from it.

His *real* object of study however is not the particular circle he has drawn, but the universal 'form' of Circle.

This form, this ideal circle, is something that does not exist in the world of particular things and is apprehended by the intellect rather than the senses. (The form of circle cannot be known through the senses, it is only known through *thought*)

<u>Science:</u>

The method of science employs hypothetical assumptions. It assumes hypotheses, e.g., 'all swans are white', 'all men are mortal' and then examines them by making deductions *down* from them.

If the hypotheses are not consistent with data and with themselves they can be rejected.

If the hypotheses are consistent with the data and themselves they are retained.

This testing and accepting or rejecting of hypotheses is the method of science.

This 'method, however, has significant limitations. The following deduction illustrates such a limitation.

- All swans are white (hypothesis)
- X is a swan
- Therefore X is white.

In this deductive argument, the universal hypothesis is *assumed* ('All swans are white'), the particular is also *assumed* ('X is a swan').

The conclusion is made to follow from these premises by the law of non-contradiction.

That is to say, 'X is *not* white' cannot follow from the first two premises above without ending up in a contradiction.

Because of the *assumptions*, however, the fact that the conclusion follows consistently according to its own deductive method means the method cannot establish knowledge.

It cannot establish that the conclusion is true because he assumptions leading to the conclusion may be false. Each premise stands in need of clear justification.

Furthermore if the same deductive method involving other assumptions is used in such justifications we are little further forward because the further assumptions will also stand in need of justification. Plato notes this point extends even to geometers who also leave some assumptions undisturbed [59]

A deduction in geometry may be consistent with itself, but it is not 'knowledge' as it makes assumptions. Euclidian geometry, relied on for 2000 years, made the assumption that parallel lines never meet. When various attempts were made to prove the principle that parallel lines never meet completely new geometries were discovered; such as that from drawing lines on a sphere, where parallel lines have to meet and where the angles of a triangle do not add up to 180 degrees.

2. Dialectic

To employ the method of <u>mathematics</u> and of <u>science</u> is to analyze the objects of knowledge, the forms indirectly as investigating the properties of a drawn circle to find out about the form of Circle

The method also involves moving *down* to conclusions on the basis of assumptions that stand in need of justification. Assumptions like 'All swans are white' or 'Parallel lines never meet'.

We must examine forms, the actual objects of knowledge, in some other way. Plato terms this other way 'dialectic'. The route to knowledge via the method of 'dialectic' is not <u>scientific</u> method, and it is not the <u>mathematical</u> method.

This alternative method to the mathematical and scientific reasoning procedures is needs to avoid moving *downward* from assumptions (such as 'parallel lines never meet', or 'all swans are white' etc.). Something is required which enables us to analyze forms directly.

Plato suggests that we should (instead of moving *down* from assumptions) proceed *up* from a hypothetical assumption as to the nature of the form to a direct analysis of the form itself.

For this purpose assumptions may still be used but as footings or underpinnings to climb *up* rather than as a point from which to move *down* to conclusions [60].

We must avoid deducing things from assumed premises. Plato says, then, we must examine forms using a different procedure – the 'dialectical' method.

Plato must not, however, say the dialectical method *is* such and such. This would make it a hypothesis or assumption, standing in need of justification.

Just to state that the dialectical method is the path to knowledge is a hypothetical assumption that demands a justification.

And if this were justified by some other method, dialectical method would forfeit its place as the ultimate path to knowledge.

Plato, then, must not and does not explicitly state what the dialectical method is.

What he might be doing in the dialogues, however, is illustrating or showing it via demonstration or display. Plato's dialogues could be viewed as a demonstration or display of the dialectical method in operation and its progress toward knowledge.

If this is so, a look at the content of the dialogues suggests that discussion and the search for definitions must be central to the dialectical method, as most of the dialogues are laid out like this.

In most of the dialogues Socrates questions a person (often a particular expert) on the meaning of a word. What he is after is an accurate definition of a 'form'.

The speaker Socrates is discoursing with is often shown via questioning not to really have *knowledge* of what he is talking about, because he does not have a precise description of the form in question.

In his conversations Socrates is shown to go from alternative definition to alternative definition, scrutinizing, rejecting and finally (sometimes) accepting one.

The investigation of alternatives is an integral part of the discourse and so perhaps of the dialectical method.

Plato sometimes talks of rubbing together alternative conflicting hypothetical assumptions to cause a 'spark'.

The truth comes like flash then because of this friction. Like, for instance, comparing a hypothetical assumption about justice in the individual with a hypothesis about justice in the state. 'Rubbing the two hypotheses together may produce a spark to illuminate what justice actually is. [61]

Plato also compares dialectic to running on a course There is no stated formula by which the end is to be reached, no path of inference laid out in advance, because this would make it an assumption standing in need of justification. The runner, the dialectician, must find his course as he runs. [62]

4

THE SIMILE OF THE SUN

We saw in the previous chapter how Plato regards deductions of scientific method and mathematical method as not being the proper path to knowledge because they use hypothetical assumptions. These assumptions stand in need of justification and could turn out to be false, as 'all swans are white' and 'parallel lines never meet' turned out to be false, although they were relied upon for a very long time by science and by mathematics respectively.

Knowledge is not something that can turn out to be false; if it is false it is not knowledge, as was explained Part I Epistemology. *Knowledge* of something it is more than *opinion* (opinion can turn out to be false)

If any of the assumptions of science or mathematics could be justified, however, then they could be saved as knowledge. That which does the justifying, though, cannot be just another hypothetical assumption that requires its own justification.

That which does the justifying needs to something that does not need justification itself from 'outside'. It must be self-justifying and the ultimate source of justification for all else.

Plato calls this ultimate source of justification the 'form of the good' and places it, appropriately, at the summit of knowing. He compares the Good's relationship to knowledge of the forms in the 'intelligible' world with the sun's relationship to the sight of things in the 'sensible' world. The sun makes the existence of things possible and by its light makes it possible to know that sun.

SUN	GOOD
in	in
VISIBLE WORLD *by its*	**INTELLIGIBLE WORLD** *by its*
LIGHT	**TRUTH**
makes possible	makes possible
SIGHT and existence of objects of sight	**KNOWLEDGE** and existence of objects of knowledge (forms)

The good is the source of is own justification and acts as ultimate justification for all knowledge. In so doing it is responsible for the creation of all knowledge.

If we can reach the good by moving *up* from hypothetical assumptions via dialectical analysis, we may be able to come back *down* as save some hypotheses as knowledge by justifying them.

One way of looking at this ascent to the good is put forward by W. T. Jones, *The Classical Mind* (1969)

If I look into a car engine I just see jumbled wires radiator containers of various kinds and more. An experienced mechanic can recognize far more parts that I and, in addition, he or she has learned how altering some parts can produce change in others or change in general. He or she is unlikely to know exactly why this change takes place – just that it has done in the past when the same alteration has occurred. To know exactly why he or she would need to move up to how the engine works according to the general laws of thermodynamics. To know exactly why and how the laws general laws of thermodynamics work would require seeing how they relate to higher principles of physics. These would the need to be seen in relation to general principles of science and what is to count as knowledge; a move up to epistemology in fact. The ascent could end when something is reached that that can be an ultimate source of knowledge and justification. This is what Plato holds is the 'Good'. [64]

If we can ascend to this source of justification via dialectical method, we can then descend again and save (or reject) some hypotheses and those below that depend on them as knowledge via their ultimate justification (or otherwise) from the Good.

The form of the good, like the sun, illuminates that below it; it is by the light of its truth (a truth that does not depend upon the truth of anything else) knowledge can exist.

Without the Good we are left only in dim light and are left relying on assumptions as to what is the case.

One of Plato's statements in the simile of the Sun is that the sun 'is the cause of sight and is seen by the sight it causes.' The Good then is the cause of knowing and is known by the knowing it causes.

There may be some reminder here of well-known religious statements. 'It is by God's light that we come to know the truth'. 'God is truth'. 'Everything depends upon God'.

The Good here seems very close to many conceptions of God. Plato's influence in this regard, therefore, is perhaps clear.

We see, then, that Plato has given much to underpin religious belief particularly as regards conceptions of God of heaven and earth, in addition to fundamentally shaping metaphysical and epistemological inquiries.

5

THE SIMILE OF THE CAVE

In this chapter the simile of the cave it outlined. It is revealed to serve two purposes: a metaphor for the epistemological ascent to knowledge and it depicts the reaction of society to the philosopher, the lover of wisdom.

The character of Socrates describes a cave where prisoners have lived since childhood. The are restrained in such a way that they can only look straight ahead. Behind them there is a fire and between the fire and the prisoners a screen has been erected a puppet show with shadow figures is always on view. As all prisoners can only see the shadows all come to regard what they see as reality. Prisoners are then thought to be released from their bonds. One stands up and turns around. He walks toward the fire but the light hurts his eyes, and he would be inclined to turn back. If he were then forced up out of the cave, the light outside would hurt his eyes and at first he would not be able to see anything. Later he would become accustomed to the light by looking at reflections and shadows of things first before turning to objects. Much later he would be able to look at the sun itself. Later still he would come to the conclusion that it is the sun which produces changing seasons and years and, in a sense, is responsible for everything. [65]

This simile of the cave here, then, appears to represent the ascent to knowledge. Recalling how the divided line had four stages, it should therefore be possible to identify the four stages in the ascent to knowledge out of the cave. These are given by Plato by Socrates saying explicitly that the similie of the cave is connected with what preceded it and that the ascent out of the cave into the sight of the world of objects corresponds to the progress of the mind from the normal world of sensation up into the intelligible realm. The final thing to be perceived in the intelligible realm (perceived not without difficulty) is the sun, the form of the Good. [66]

What more can be said of the cave dwellers? These are happy in their ignorance, which they do not recognize as ignorance. They can construct science by predicting the sequences of shadows, as a mechanic can discover a way of stopping a rattle in the engine without explicit knowledge of why the rattle occurs or why it disappears. This science is *useful*, but it is not knowledge.

6

EVALUATING PLATO

1. The Problem of Matching the Similes:-

One long-standing issue in the *Republic* surrounds the difficulty of making the sun, line and cave similes consistent with each other. This belongs to the province of scholars of Plato, but brief consideration of the issue can be illuminating.

To appreciate this consistency issue we need to have in mind the three similes. First, then, a quick reminder.

The simile of the sun:

The sun, supreme in the visible realm, corresponds to the good, supreme in the realm of thought. It enables the objects of knowledge to be known be the mind, as objects of sight are seen by the eye because of the sun.

The simile of the divided line:

Plato continues the division of the visible/sensible and the intelligible realms in the simile of the divided line. The main division is between the visible world and the intelligible world. The visible world is the lower world divided into physical objects and images and shadows of these. This is the world of opinion where belief and illusion are the modes of cognition.

The intelligible world is the higher world of knowledge, divided into the objects of pure thought (the forms) and the physical objects used for the purposes of mathematical reasoning (like the drawn circle is used to examine the form of Circle). Plato is also setting out in the divided line an epistemological progression from opinion to knowledge.

The simile of the cave:

Plato has Socrates ask us to imagine prisoners in an underground cave with a fire behind them, bound so that they can only see shadows on the wall in front of them, cast by puppets manipulated on a wall behind them.

The released prisoner is made first to turn around and see the fire and puppets, and then ascend to the outside world. Here, in the blinding light, he first sees shadows and reflections, and then real objects of which these are images, finally he is able to see the sun itself.

Each stage, from darkness to light in increasing degrees is painful for the prisoner and symbolizes the progression from opinion to knowledge. The realm inside the cave corresponds to the visible world, and the world outside to the intelligible realm.

Connecting the similes?

It is tempting to regard the relation between the sections of the line with knowledge at the top and opinion below, and the stages of ascendance up out of the cave from darkness to light as one of direct correspondence. What else could Plato have been intending when Socrates tells Glaucon that 'it must be applied as a whole to what has gone before'? One stage at a time, then, we have the following:

1. The cave the state of the bound prisoners accepting the shadows as reality should then correspond to the lowest section of the divided line, *illusion*.

2. The state of the freed prisoner who sees the fire and the puppets which cause the shadows correspond therefore to the next section of the divided line *belief.*

3. Seeing reflections in the outside world must correspond to the next section of the divided line, stage of *reasoning*

4. The sight of the objects themselves must represent the next stage of the divided line, *dialectic.*

5. Finally, the sight of the sun represents a vision of the form of the good that stands over all forms.

There are significant problems, however with attempting to maintain such a correspondence between the stages of the divided line and cave similes. This sort of problem is, as just mentioned, the concern of scholars of Plato. One such is considered here, though, for illustration.

How can the sight of shadows of *normal* existence in cave life correspond to illusions in lowest section of the line?

Plato says the prisoners in the cave who are forced to look at shadows are 'like us': they represent a person's ordinary state of belief about the physical world. But in the divided line simile, it is the second section of the lower part that seems to correspond more naturally with the general state of the ordinary person seeing objects.

It is not the bottom section of the divided line, of images of objects and shadows and reflections, which is our 'normal' state, although the cave simile suggests that is our 'normal' state

Indeed, Plato explicitly regards the level of cognition in the lower section in the divided line as illusion and in the next section up in fact as belief. But surely we are 'normally' in a state of *belief* – in the second section of the line and not at the very bottom.

In the simile of the sun too shadows are not interesting in themselves, only as an analogy. The objects that we 'normally' see are illuminated by the sun analogous to forms being illuminated by the Good.

In the cave, this (normal) level of cognition seems to correspond more closely to the experience of the freed prisoner on seeing the puppets and fire that cast the shadows. But Plato explicitly regards the initial looking at shadows stage of the cave simile as the 'normal' state of the ordinary person, like us.

A solution to the sun, cave and divided line mismatch?

One solution to this apparent confusion is to see the cave simile as primarily concerned with *moral* education. The cave world of people 'like us' could represent political conformists, manipulated by the state and media by being encouraged to care only about images and values which are presented to them.

We do not see the images and values they care about as *presented* and, in this sense, are prisoners. The first step in constructing their own moral awareness is to (turn around and) see that these images and values are presented to us.

In the movie 'Fight Club' Brad Pitt's character makes a speech suggesting to his male audience that advertisers plant desires in us, so we go out to work hard to gain money to buy these things, and later we realize we don't need them. The way to break out of this circle is to recognize (to turn around and see) that the things we 'normally' value do not come from us but are presented to us.

This could now correspond with the 'illusion' of the bottom section of the line, as the general state of the ordinary person is to accept unreflectively the images and values presented to him; and to be watching the shadows of puppets as presented in the cave simile. The divided line concept of illusion being taken at this level to refer to unreflective acceptance of what is presented (by advertisers or popular culture etc.) as being real.

Despite the above possible solution to one problem of matching the sun, line and cave, their exact connection still remains a matter of debate.

Difficulties such as these show that Plato may still not be fully understood in all respects

Improving such understanding may lead to further development of present day understanding of metaphysics, epistemology and much more. Such exegetical work, of course, is the province of scholars of Plato.

2. Forms and the Third Man Argument:-

Plato's theory of forms has been attacked using what has become known as the 'Third Man' argument. This argument is often cited and usually attributed to Plato's pupil Aristotle. The argument runs as follows:

- In order to explain the similarity between two men, we must posit a third man, the form of Man.
- Now, however, we might want to explain the similarity between the first two men and the form of Man.
- To do this, though, we need to posit another; a *third* man to explain the commonality between Form Man and particular man.
- The process of positing third men will have to continue without end to account for all the similarities between the posited men or between men and the form of Man

Is the Third Man attack on Plato's theory of forms a fair one?

The attack might be avoided by suggesting that the original third man, the form Man, does not possesses the features which particular men possess e.g., having two legs.

So particular men and the form of Man are not really 'similar' and don't have to be explained as such.

Only particular men are 'similar', because they both participate the form Man.

Perhaps as important here is the point that the third man argument, often attributed to Aristotle, appears to owe its origin to Plato.

Plato raises the problem himself in his dialogue *Parmenides* (130b-132b), so it is clear that he was well aware of it, and likely therefore not to have left himself vulnerable to it. The importance of gaining a correct interpretation and understanding of Plato is again made apparent.

Aristotle's theory of forms:

As Plato was a student of Socrates and developed his ideas, so Aristotle was the student of Plato and developed his ideas. Where Plato promoted the ideas of Socrates, however, Aristotle challenged his teacher. In particular, he criticized Plato's theory of forms and proposed his own theory, although it lies well within the conceptual framework left by his teacher.

Aristotle objected to the idea of transcendent forms. He argued that forms must be *in* things, not located somewhere else. There is 'matter' and it is given 'form' to become particular things. Matter does not exist except in some form and, similarly, form does not exist separate from particular things.

There is not for Aristotle therefore any separately existing form Circle, for instance, just particular circles; and these embody the form of Circle. The form or essence of Circle only exists *in* the particular circles.

The difference between Aristotle and Plato shows up in their discussions of art. Plato is dismissive of art. He thinks a painting, for example, is thrice removed from reality. A painting is an imperfect representation or copy of a particular thing that, in turn, is an imperfect copy of what is real – a form.

Aristotle draws the opposite conclusion about art. Because he thinks the essence or form of things are embodied in those things, an artistic representation can bring us closer to reality (not take us further away). A painting of a particular thing might capture its essence or form. In a painting of a hero, for example may capture the form of heroism, that which makes someone a hero; the essence of what it is to be a hero. It still represents something 'beyond' any particular embodiment of heroism, but not something that exists in a separate realm.

Knowledge for Aristotle, then, knowledge of the form of heroism, say, can be given to us via art – art can be a source of knowledge.

3. Wittgenstein: Can the notion of 'form' be rejected altogether?

Plato and Aristotle's theories can still be viewed as similar. Both identify the true reality of some particular thing with its 'form' or *essence*. They just differ as to where the form is located. For both it is still the form of man, for example, that makes man (essentially) different from other animals, and so identifiable as different from other animals.

We may, for example, call several things 'bee'. We normally think the reason that we do this is because they have something in common. The essence of 'bee'; the definition of 'bee'; 'bee-ness'.

Plato places this form of bee in a realm separate from this world, a realm of perfections – a heaven. Aristotle, places the form of a bee in particular bees (form which might be shown to us at least in part by a work of art).

Both Plato and Aristotle, however, regard forms as objects of knowledge. What is it that makes a bee a bee? What makes a particular man a man? The answer to the first question is that it embodies the form of 'bee'. The answer to the second question it that it embodies the form of 'man'. Such a form or essence might be captured by a definition (or, for Aristotle depicted in art if the 'right' words cannot be found).

Ludwig Wittgenstein (1889-1951) views this whole approach – an approach that has dominated thinking for the many centuries since Plato and Aristotle– as a mistake. He sees it as an error resulting from a failure to understand how language works.

Wittgenstein's analysis of how language works rejects this view that the particular things like bees described by the same word 'bee' necessarily have something in common, a bee-ness, a form of bee.

If we take a piece of rope, for example, and look at each end we would say that each end belonged to the *same* piece of rope.

It is not necessary, however, that there be something running all the way through the rope joining each end to make them part of the *same* rope.

Nor is it necessary, by analogy, that all the different uses of the word 'bee' need have something in common, something (some 'thread' that runs through them all). The same applies to uses of the word 'man'

The different uses of the *same* word need only be connected, like different ends of the *same* rope, by overlapping links.

For example, something in one use of a word 'table' will be like that of another use of the same word and that second use may have something in common with a third use. But all three uses need not have the *same* thing in common (a common essence or thread).

There is probably a whole spectrum of things we call 'table' ranging perhaps from made of wood with four legs, to made of plastic with no legs, to made of glass and hanging from the ceiling, and so on. They might all reasonably be called 'table' because they are linked in various ways. But they need not all have the *same* thing in common (a common essence), as the ends of the *same* piece of rope do not have to be joined by one piece of thread running from end to end.

If Wittgenstein is right, the whole project of looking for essences is based on a misunderstanding of how language works. As such, the theory of forms (both Plato's and Aristotle's later version), together with all the vast intellectual history that rests upon it, is also based on a misunderstanding of language.

There is no common essence of, say, 'justice' that all just acts possess, no essence of 'beauty', or 'heroism', no essence of what 'human existence' is, and so on.

The latter strikes at the heart of the whole literary and philosophical movement of 'existentialism', a movement whose contributors are aiming to convey the through literature, art and philosophy the essence of what it is to exist.

Post Wittgenstein, there is no need to find a a common thread or essenceof what it is to exist, just as there is no need for a common thread running through *all* acts of justice, or *all* objects of beauty or indeed with very particular relevance to this story, all uses of the word 'knowledge'.

The Value of Philosophy?

It is perhaps as well to stop here at this (disturbing?) point with a comment about the value of philosophy.

Bertrand Russell in *The Problems of Philosophy* (1912) notes that Philosophy is of value because it is able to suggest a greater range of possibilities, so to enlarge our thinking and free us from the tyranny of custom.

As such it is a source of power and, for the questions it exposes, it is also able to keep alive our sense of wonder.

If some of these values have been conveyed in this book, then it will have been worth the effort of writing, and (hopefully) worth the effort of reading.

NOTES

[1]   H. H. Price, 'The Permanent Significance of Hume's Philosophy', Philosophy 15 (1940), pp. 1036

[2]   see René Descartes: 'The Meditations', Meditation Two. In, for example, Descartes: Philosophical Writings E. Anscombe trans. (1954) Nelson & Sons.

[3]   See David Hume: Enquiries Concerning Human Understanding and Concerning the Principles of Morals, section 12.

[4]   See David Hume: Enquiries Concerning Human Understanding and Concerning the Principles of Morals, section 4

[5]   Ibid.

[6]   Ibid

[7]   See David Hume: Enquiries Concerning Human Understanding and Concerning the Principles of Morals, section 12.

[8]   See David Hume: A Treatise on Human Nature Book I, Part 4, Section 6.

[9]   Ibid.

[10] See David Hume: A Treatise on Human Nature Book I, Part 4, Section 2.

[11] See, for example, Immanuel Kant: Prolegomena for Any Future Metaphysics, trans. L. Beck. (1950) Bobbs Merrill

[12] See, for example, Immanuel Kant: Critique of pure Reason Transcendental Aesthetic, Section I. trans. N. Kemp Smith (1929) MacMillan & co

[13] See David Hume: 'Enquiries Concerning Human Understanding', Section 12.

[14] See John Locke: Essay concerning Human Understanding, Book IV. Ed.

[15] See A. N. Whitehead: Science and the Modern World (1925)

[16] See Bertrand Russell: The Problems of Philosophy, chapter 2.

[17] See, George Berkeley: The Principles of Human Knowledge and Three Dialogues between Hylas and Philonous.

[18] Ibid.

[19] See Bertrand Russell: The Problems of Philosophy, chapter 2.

[20] See John Leslie: Physical Cosmology & Philosophy (1990) Prentice Hall

[21] See David Hume: Dialogues Concerning Natural Religion

[22] See, for example, Fyodor Dostoevsky: The Brothers Karamazov 1984 Bantam

Classics

[23] See René Descartes: 'The Meditations', Meditation Five. In, for example, Descartes: Philosophical Writings E. Anscombe trans. (1954) Nelson & Sons.

[24] See Gottfried Leibniz: 'Philosophical Studies 34'. In, for example, Leibniz: Critical and Interpretive Essays Michael Hooker Ed. (1982) Manchester University Press

[25] David Hume: A Treatise on Human Nature Book I, Part 3, Section 7.

[26] See, for example, Immanuel Kant: Critique of pure Reason Section IV trans. N. Kemp Smith (1929) MacMillan & co

[27] René Descartes: 'The Meditations', Meditation Three. In, for example, Descartes: Philosophical Writings E. Anscombe trans. (1954) Nelson & Sons.

[28] See John Locke: Essay concerning Human Understanding, Book I, chapter IV.

[29] See Ibid., Book IV chapter X

[30] See David Hume: Enquiries Concerning Human Understanding and Concerning the Principles of Morals, section 7.

[31] See, for example, William Paley: Natural Theology M. D. Eddy Ed. (2008) Oxford World's Classics

[32] See, for example, David Hume: Dialogues Concerning Natural Religion, and The Natural History of Religion G. A. Gaskin Ed. (2008) Oxford World's Classics

[33] See Ibid

[34] See Sigmund Freud: 'The Future of an Illusion' Chapter IV. In, for example, The Complete Psychological Works of Sigmund Freud Series James Strachey Ed. (2009) Vintage Classics

[35] See A. J. Ayer: Language Truth and Logic (1952) Dover Books

[36] See Ibid.

[37] See René Descartes: 'The Meditations', Meditation Six. In, for example, Descartes: Philosophical Writings E. Anscombe trans. (1954) Nelson & Sons.

[38] Ibid.

[39] See, for example, Austrian Philosophy: The Legacy of Franz Brentano Barry Smith (1995) Open Court Pub.

[40] Johansson et al (1978) 'Social psychological and neuroendocrine stress reactions in highly mechanised work.' Ergonomics 21.8 (1978)

[41] 'Stress and open-office noise'. Evans, G W. Journal of Applied Psychology (2000)

[42] See René Descartes: 'The Meditations', Meditation Six. In, for example, Descartes: Philosophical Writings E. Anscombe trans. (1954) Nelson & Sons.

[43] See Peter Strawson: Individuals: An Essay in Descriptive Metaphysics chapter 3

(1959) Macmillan.

[44] See G. Ryle: The Concept of Mind (1964) Peregrine Books

[45] Turing, A.M., 'Computing machinery and intelligence'. Mind, 59 (1950)

[46] See John Searle: 'The myth of the computer' In, for example, Minds, Brains and Science (1984 BBC Reith Lectures) (1984) Harvard University Press

[47] Ibid.

[48] See, for example, John Stuart Mill: An Examination of Sir William Hamilton's Philosophy, Ed. John M. Robson (2012) Penguin

[49] See Ludwig Wittgenstein: Philosophical Investigations Part I 1973 Blackwell

[50] See, for example, Peter Strawson: Individuals: An Essay in Descriptive Metaphysics chapter 3 (1959) Macmillan.

[51] See David Hume: Enquiries Concerning Human Understanding and Concerning the Principles of Morals, section 8.

[52] See John Locke: Essay concerning Human Understanding, Book II, chapter XXVII.

[53] 'The formation of false memories' Loftus, E.F. & Pickrell, J.E. (1995), Psychiatric Annals, 25, pp720-725.

[53] See René Descartes: 'The Meditations', Meditation Six. In, for example, Descartes: Philosophical Writings E. Anscombe trans. (1954) Nelson & Sons.

[54] See Plato: The Republic 493a-c

[55] See Cratylus (439c-440a) in, for example, The Dialogues of Plato trans. B Jowett (1875) Clarendon Press.

[56] See Meno, (71e-72d) in, for example, The Dialogues of Plato trans. B. Jowett (1875) Clarendon Press.

[57] See Phaedo, (74a-77a) in, for example, The Dialogues of Plato trans. B. Jowett (1875) Clarendon Press.

[58] See Plato: The Republic (509d-511e)

[59] Plato notes this at 533c of The Republic

[60] See Plato: The Republic 511a

[61] See Ibid. (435a)

[62] See Ibid. (532b).

[63] See Ibid. (507b-508e)

[64] See, for example, The Classical Mind W. T Jones (1969) Harcourt

[65] See Plato: The Republic (514a-516c)

[66] See Ibid. (517a-c)

INDEX

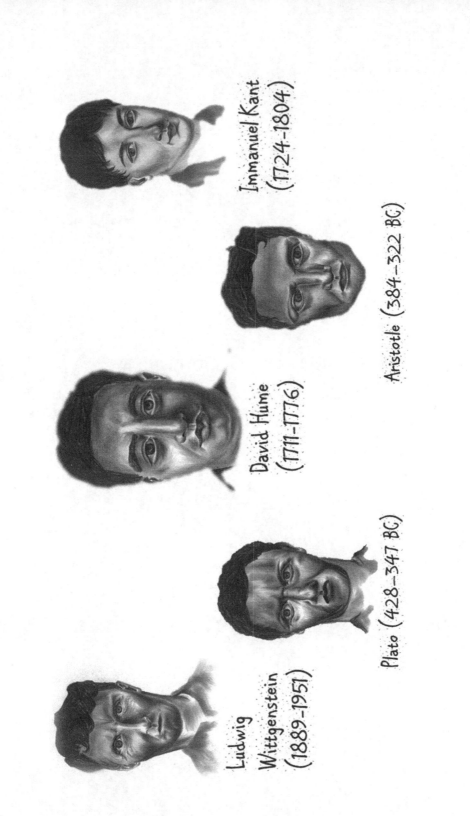

Immanuel Kant (1724–1804)

Aristotle (384–322 BC)

David Hume (1711–1776)

Plato (428–347 BC)

Ludwig Wittgenstein (1889–1951)

Printed in the United States
By Bookmasters